Education and Psychology in Interaction

The fields of education and psychology have attracted an increasing volume of attention in recent years. The profile of psychology and psychologists has risen in societies which are eager to understand the nature of human well-being and the conditions which can promote it. Education, for its part, has become a central element of social and economic policy across the globe, in line with changes in the technological basis of the economy, and in society and the family.

This book takes an in-depth look at how education and psychology have related to each other, and at the current state of this relationship. Through thorough analysis of the ideological, historical, social and professional contexts of this interaction, the author develops the theme that, despite basic differences in aims, the fields are interconnected. Indeed, neither can realise its aims without recognising this inter-dependence.

Education and Psychology in Interaction is therefore a text of fundamental importance for teachers, educationalists and psychologists, with vital implications for both theory and practice.

Brahm Norwich is Professor of Educational Psychology and Special Educational Needs at the School of Education, University of Exeter. He has worked as a teacher, professional educational psychologist and teacher trainer and researcher.

Routledge Research in Education

Education and Psychology in Interaction

Working with uncertainty in interconnected fields

Brahm Norwich

London and New York

First published 2000 by Routledge
11 New Fetter Lane, London EC4P 4EE

Simultaneously published in the USA and Canada
by Routledge
29 West 35th Street, New York, NY 10001

Reprinted 2001

Routledge is an imprint of the Taylor & Francis Group

© 2000 Brahm Norwich

Typeset in Garamond by
The Running Head Limited, www.therunninghead.com
Printed and bound in Great Britain by
Biddles Short Run Books, King's Lynn

British Library Cataloguing in Publication Data
A catalogue record for this book is available
from the British Library

Library of Congress Cataloging in Publication Data
Norwich, Brahm
    Education and psychology in interaction: working with uncertainty
in interconnected fields / Brahm Norwich.
    Includes bibliographical references and index.
    1. Educational psychology. I. Title
LB1051.N645 2000
370.15 – dc21   99–44824   CIP

ISBN 0–415–22431–4

Contents

Tables and figures

Tables

Figures

Preface

A preface is an opportunity to say something personal about the book, to present it to the reader from a different perspective. Although I include a personal angle in the introductory and concluding chapters, I feel it is worth making some of these points at the start of the book.

This book has taken several years to write. This is partly the usual problem of finding time to write while teaching, researching and carrying out administrative responsibilities. But it has also taken time to put together the ideas so as to form a broad overview. This has meant revisiting familiar work, and searching out new work from other fields that bear on the themes examined here.

What prompted me specifically to start the book was the extent of the decline in the position and value placed on educational psychology in university departments and institutes of education in the mid-1990s. This was impressed on me at a meeting of the Education Section of the British Psychological Society about that time. Someone remarked that professorial chairs in educational psychology at well-regarded schools of education were not being filled. This passing remark captured the significance of the widely recognised issues faced by educational psychology as both a theoretical and a practitioner field over a longer period.

What has been the relationship between psychology and education in the changing social and political context? What is the basis for a constructive future relationship? Though much has been written and said about this, little has been done that is based on a fundamental analysis of issues and questions. One of the continuing questions for me was whether psychology had already been 'given away', to use the phrase current in the 1970s. Do psychologists working in education have a continuing and distinctive contribution to make? For example, have the empirical and systematic methods of research and evaluation which psychology has contributed been taken over and developed by non-psychologist educational researchers? Have the ideas and practices which have been developed by practitioner psychologists been adopted by teachers and educationalists, leaving psychologists with no distinctive contribution to make?

My plan was to write a book that analysed the ideological, historical, social and professional contexts of the interaction of psychology and education. Its main theme is that, despite important differences in aims, the two fields are basically interconnected. This means that their respective aims and contributions cannot be understood without recognising this interdependence. The message of the book is therefore to urge a nurturing of this interconnection. In dealing with these questions and issues I hope that the book will appeal to a broad range of professional groups: teachers, educational researchers, teacher educators, research and practitioner psychologists and philosophers, and social scientists interested in education and psychology.

Much of the content of the book has been stimulated through my work at the Institute of Education, London University. This has been through contacts with students and colleagues. From some, I have learned insights and so developed my understanding. From others, I have gained from making sense of differences in perspective. Both ways, this book has depended on having the opportunity to discuss and debate. I appreciate the privilege of being able to do so.

1　Introduction

> If you take the notion of the perfect product and apply it to schools, you join
> the search for the effective school, the excellent leader, the perfect teacher,
> the National Curriculum . . . The danger of universalism is a constant quest
> for the right answer, the exemplary set of rules, the perfect plan.
>
> MacBeath (1998, p. 68)

Rationale of this book

Education has been pushed to the forefront of social and political agendas in
our fast-changing world. In Great Britain the current Labour Government
has placed education at the top of its priorities, hoping to shape a society
better equipped and prepared for the future. This has been expressed in
terms of raising standards for all pupils in schools and establishing systems
to support life-long learning. Parents and teachers have a special responsibility to promote learning and attainment. The culture of education has
become dominated by the brave new language of high expectations, challenge,
targets and effectiveness. Teachers are expected to become more expert in the
processes of teaching and learning. We hear evocative phrases like 'pedagogical wizards' and 'alchemists of the mind' to describe the challenges of finding new and more effective pedagogies. When teachers are being exhorted to
adopt new pedagogies which make use of what we know about the brain and
learning processes, it is timely to review the relationship between psychology and education. Current debates are about education becoming a more
research-based profession supported by evidence-based teaching. This raises
long-standing questions about a science of education and psychology's relationship to education. From its inception as an independent field of study
and practice, psychology has been promoted as a foundation science for
education. In this context it is useful to reappraise the relationship between
education and psychology.

From the education perspective, we are living through a period when
Western industrialised societies are undergoing major social and economic
changes. These are times of major technological development, following
great international political changes. This has stimulated widespread con-

cern about the quality of education and training for the population overall. A common view in the UK, which was well expressed by the National Commission on Education (1993), was that the abilities of the majority of young people were not being valued and developed sufficiently. The overall effect has been a considerable growth of interest in what education is about and how it relates to and serves the wider society and public interest. It has been an occasion for political interest groups to pursue their respective policy positions and values. For the first time for many years, education came to be a central issue in the 1997 British election campaign. Debate in the media and in politics has focused on whether standards of literacy and numeracy have declined or not, on the quality of teaching in schools and so on. Research has been conducted and used to clarify the nature and the extent of these gaps and shortfalls. In situations like these, international league tables are used to identify how Britain rates in comparison with similar countries (Reynolds and Farrell, 1996). In these comparisons Britain did significantly less well than its major European partners, for example, in the proportion of students reaching grades A to C at GCSE (the main national qualification for 16-year-olds) or equivalent, and in vocational qualifications (National Commission on Education, 1993). The low literacy and numeracy standards of a significant minority of young adults have also been a focus of concern (Dearing, 1993; Barber, 1996).

It is interesting that political interest in reforming the education system came at a time when evidence was indicating that some standards were improving, such as the numbers achieving five good passes at GCSE. However, there have been continuing concerns about literacy and numeracy standards as targets in primary schools, which has prompted the Labour Government to set very challenging targets for 11-year-olds. What has happened is that the education system has become the arena for seeking solutions to deeper social and economic problems and wider anxieties about the future. The recent restructuring of the education system, with its market-style arrangements, central directives and systems of accountability, has become part of a policy solution to wider problems. What has actually been going on in schools, and what teachers have or have not been doing, has become less important than the wider imperatives which drive education policy. One imperative has been the need in the economy for more adaptable, skilled and suitably qualified people. Disappointment about Britain's economic performance and growth has been decisive in setting the political agenda. The situation has been aggravated by changes accompanying the emergence of the global economy and the new information technologies. The challenge has been to respond to the skill demands posed by these developing information technologies. Analyses of these problems have pointed to a skills gap in the working population, amongst other factors, and have led to expectations of how the education system can contribute to enhancing the country's economic well-being. The economy has been seen as trapped in a low-skill equilibrium (Finegold, 1993). The quality of educational provision and training and industrial success are seen to mutually reinforce each other, in a way which has been inadequate to match aspirations for the country's current and future social and economic well-being.

There have also been major social changes in families, the position of women, individual rights and employment patterns that have led to calls for solutions which involve an increased role for the education system. Unemployment has been a persistent problem in the context of changing work patterns and people's growing preparedness to do several different jobs over their working life. Changes have also taken place in the patterns of family life and child rearing, and these are thought to have considerable influence on children and young people. There is more divorce, more lone parents and reconstituted families and more women in paid employment. These are considered to be important trends as they affect the nature of home life, which is seen to be critical for the development and learning of children. There has also been an increase in the number of young offenders, as shown by increasing crime convictions, while children and young people have been exposed more to the dangers of drugs and even violent crime.

These changes have prompted the build up of interest over the last decade, which came from various parts of society in response to the general perception of the inadequacy of educational and training provision in Britain. The strong support given to the independent National Commission on Education by many interested parties showed that there was a widespread view across the political spectrum that all was not well with education and training in the country. The vision expressed by the National Commission also captured some consensus that knowledge and skill would increasingly become the key to a nation's economic and social prosperity in the development of an interlinking global economy (Reich, 1991). Economic investment by multi-national corporations is now seen to depend to a significant extent on the degree of knowledge and skill in the working population. Capital in this fast-changing global economy will increasingly be identified with the quality of human resources in the production and service sectors of the economy.

The increasing emphasis on knowledge and in what has been called applied intelligence represents a fundamental challenge to nations in how they manage their educational and training systems. It also has an inevitable bearing on the structure of employment and job availability. These technological and economic changes will have a continuing impact on the patterns and distribution of work and unemployment in society. With a decline in the number of less-skilled jobs, unemployment may become endemic in certain sections of the population and contribute to the widening income gap between the more and less wealthy members of society. The overall effect of this will be to threaten the cohesion of society by widening the difference in employment opportunities between the better and worse off members of society. We hear about the risks of a developing 'under-class' of people outside the mainstream of society who are alienated and pose threats to it. This situation has led to the vision of a society in which the overall standards of knowledge and skill are increased, so that all sections of the population can better match the demands of changing technology and patterns of service and production. This is a society in which people are more flexible about work patterns and job retraining, in which continuous learning is a major feature of people's lives – what has come to be called a learning society.

However, a vision of education and training which was dominated by the needs of the economy would be seriously impoverished and counter-productive. Education in the home and school and in the wider society through the media is also about moral, spiritual and aesthetic experience. Education also needs a vision which includes ways of promoting all-round human dispositions, virtues and values, including those focused on develop-ing individual qualities supportive of social and organisational arrangements. In the context of major social changes this means that a state, through its education and other systems, will need to find better ways of enabling children and young people to come to act as responsible and active contrib-uting members of society. The tendency is to look to the school system as the arena in which social problems might be prevented and social change facilitated. Much then is required of schools and teachers to enable children and young people to adjust to changes and cope with social problems.

One response to these increased demands on the education system has been the introduction of a National Curriculum and a system of assessing attainments at various stages of schooling. But changes have also been intro-duced to the processes and systems of schooling. The training of teachers and the inspection of schools have been revised as part of a move to adopt more purposive management systems in education. The ethos has become one of school reform: school improvement is sought through a better under-standing of what makes for an effective school. Work in the areas of school effectiveness and improvement has come to stimulate and shape the govern-ment's political agendas for education, but also to serve these agendas in supporting policy and practices to raise educational standards. The search then is to find out what works best in organisational procedures and teach-ing strategies in order to improve learning outcomes.

The search for greater educational effectiveness, which goes beyond a focus on any particular level or setting which affects learning outcomes, has most recently centred on the internal processes of schools as semi-autonomous organisations. But the search for effectiveness has a long history in edu-cation, being associated with a technical approach to education that has been dominant throughout this century. It is an approach which has been seriously criticised in some quarters for its lack of appropriateness to education and human affairs. It is interesting that many of the current critiques of school effectiveness knowledge reflect many of the same points used in previous critiques of a technical model of education (White and Barber, 1997). These are about the unexamined value assumptions underlying the identification of effective techniques and the limited conceptions of educational aims. They are also about the importance of the particular context, problems in generalising, and the dehumanising effects of scientific methods that reduce learning to quantitative variables. These continuities indicate that the current interest in school effectiveness research and knowledge is a further expression of the longer-standing technical tradition. It is an approach in which credibility is based on the authority of a science of education. This idea of a science of education and teaching is a modern one in the sense that it has gained prominence with the growth and successes of the natural and biological sciences. The hope has been that the social and psychological sciences in general, and also specific versions of them, such as educational science, can provide the base of knowledge and understanding of learning and teaching processes, from which can be derived well-founded and effective educational techniques and procedures. Psychology as a scientific discipline has been seen for over a century as offering or having the potential to offer a foundation of knowledge and understanding for education.

Despite these claims and promises, the status of psychology in relation to education has declined in Britain. This is evident in several respects in the education and training of teachers, in educational research and development and in the role of professional educational psychologists in the education service and of academic psychologists in university departments of education. In the initial training of teachers, psychology has had a long involvement going back over a century. It made a renewed contribution when teacher training became a degree course. However, more recently, with greater emphasis on practical experience and competence in teaching, the usefulness of knowledge and understanding about learning and development has been questioned as being too theoretical. So psychology and psychologists, as such, have played a decreasing role in the initial preparation of teachers. However, researchers with a training in psychology have played a continuing and major role in educational research. Yet many of these researchers would not see their research as being in either basic or applied psychology. Their research methods may originate from psychological methods of inquiry, but quantitative research now has an established position in educational research outside psychology. There has been a marginal use of psychology as a field which provides a resource and perspective on the conditions and processes of learning. And when knowledge and understanding from psychology have been applied in educational research and development, this has been done without thorough practice development and evaluation work. The temptation has been to go for quick adoption and implementation, for a naive and sometimes mindless technological approach.

Psychology has been applied and used in the education service, particularly in relation to provision for those with difficulties and disabilities, by professional educational psychologists. Though formal evaluations indicate that educational psychologists have been making useful contributions to the education service, there have been continuing problems. This is the issue of whether educational psychologists have been using psychology in their practice to meet a wide range of service needs or whether they have been acting mainly as advisory teachers for children and young people with difficulties and disabilities. It has raised questions about the value of different kinds of psychology; such questions have been associated with crises of confidence about its individual focus since the 1970s. These bouts of professional doubt have been in response to the growth of political and social science criticisms of the theoretical assumptions and technical practices involved in the measuring of psychological characteristics such as intelligence. Psychometrics came to be identified as psychology's main contribution and as a practice which discriminated against those with less social and economic power. This prompted moves from some professional educational psychologists to abandon assessments of children and young people which focused on individual characteristics. Yet psychological assessment of individuals' characteristics and their needs has been a core function of professional educational psychologists in the service of Local Education Authorities (LEAs). The refocusing of professional educational psychology has been in different but related directions. These moves have included the adoption of conceptual schemes which have directed analysis away from individual general characteristics in two directions. One direction has been to analyse observable behaviours in specific contexts; the other has been to analyse larger units or systems, such as the classroom, the school and the school–family system. All this has left educational psychology in a state of some uncertainty about its primary aims and functions.

Ideological context and social and political values

The recent state of uncertainty about psychology in education needs to be understood within the broader social and ideological context of education after the Second World War. Equality and equality of opportunity became dominant educational policy values. Egalitarian strategies came into the centre of political debate about education in the wake of questions about diverse kinds of schools for different educational needs. Political opinion has long debated whether organisational diversity, in the form of selective schools, is compatible with equality. This debate has been about how the allocation of educational opportunities and variations in attainments relate to the organisation of schooling. There was some consensus between the main political parties over the move to comprehensive secondary schooling and later about the principle of integrating pupils from special schools. But the underlying tensions within the consensus emerged when the last Conservative Government revived market-style principles and school diversity in its educational policies in the 1980s. The main aim of the restructuring which started with the Education Reform Act (1988) was to raise educational standards by giving parents more client information about schools and allowing them to state school preferences. Schools were given more autonomy from LEAs and enabled to change their funding base and character, including the piecemeal introduction of ability selection as part of a policy to develop a greater diversity of schools. The Labour Government has built on these changes but tried to focus more on how schooling functions than on its structure. Raising standards has continued to be the driving policy aim and has been supplemented by central directives about target setting in primary schools. This is where the Labour Government has introduced its progressive agenda in terms of the values of social cohesion with an egalitarian strand, which is presented in terms of pursuing inclusive values. Excellence is not supposed to be just for the few, but for all – even for those with special educational needs, as the policy statements put it. But whether target setting for 75–80 per cent of children will have spin-offs for the minority not covered by these targets is still to be seen. We also wait to find out how far the investment of money and effort to improve schools and raise standards without addressing the structure of schooling is compatible with inclusive aims. The government is seeking both inclusion and educational excellence. Experience will show whether the potential tensions between these aims will surface over time.

Egalitarian principles have had a major setback in political agendas internationally. With the demise of Soviet communism and the spread of capitalist market systems, there has been a rise in the values of liberty and individualism. The growth of centre-left politics in the USA and UK represents the search for a third way between old-style socialist principles, which embraced equality as a guiding principle, and more laissez-faire individualism. If equality is supported by this version of progressive politics, it is more about providing equal opportunities than about seeking more equal outcomes. By incorporating equal opportunities into the values of inclusion, the current government is trying to shift the basis of progressive political values away from traditional egalitarian redistributive policies. But the old ideological debates within educational policy about excellence and equality have been refocused on the relationship between excellence and inclusion. Underlying these debates are differing positions about the origins of differences in educational attainments. The commitment to excellence has often been associated with the assumption that people differ in abilities and that differences are not easily altered, whatever their underlying causes. Making the best of these abilities will involve identifying these abilities and making appropriate and differential provision. This may require different classes or schools, with the consequence that different attainment levels become associated with social separation. Through a process like this, excellence can lead to less inclusion. By comparison, the commitment to inclusion and greater equality of outcomes, if only at primary school level, has usually assumed that attainment differences arise from different opportunities at home and/or in the quality of school teaching. Ability differences tend to be attributed more to alterable environmental factors than to less alterable factors and innate potential. But improving schools and teaching to allow the majority to reach challenging levels may draw investment and attention away from those who are above this level and those not likely to reach it. This could have the result of limiting individual excellence. Through a process like this, more inclusion can lead to less excellence.

It is possible to pursue excellence for all and inclusion to some extent, but there are limits that are set by one aim on the other. The policy rhetoric of raising standards for all needs to be seen to involve a balance between raising the mean level, which takes account of each person's standard, and reducing the variation between the highest and lowest levels. The more the mean level is raised, the greater the variation in levels. The more the variation in levels is reduced, the lower the mean level. This arises from the individual differences in abilities to learn and attain and the greater investment of teaching effort needed to raise levels for lower attainers. The point of this analysis of policy aims, processes and likely consequences is to highlight the significance of what can be called learning resources for attainment. These resources involve both the environment at home and at school, and the resources of learners. My aim is to show the significance of concepts of individual capacity or competence in educational policy positions. Decisions about educational opportunities and provision are influenced fundamentally by assumptions made about children's and young people's abilities or potential to learn. This is well illustrated by the Government's primary school literacy and numeracy targets for 11-year-old pupils. The national programmes that work towards having 75 per cent and 80 per cent of pupils reaching National Curriculum Level 4 in numeracy and literacy respectively assume that lower attainment has arisen in the past from alterable environmental factors rather than fixed ability factors.

Underlying these belief and value systems are the long-running debates about the relative effects of nature-genetic and nurture-environmental factors on human behaviour and achievement. Psychology has been dominated by this debate in one form or another since its emergence as a distinct discipline and professional field. It is a basic social issue which goes back to the origins of Western social thinking, when Plato adopted a position in his proposal for a good state. It has had especial contemporary relevance to the focus of theoretical endeavour and inquiry within psychology, particularly within British educational psychology. This will be discussed in chapter 3 in the context of the work of Cyril Burt, one of the founders of British educational psychology, on the origins of differences in intellectual functioning. But for the purposes of introducing this book, the relevance of this analysis is that psychological assumptions and positions are connected to social value and education policy issues. Though psychology might be expected to provide the knowledge which informs policy making and implementation, social and political values have a pervasive and continuing influence on the nature of psychology and its relationship with education. One of the main themes of this book is that the relationship between psychology and education needs to be understood in terms of their relationship with social and political values. There is therefore a three-way relationship between psychology, education and basic social and political values. These social and political values can be characterised in the simple and broad terms of the interplay between conservative and progressive positions. However, these are relative and changing positions which depend on more specific social and political agendas. The distinction is not a tight dichotomy, because some positions can have both progressive and conservative elements. Though progressive positions have been associated with support for the interests of the disadvantaged and oppressed members of society, I am taking them as positions which aim for social and political change based on the belief that improvements can be made. By contrast, conservative positions aim to retain what is currently judged to be good, based on the belief that change is less possible. This is the difference between a more hopeful and a more resigned perspective, between one which sees potential and rejects limits to human fulfilment and one which accepts limits.

So, even though educational psychology does not focus explicitly on these social value and policy matters, I contend that its interests and agendas are nevertheless strongly influenced by them. For example, within professional educational psychology there was, starting in the 1970s, a move away from generalised ability-based models of assessment, such as the IQ test, towards more contextualised and behaviour-focused assessment models. This was justified in terms of problems with what have been called 'within-child' deficit models, arising from critiques of their over-emphasis on human limitations and their discriminatory use with children from ethnic minority or working class backgrounds. Models which focused on the environment came to be preferred by some psychologists. The discourse switched to one of conceptualising the environmental conditions in the classroom, school and home which can lead to gains in educational attainments. The influence here from the progressive and egalitarian beliefs and values is clear.

Another example of how the policy context and social values influence the changing interests in different theoretical positions in psychology can be found in the renewed interest in and contemporary influence of Vygotskian ideas in psychology and education (Vygotsky, 1978). These ideas emphasise the teacher's role in mediating learning and the social nature of learning. They have been promoted by proponents in terms of their difference to Piagetian ideas which portray the child as learning and developing as an individual in direct relation to the environment. The Piagetian framework is represented as individualised and biological, assuming fixed stages and sequences of development, less interested in the social environment and the potential for change in psychological development. Vygotskian ideas have also been contrasted with behaviourist psychological ideas, which have had a longer influence on education, particularly through educational psychology practice. Behaviourist ideas include ones about the context of learning, the stimulus setting of learning and the cueing and shaping of learning responses by adults. There are clear similarities with neo-Vygotskian ideas about situated development, assisted learning and the potential for change. But it is interesting that it is not the similarities which are highlighted, but the differences between behaviourist and neo-Vygotskian social constructionist approaches. My point is that Vygotskian proponents emphasise the differences because of the influence of progressive beliefs and values. The distancing from behaviourism by the neo-Vygotksian tradition fits with progressive-egalitarian values. Behaviourist theories have their origin in animal experimentation associated with biological and mechanistic assumptions that there are common principles of learning across different species. This contrasts with neo-Vygotskian social constructionist theories which are more holistic in seeing the individual as intimately related to the social environment. Learning in these theories is intrinsically linked to the development of speech and language, which are social and public phenomena. The implication is that psychological functioning and development is at bottom social, and that individual characteristics reflect this social process rather than biological processes. The avoidance of the biological, with its associations of what is fixed and unalterable, in the strongly socialised neo-Vygotskian view of psychological functioning can be seen to reflect a progressive-egalitarian emphasis on social environment and change.

The focus

This book takes a broad overview of the relationship between psychology and education. Unlike other books about educational psychology, it is not a textbook covering relevant topics on learning, memory, motivation and classroom process, nor is it a summary of current knowledge and understanding of a particular topic. It is not a book which intends to illustrate the specific ways in which psychological concepts and theories can inform an understanding of the educational process and be applied to practice. It is a book about the nature of psychology and education and the interdependence between these two fields of study and practice. Psychological ideas and assumptions have played a central role historically in educational theories and practical schemes. Educational questions led to psychological thinking and the development of psychology. As mentioned above, this relationship has a long history which dates back to the time of the Greek philosophers, and can be found in Plato's educational philosophy (Egan, 1983). These links between psychological ideas and assumptions within philosophy and educational thinking and practice continued till the nineteenth century. Then in the late nineteenth century, when psychology became established as a distinct university-based discipline, it assumed a scientific mode of operation and this opened up a new form of relationship with education.

This book focuses mainly on the recent relationship over the last century, though it is informed by an understanding of the longer continuities between psychological and educational thinking and practices. One of the main messages of the book is that a contemporary understanding of the relationship between psychology and education has to be strongly informed by an awareness of historical and philosophical questions about the nature of theoretical and practical knowledge and the relationships between values and knowledge. The book will therefore be focused on differing notions about the nature of psychology and education and how these relate and mutually interconnect. This will require some analysis of how psychology and education differ in terms of their basic aims and assumptions. The main force of the argument in the book will be that despite fundamental differences in the aims of psychology and education, as distinct disciplines or activities they depend on each other and are connected specialisms. From the perspective of education, with its ideas and practices concerned with how to promote learning and development, there is a need for clear and explicit assumptions about the nature of learning, how it takes place and what conditions support it. Some of these assumptions are psychological and therefore call for a working relationship with psychology. From the perspective of psychology, which seeks to describe and explain the many interrelated facets of personal experience and action, there is a need to address areas which are significant in terms of what is worthwhile for human aspirations and fulfilment. Education provides such an area for inquiry and explanation. A vibrant and relevant psychology needs therefore to relate dynamically to education. The contemporary relationship between psychology and education is complex. This is evident in the different terms which are used to refer to the relationship. We hear about educational psychology, psychology of education, psycho-education, psycho-pedagogy and psychology in education. These references are associated with different perspectives and commitments. They are connected to differences between theoretical and applied psychology, between academic and professional psychology. This book will be about these differing perspectives, their aims, assumptions and methods on one hand, and the social and professional context of these practices on the other.

Themes and perspectives

If the decline of educational psychology is going to be understood in the context of education policy and practices and basic social and political values, then various themes and perspectives need to be explored. This calls for a thorough examination of the knowledge bases and value orientations associated with psychology and education. Examining the knowledge base will open up questions about the nature of psychological knowledge and understanding, what are called epistemological questions. Linked to these are questions about the relationships between different social sciences, like psychology and sociology; between social and biological sciences; and between all these sciences and fields like education. Examining value orientations also opens up questions about different aims, assumptions and methods in the social sciences. These are linked to different epistemological models and methods of inquiry. And, as the introductory discussion has illustrated, there is a relationship between value orientations and different schools of thought and explanation in psychology. This book will deal with these matters drawing on the following key themes and perspectives.

Educational practitioners' interests

To understand teachers' perspectives on theoretical knowledge and research related to education, it needs to be appreciated that practitioners are strongly interested in practical techniques and procedures which are seen to be practically feasible and work well. Teaching is often considered to be a craft occupation in the sense that its activities and procedures can be (and often are) learned in the context of doing without the need for an underlying knowledge of the processes of teaching and learning. It is in the nature of teaching that it involves practical strategies and skills, and when teachers emphasise these aspects, we need to remember that this originates in and is reinforced by their working conditions in schools. There is constant face-to-face contact with pupils, which leaves little time for reflective analysis of teaching problems. The effect of these teacher interests is that theoretical knowledge about education is likely to be judged mostly in terms of its practical usefulness rather than its coherence and validity. And under prevailing working conditions, teachers are likely to be little interested in theoretical knowledge unless this can come to inform practical strategies.

Nature of teaching and education

It is a commonplace to describe teaching as an art. This is expressed sometimes as teaching being a craft activity and sometimes as its being a practical art. Reference to a craft or practical activities qualifies the kind of art involved in teaching. It is to distinguish it from a fine art such as sculpture. But the main point of identifying its artistic nature is to define its procedures as too complex to be reduced to systematic formulae or rules. This arises because teaching relies on spontaneous and creative combinations of actions. But this position about the artistic nature of teaching can be opposed to seeing teaching as an applied science. Many teachers who consider education and their teaching to be a practical art or craft will have difficulties with the idea that what they do is an applied science in general, or an applied scientific psychology in particular. This means that any analysis of the relationship between psychology and education needs to consider the art–science question about the nature of teaching. These issues will be dealt with in the next and subsequent chapters.

Sources of knowledge and understanding in education and teaching

Some of the main sources of knowledge and understanding in education have come from those who have had limited or little practical experience of school teaching. In this sense they have been interested outsiders or have taken outsider perspectives, if only because the nature of working conditions in schools had not enabled teachers to undertake the necessary inquiry and conceptual work. The foundations of thinking about education and teaching have tended historically to be based on values, ideas and theories from outside the practical occupation of school teaching. Since psychology has developed as a scientific discipline, it has come as a foundation discipline to be used in education as an applied science in this way. But psychology has not been the only social discipline applied to education. Sociology also has a long tradition of being used to make sense of education and to inform policy and organisational aspects of schooling. Those disciplines which have been treated traditionally as foundations of education have been history and philosophy, especially philosophy with its original interests in human and social values and the nature and basis of human knowledge.

The decline of psychology in education can be partly attributed to sociologically based critiques of psychology's individualist and biological basis and its associations with conservative political values. But it has also been associated with the growth of interest among teachers, teacher educators and trainers themselves in developing and understanding the processes of teaching and learning. These moves for teachers to take more responsibility for undertaking educational research and developing their own educational knowledge are associated with an increased professionalisation of teaching. The growth and establishment of educational research represents a greater professionalisation of teaching as an occupation. It raises important questions about who does educational research and how it is done. How does the knowledge and understanding derived by teachers from their own practice and experience relate to knowledge constructed by teacher educators and trainers? And how do these forms of knowledge and understanding relate to the knowledge constructed by psychologists in their theoretical and applied research and in their professional practice?

Education's need for knowledge and understanding about teaching and learning

Teaching involves decisions about what is worth learning, how to plan and arrange activities to enable learning and how to assess progress and attainments. This involves thinking about these activities at different levels, from the large scale of national and regional education systems to the middle levels of school organisations to the level of face-to-face group and individual teaching and learning. To make effective decisions, there is a need for ways of thinking in detail about aims and strategies, ends and means. Thinking about ends involves decisions about values and purposes. This requires consideration and clarification of the nature and balance between different values. This inevitably raises empirical questions about the practicality of realising complex and multiple ends. So the centrality of values in education is not in opposition to the role of empirical considerations. Value clarification and commitment depends on what can and does happen; ends depend on means. But means also depend on ends. Once values and goals have been established, ways and means can be sought to better achieve these ends, that is, research into what works and how it works. Complex empirical relationships between contexts, actions, and their consequences will be basic to the kind of educational knowledge required in education and for teaching.

I argue that in education these evaluative, conceptual and empirical aspects need to be kept interconnected. Each aspect depends on the others for its clarification and determination. This requires that each aspect be fully developed in its connection with the other aspects. Education therefore needs not just the inspiration of ideals and vision, but also conceptual assumptions and interpretations about the nature of teaching and learning included in psychology. These theories or interpretations need to be well-founded, in the sense either of withstanding empirical testing or of having useful consequences. Such resources of knowledge may arise from different sources. They may be induced from the practical experiences of teachers and activities in schools by teachers or educational researchers; they may arise from experiences and activities in other social areas, or from translating and developing general theoretical schemes into practical procedures and techniques. The point is that educational knowledge would become restricted and impoverished were it to draw on limited sources. Psychology and other social science disciplines, it will be argued, are important resources of knowledge and understanding for education.

Psychology's need for a field like education

It is easier to characterise psychology in general than in specific terms. This uncertainty stems from fundamental differences about whether psychology is a scientific discipline in the sense that physics or biology are taken to be. It is connected with the way that the aims and methods of any study puts limits on what is counted as a legitimate subject matter for study. Nevertheless, it is widely agreed that psychology seeks to understand and explain human experience and behaviour. Yet even at this degree of generality there are differing interpretations about what counts as understanding and explanation and whether psychology can study and generalise what is common to individuals or study what is individual to each person. There are differing perspectives on whether psychology is seeking to generalise in terms of causal relations that enable prediction or is seeking to understand how individual people make sense of their worlds and to identify their motives as a way of understanding their particular behaviour and experiences. There are also differences about what counts as evidence, whether it needs to be publicly observable and measurable or can be private and about meanings. Psychology's relationship with allied fields is also a major preoccupation: whether its subject matter is distinct from biology and physiology on one hand, and how it relates to the study of collections of individuals in groups, organisations and states – how it relates to sociology – on the other hand.

Despite these differing opinions about understanding and explanation, psychology can be seen as a science in the widest sense, whether a natural science like physics or an interpretive science. Science in this sense is about making sense, it is about satisfying curiosity about human experience and behaviour. Psychology is basically a theoretical activity which develops ideas, schemes and theories to promote understanding and knowledge of individual functioning in this general but significant sense. If it is defined as seeking to enhance human experience and fulfilment, then the aim of seeking understanding is a precondition of this aim. Its primary aim is not about bringing about change and improving human welfare, even if this derivative aim is included in its definition. One line of argument is that psychology should focus on practical real-life problems as the focus for seeking understanding and explanation. This is an important position for ensuring that psychology is relevant to practical uses and applications. But care should be taken not to play down the basic theoretical aim by implying that psychology is primarily about seeking practical solutions to immediate practical problems.

What is at issue here is what counts as a problem, whose problem it is and what attitude is taken to the problem. Psychologists have been interested in general and long-standing, rather than particular and local, problems and questions. These general and long-standing problems may have been problems for those in national administration and government, but they may have also sprung from wider problems in education, crime, mental health and questions concerned with religion, ethics and the origins of mind in biology and society. Problems also differ in terms of whether they call for particular techniques to achieve certain solutions or whether they call for general ideas and schemes which solve explanatory or interpretive problems by providing understanding. Psychology, from what has just been said, is basically about the latter problems. But ideas and theories, and research methods used to develop and test them, can be used to address practical problems. There is psychology as an explanatory-theoretical endeavour and there is applied psychology when psychology is used to deal with particular practical matters.

The distinction between psychology and applied psychology seems to correspond to the distinction between science and technology. There is a problem, however, in aligning psychology with science and applied psychology with technology. It is the assumption that there is a close historical relationship between science and technology, whether in the fields of physical science and engineering, or in the social sciences and practical fields like education and mental health. In fact, technology has had a fairly independent and long-standing existence predating the growth of the physical sciences. Scientific knowledge has been used only over the last two centuries to enhance technology, and much of the status and authority of science derives from the success of these applications (Wolpert, 1992). A similar point can be made about the relationship between a human/social science like psychology and the techniques and strategies used in a field like education.

Educational strategies and techniques have arisen from practical attempts to better achieve educational aims over many centuries. These may have also been informed by philosophical and theological ideas, but the development of educational techniques preceded them and had its own independent existence well before the emergence of modern scientific psychology and the idea of an applied scientific psychology.

There is a strong tradition within contemporary psychology which promotes and is sustained by the belief that scientific psychology can benefit fields like education and mental health. I will discuss this tradition in more detail in chapter 3, but for the present I want to point out that in this view education is expected to be the grateful recipient of the goods from applied psychology. The idea that there might be some mutuality in the relationship between psychology and education does not fit well with this tradition. I oppose this one-way perspective even in its sophisticated versions, arguing that psychology and education are interdependent. Psychology has as much to gain from its contacts and close working relationship with education as the other way round. The reasons for this are to do with the nature of psychology and its need to find stimulating problems in important and practical activities like education. This is not just about focusing theory and inquiry on topics which might have fruitful applications, but about maintaining links with activities which can genuinely stimulate curiosity. Psychology can tend to become isolated from thinking and perspectives in allied fields like education and can also benefit considerably from learning about the theoretical and practical perspectives of educators. By associating with education, psychology also comes into contact with the applications of other disciplines such as sociology, history and philosophy, which can offer alternative, and sometimes rival, perspectives on education. This can challenge the position and contribution of psychology to education, and can be seen as a spur for psychology to relate and co-ordinate its theoretical sphere and perspective with these other disciplines. This interdisciplinary contact is especially valuable for understanding the internal theoretical differences within psychology. It is sometimes easier to co-ordinate a particular psychological theoretical approach with one from another discipline than with a different psychological approach. Relating closely to educationalists can offer psychologists this chance to consider their own particular version of psychology in terms of others' perspectives.

The institutional and professional context

The relationship between psychology and education cannot be fully understood without considering the institutional and professional contexts in which psychologists and educators work. Teachers are most likely to come across psychologists who work in the applied field of professional educational psychology. This is usually in the context of identification of and support for pupils with difficulties in learning and assessments for decisions about additional or different provision. Whether teachers become aware of what is psychological about the contribution of psychologists is a point to be discussed in a later chapter. Teachers may also have had some contact with psychology in their initial teaching preparation. This has become less evident with the moves towards more school-based initial training with a focus on practical competencies. Psychology might appear to beginning teachers to have insights and approaches to offer, but whether this promise has been realised is an important question for the relationship between psychology and education.

Psychology students may learn as part of their undergraduate courses about the processes of cognitive development, learning theory, models of memory and thinking and different personality theories, in addition to theories about various childhood emotional, behavioural and intellectual difficulties. But whether these theories are applicable or, if applicable in principle, are presented with a view to their applicability to educational and other practical spheres is often open to doubt. It might be thought that the relationship between psychology and education would be at its best in the field of educational psychology, as one of the applied fields of psychology. But even here there is a tendency for groups to become locked into their own ways and not relate outwards to psychology and education. So it is not uncommon to find that many psychology graduates who have chosen to specialise and train as professional educational psychologists come to see a distance between psychology and education. They come to see themselves as learning how to think and work as local authority psychological service professionals. This is approached as learning practical knowledge and skills, with the tendency to leave theoretical considerations behind. Coming from or via teaching to their professional psychology training, they are similarly keen to leave educational and teaching matters behind as they become involved in their chosen professional work. To complicate the matter, there has been a considerable gap between educational psychology as practised by professionally trained applied psychologists, and as a research-teaching activity practised by psychologists and sometimes educationalists in university departments of education. These differences will be explored in more detail in chapter 4, but they are mentioned now because they underline divisions in the institutional relationship between psychology and education.

The uncertain nature of psychology and implications for applied psychology

Study of such diverse fields and topics, from physiological to group and organisational processes, comes under the broad umbrella of psychology. Approaches to inquiry and theory include different and sometimes contradictory assumptions about what is involved in seeking psychological knowledge and understanding. These range from the natural science model – what has been called positivist science, with its assumptions of mechanism,

atomism, cause and effect – to the organismic-structural model with assumptions of holism and structures which account for functions. It includes
hermeneutic-interpretative models which assume the inherent ambiguity of
human communication and use interpretations to identify and clarify meanings; and critical or emancipatory models which aim to expose discriminatory and oppressive conditions with a view to supporting and enabling
emancipation.

These diverse approaches do not differ in ways that are simply resolvable
by reference to criticism and determining evidence. Their differences are at
the more basic level of the aims of the inquiry and theoretical construction.
This involves assumptions about the subject matter of the inquiry, what can
be known and what counts as evidence. It leaves one looking for ways of
choosing between these approaches or synthesising them, seeking some coherence or foundation from which to work. These complex matters are central and crucial to the nature of psychology and inevitably bear on applying
or using psychology. Within each broad model or approach in psychology
there are implicit and often quite explicit applications and uses. In some
approaches the application is built into the model, something which depends on the aims of the model and the kind of values which are associated
with its aims. What has been called the emancipatory approach overtly
endorses certain social values, while the mechanistic natural-science model
claims to be value neutral. The neutrality claim does not mean that values
are unimportant. It means rather that social and political values like seeking
equality or liberty are not part of the aims. The values of impartiality,
openness and respect for the integrity and implications of evidence are central to the aims in this tradition.

Different approaches can be taken to this diversity of models in psychology. One is to ignore the basic differences between the models and draw on
whatever applications and uses can be derived from them. This is a kind of
eclecticism which mixes procedures and techniques from different theoretical sources according to the needs of the situation. It has the advantage of
flexibility, adopting what might work, but overlooks the incompatibility
between the models and uncertainties about the appropriateness of different
techniques. The other approach is to adopt one particular model, which may
not be as restrictive as it appears, as some models have great diversity within
them. But it does still limit the range of applications and uses compared to
the eclectic approach. This analysis of the uncertain nature of psychology,
and the implications for its relationship with education, will be discussed
further in chapter 4.

The possibility of a constructive relationship between psychology and education

Despite the uncertainties discussed above about psychology and its applications, it will be argued that this state of affairs does not undermine the benefits

of the relationship between education and psychology. One reason for this is that uncertainties and diversities of assumption and approach are not confined to psychology. In education itself there is a similar diversity of approaches. And, as will be discussed more fully in the next chapter, these internal differences within both psychology and education are linked and related to each other. So, an awareness of these diversities and incompatibilities is important for understanding how psychology and education interact. And, as mentioned above, the mutuality of the relationship between psychology and education needs to be recognised, especially from the side of psychology. This means not just that education can provide psychology with stimulating questions and problems, but also that psychology in its contact with education has to relate to and co-ordinate itself with other allied disciplines. This interchange and collaboration across disciplinary boundaries assists psychologists to develop a more balanced perspective on the relative contribution of their field.

Outline of chapter contents

The book is organised into five chapters. After the introduction in this chapter, I will look at education as the context for a relationship between psychology and education in chapter 2. In this chapter I examine education as a field of practice which requires practical theory. I also examine whether there are grounds for seeking a scientific basis for education. I argue that multiple values are intrinsic to education and its aims and that different educational theories are interconnected. I also show that different educational theories assume different models of the learner and learning. I conclude that education cannot operate without assumptions of a psychological nature. In chapter 3, I will look at psychology in the context of the relationship between education and psychology. Psychology is examined as a study of humanity and as a science. In this chapter I examine the divided nature of psychology, its different models and proposals for maintaining its breadth and coherence. I conclude the chapter with a case for supporting a co-existence of different kinds of psychology and for a conception which connects it to biological and social levels of analysis. I also argue for a dual conception which includes and connects theoretical and applied aspects, with the theoretical as the precondition for the applied and practitioner aspects. This leads into chapter 4 in which I will examine the special relationship between psychology and education in the field of educational psychology. A historical perspective is used to provide the background to the contemporary difficulties in the research-teaching and practitioner branches of educational psychology. The chapter explores the tensions in the scientist-practitioner role and the pressures from the education service on educational psychologists to have technical knowledge to meet service needs and problems when there is no adequately developed theoretical and technical base.

This chapter concludes with a call for greater recognition of the similarities between practitioner and academic educational psychologists, especially in their work with teachers, and for making psychology applicable to teachers' practical needs. In the final chapter I will summarise the key points from each of chapters two, three and four. I also draw on two social analyses which are relevant to the relationship between psychology and education. The main themes of the book are then pulled together in the final sections, namely: psychology and education as connective specialisms; education as involving multiple values which require balancing, confronting ideological dilemmas and impurity; the diverse natures of education and psychology arising from epistemological uncertainty; and the value of epistemological co-existence.

2 Education as theory and practice

Does it need a scientific basis?

we are likely to look back on the current list of prescriptions to cure education's ills as irrelevant because they, too, fail to identify the real cause of the problem ... The trouble is not caused by the usual suspects ... it stems from a fundamentally incoherent conception of education.

Egan (1997, p. 2)

Introduction

Education is often taken to mean schooling, as school is the main formal educational institution in society. This can lead to a situation where education thinking and practice becomes the professional and specialist preserve of school teachers. But of course education is broader than schooling and involves parents, policy makers, religious organisations and many other interested parties. Education is an intensely personal as well as a social and political matter. Like matters of national defence which are too important to be left to the armed services, education is too central to the well-being of individuals, institutions and the state to be left solely to professional educators. With such a broadly based stake and involvement in educational outcomes we would expect differing and conflicting ideas about educational aims and methods. Authoritative perspectives about the nature of education might be expected from professionals who specialise in a field. But in the case of teachers and teaching, the daily personal demands of the work and the tight professional conditions of work lead many teachers to adopt a 'practicality ethic' in their approach to educational thinking and research (Doyle and Ponder, 1977).

As for policy makers in schools and in local and central government, they find themselves confronting questions about basic educational aims and methods, but even here the context is one of pressing practical policy review and developments. For example, the design of the UK National Curriculum in the late 1980s involved little basic questioning and analysis about the nature, aims and methods implicit in such a curriculum (White, 1993). It is academic educationalists who have the time and opportunity to delve into and specialise in ideas and assumptions about the nature of education. But this calls for analysis and theorising of an ethical, philosophical, social, psychological and historical nature. The implication is that such thinking and theorising requires interconnections between different academic special-isms. This chapter is concerned with various questions and issues about the nature of thinking and theory in education and the origins of this theory, especially in relation to psychological ideas. These are complex matters relating to the content of theories and the functions of education theories. As would be expected, there are major differences of view over these matters which need to be addressed. They bear directly on the relationship between psychology and education, as psychology has been characterised as a founda-tion discipline of education.

This chapter deals with the place of theory in education. I address ques-tions about what an educational theory is and how it compares and contrasts with explanatory theory from the social and psychological sciences. I then consider different kinds of educational theory in terms of basic underlying beliefs and values or ideologies about teaching and learning. These ideolo-gies relate to different perspectives on education; from society's and from the individual person's perspectives, from the perspective of conserving the her-itage and constructing the future, and from active agent and passive object perspectives. I then argue that educational theories require some psychologi-cal position, what are called meta-psychological assumptions. These meta-psychological assumptions are the bridge between psychology and education which is explored in the middle of the chapter. These different ideologies are then examined in the question of whether teaching is an art or an applied science. This leads on to the related question of whether teaching can have a scientific basis which involves a critical discussion of different conceptions of science and its aims. The chapter concludes with an analysis of the rela-tionship between the professional knowledge of teachers and a science of education and teaching.

What is theory in education for?

To get started it will be useful to define broadly some of the key terms in this discussion. The intention is not to begin or end with some precise set of definitions but to clear some of the ground by clarifying what is under consideration. Education will be understood to be about promoting learning and development in the widest sense. This leaves open important questions of what is worth learning and development in which directions. But it makes clear that education will be taken to be a practical goal-directed activity. This has implications for what a theory of education might be about. A theory of education would need to include some notions about the purposes or goals to which the activity would be directed. There are many and varied notions about these. I do not intend to consider them directly at this stage, except to point out that educational goals represent value judgements about what is worthwhile in life, or what is sometimes called conceptions of the good life. This can be seen, for example, by considering the following statement of educational goals:

> to enlarge a child's knowledge, experience and imaginative understanding, and thus his awareness of moral values and capacity for enjoyment, and to enable him to enter the world after formal education is over as an active participant in society and responsible contributor to it.
>
> (Warnock Report, 1978)

A theory of education would need to include ideas and justifications for the goals chosen to be promoted by practical activity. This interpretation of educational theory focuses on both the ends and means of education as a practical activity and in so doing is about formulating principles of action. In this sense, education theory is about practical knowledge as distinct from theoretical knowledge, even if this practical knowledge is influenced by theoretical knowledge. This distinction between theoretical and practical knowledge is important as it bears on the nature of educational theory and knowledge. Theoretical knowledge is often taken, as in the natural sciences, to consist of systems of beliefs and hypotheses which are confirmed by empirical evidence. It functions as an explanation of phenomena and enables prediction. By contrast, practical knowledge, consisting of principles of action, functions to guide practice.

It can be and has been argued (O'Connor, 1957) that using the term 'theory' in educational contexts is a mere courtesy, as it is only justified when applying theoretical knowledge from social sciences like psychology and sociology. This restrictive usage of theory is intended to exclude accounts which are not causal in the sense that the sciences are causal. This position has been criticised by those who wish to see theory in education include not just explanations of human activities, but also justifications of beliefs and values which relate to the educational endeavour (Hirst, 1983). The two perspectives are similar in seeing theory in education as concerned with causes, but they differ over whether theory is also concerned with reasons and justifications for values and beliefs.

Contributory or foundation disciplines?

There is another way of looking at this critical matter which bears directly on the relationship between psychology and education, and that is whether educational theory is primarily about principles for educational practice. Theory in education can be about educational practices and processes treated as phenomena, with no direct focus on guiding practices. This difference can be characterised in terms of whether theories are *for education* or *of education*. It might be argued, however, that theories of education can then be used to inform practical principles and therefore theories for education. In other words, theories of education and theories for education are linked. This might be so, and it is something we will return to later; but there is still the question of whether theory in education derives from within education and has an educational origin, or whether it is put together from theories which derive from its contributory disciplines.

Hirst (1983) has raised serious doubts about whether and how the contributory disciplines are related to the needed practical principles in education. The contributory disciplines have their distinct agendas and concepts and ask their own distinctive questions. Conclusions reached in these fields, however focused they may be on educational practices, are not themselves practical principles. They may be generalisations about the relationship between variables which bear on the means and ends of education, but they simply cannot determine practice. What is being criticised here is the often assumed *foundation model* of the relationship between contributory disciplines and education. This model assumes that the contributory disciplines, in keeping with their representation as foundation disciplines, provide the basis for principles of practice which then justify and guide educational practice. Hirst's argument, and it is one which is in tune with current developments in educational circles, is that the very character of the disciplines is inadequate as a basis for practical principles. It is not just that these disciplines are too undeveloped and contain basic theoretical differences. Such considerations are relevant to whether it is practical for the foundation model to provide the basis for principles of practice. But they do not connect with the key and radical case against the foundation model. The argument is that practical principles need to be derived from practice itself, drawing on the rules and principles which good practice embodies. They need to derive from the knowledge and principles which practitioners use themselves.

However, it has been argued as a counter that theory in education cannot derive simply from good practice, as this prejudges what is to count as good in educational practice. If rules and principles of practice are to be derived from this source, then there is a need for some criteria of which practice to derive principles from. This calls for some value judgements about the aims of education, which brings us back to general questions about ideals and values. This argument leads to the view that deriving principles of practice cannot be separated from ethical and philosophical considerations. It indicates that education theory, taken as principles of practice, even if they cannot be derived from theoretical knowledge in the social sciences, does need to draw on philosophical positions. This may be where there is a difference between the contributory disciplines of psychology and sociology, as social sciences, on one hand, and philosophy on the other.

I have supported the view that to derive practical principles from, and base them on, theoretical knowledge in the social sciences is to make a false assumption about rational action. The false assumption is that rational action necessarily depends on prior reflection and premeditation. However, knowing how to do something does not necessarily require knowing the relevant underlying theoretical principles. This applies in many craft or technical areas of activity including teaching. For example, bridges were built and metals were made for centuries without the benefit of the underlying scientific, mechanical and chemical principles. Developments were made through trial and error, and people learned these skills without having to draw on or justify them in terms of scientific theoretical knowledge. This shows that there is a difference between practical know-how, techniques or craft skills and knowledge, and the application of scientific knowledge to practical tasks and matters. This point has very important implications for education and teaching. Formerly, people taught and others learned without having any theoretical knowledge of the underlying processes of teaching and learning. However, this does not mean that theoretical principles from disciplines like psychology do not have a significant role in education theory. They can contribute indirectly, rather than act as the rational foundations for education theory or sources of practical principles. Their role, from this perspective, is one of providing a means of criticising and extending practical principles. Where forms of practice may be derived from theoretical knowledge and principles, these have to be treated as a resource for trialing, developing and evaluating practices and then adapting them. Theoretical knowledge derived from outside a practical domain like education and teaching is not a direct foundation or sole source of practical principles.

Curriculum studies as a source of educational theory

Curriculum studies has become an influential area of education study and has been promoted as dealing directly with education's need for practical theory. It has become a specialism within education studies with an interest in different kinds of curriculum theories (Lawton, 1989). The significance of the curriculum studies approach to educational theory is that it emerged partly to overcome the difficulties of basing education theory on the foundation disciplines. This approach has offered the prospect of dealing with educational theory in an interdisciplinary way. As mentioned above, approaching education questions and theory from particular discipline perspectives has run the risk of considering only partial and limited aspects of educational problems and issues. It has also let the explanatory agendas of these disciplines dominate theoretical needs in education (Kelly, 1989). Kelly puts this in terms of the contributory disciplines being descriptive rather than prescriptive: the latter is the concern of education theory.

As many educationalists have pointed out, when social scientists have attempted to be prescriptive they have overstepped their brief and the limits of their discipline. What is needed, therefore, from the curriculum studies perspective, is studies leading to theory which go beyond the descriptive-explanatory level to the practical-prescriptive one without losing the rigour and methodology exemplified in the contributory disciplines. The curriculum studies perspective is also one which recognises that too much educational practice has been based on intuition and hunch. It is one which sees the need for theory in education but in its wider sense. It is strongly opposed to the strand of opinion found amongst some educational practitioners which claims that they neither have nor need any theory. The aim is to bridge the theory–practice gap, but in a different way from the direct use of the contributory disciplines.

There are different aspects to curriculum studies which reflect different value orientations and different foci of interest. There has been much interest in the procedures of curriculum planning, development, evaluation and innovation. But there has also been an interest in more fundamental questions about the assumptions, concepts and values underlying practical principles. This has called for the justification of the values implicit in educational prescriptions. However, much of the thinking in curriculum studies has been based round the notion of a curriculum. This is understandable as this concept has formed the centrepiece of a field which is interested in the planning of teaching, but there are continuing uncertainties about what is included in an education or curriculum theory. This point links back to the previous discussion of the nature of theory in education. One of the reasons for uncertainty about what characterises an educational theory is that educationalists have tended to use and rely on theory from the contributory disciplines. This may be because theory from psychology or sociology may be seen to be 'real' theory and to be more dependable than anything which is derived from within education and by educationalists. Egan (1983), for example, has been very critical of the dearth of educational theory, and the excessive and damaging reliance by educationalists on theory from disciplines like psychology. His position reflects some of the arguments outlined above about the differences and gap between the practical theory needed by education and the theoretical knowledge provided by the contributory disciplines in the social sciences. His central point is that guidance for educational practice can only come from educational theory, and that theoretical knowledge from the contributory disciplines has no value outside an educational theory. It is on this basis that a strong case can be made for educationalists' asserting their own identity and resisting the dominance of the contributory disciplines.

What is interesting about Egan's position is that he tries to outline not only the functions of an educational theory as prescriptive, but what an educational theory would include in more specific terms. Such a theory, according to his analysis, would provide answers to questions about what should be taught, how it should be taught, when it should be taught and what the end-product or outcome would be like. In other words, an education theory would lead to a programme or curriculum which prescribes the 'what', 'how' and 'when' of teaching: a programme which could be expected realistically to lead to certain learner outcomes. This means that the agenda for educational theory is to find the best ways of attaining valued outcomes. It is not, like psychological theory, about phenomena and their explanation or interpretation. That is not to say, according to Egan, that educational prescriptions do not take account of what is either logically or empirically possible. But from an educational perspective, the constraints which need to be taken into account should be those which are dependable and not those which might be alterable. Egan bases much of his criticism of the contribution of psychology to education on the uncertainties about what regularities and constraints are provided by the discipline.

It might be wondered whether the prescriptive nature of educational theory implies that there is no empirical base and no way of testing such a theory. This does not follow, however, as practical principles constitute a speculation that undertaking certain actions leads to certain outcomes. This might lead to some questions about whether to call this 'theory' at all. But that would be to over-restrict the use of the term 'theory' to theoretical knowledge, and ignore the fact that educational theory can itself be subject to some empirical testing and falsification. Its empirical content is in the assertion that if you teach certain things in certain ways then you will produce a person with certain characteristics. An educational theory can be seen, therefore, as presenting certain predictions about outcomes. So if a theory leads to predictions of certain learning outcomes which are not fulfilled, then this could be taken, other things being equal, to cast doubt on the theory and its associated curriculum programme. This feature of educational theories, according to Egan's formulation, does not imply that they explain learning in the sense in which a psychological theory might claim to. Yet, by claiming that certain means lead to certain ends, educational theories are making some causal claims, although that is not their main function. It is implicit in the nature of practical principles that they assume links between means and ends. Educational theories are also more speculative than the explanatory theories of a discipline like psychology. This follows from the difficulties of empirically testing whether the ends resulted from the means. Educational programmes are complex and take place over a long period. This complicates the relationship between means and ends, with short-term ends becoming means to subsequent ends. The most general outcomes may also be difficult to test empirically because of their breadth and complexity.

The relevant issue in this discussion is that if a discipline like psychology is going to have significance for educational theory and practice, then well-formulated educational theories are essential. For knowledge about constraints and regularities, whether logical or empirical, only becomes useful when it is incorporated into an educational theory. A similar position, though expressed in somewhat different terms, was presented many years ago by Dewey (1929). Dewey was then concerned with the question of whether there was or could be a science of education. A fuller exposition of Dewey's ideas will be discussed later. The present discussion will centre on his views about the relation between empirically based facts and regularities and their educational significance. Dewey took a more positive view than Egan about the potential value of regularities and constraints identified in the social sciences for education. But like Egan's, his concern was with the dominance of educational practice and thinking by scientific findings. Dewey was aware of the pressure to invoke scientific disciplines like psychology in order to lend prestige and credibility to educational practices. He saw this as a distorting and negative influence on educational interests and teaching practices. Scientific research could not be converted, according to him, into immediate rules of action because of the complexity of factors involved in educational practice. Dewey, like Egan, is trying to assert the importance of educational criteria and considerations in judging the value of scientific results. Regularities derived from psychology, for example, need to be judged by those who are engaged in educational practices. They should not be considered, he argues, as yielding rules of action directly – to use his phrase – or practical principles – to use the phrase introduced above. Their value or potential value, which Dewey did not doubt, was to draw the attention of educators, in both observation and reflection to conditions and relationships which they might otherwise overlook. To quote Dewey (1929, p. 30): 'If we retain the word "rule" at all, we must say that scientific results furnish a rule for the conduct of observations and inquiries, not for overt action.'

Dewey's emphasis here was not on the nature and formulation of educational or curriculum theory, but on protecting the role and independence of educators. From this perspective, the contributory disciplines should not determine or dominate educational thinking or practice. Their role is to enable educators to see and think more clearly and deeply about whatever is being done. The chief point for Dewey was that the influence of outside fields, however scientific and supposedly authoritative their sources, was to be judged by and operate through educators in relation to educational aims and schemes.

Different kinds of educational theory

Planning in education and teaching, sometimes called curriculum planning, involves putting some theory into operation, as Lawton (1989) has pointed out. This is a critical point, as it is through the planning process that educational theory connects with educational practice. However, explicit and systematic theorising has not traditionally been highly valued amongst even well-regarded teachers. Teachers often see themselves as practical people who are concerned with the immediate and pressing matters which arise in schools. This has been called their 'practicality ethic' (Doyle and Ponder, 1977). This suspicion of education theory is understandable even if it weakens teaching and education. The working conditions in schools are such that teachers have to confront many, varied and pressing matters which require instant decisions and actions. The occupational climate is not one which encourages in-depth analysis and reflection. Teachers also know that effective teaching is about skill, technique and procedural knowledge, which are learned from experience and practice. It does not have to wait for derivation from more abstract and fundamental theory. As several educational theorists have pointed out (Hirst, 1983; Lawton, 1989) practice has and can precede theory in education, as it has and does in many other practical fields, such as engineering and medicine. However, recognising this precedence is consistent with the position that theory can and does have an important part in guiding practices. Nor does it deny that any practice presupposes some assumptions and values. The point is that the links between fundamental educational theory and educational practices are two-way and rather tenuous. The links are tenuous because of the conflicting nature of fundamental educational theorising. Much of what passes as educational theory relates to basic beliefs, assumptions and values over which there is much scope for disagreement. Engaging in theoretical debates and attempted resolutions of differences is understandably distant from the pressing concerns of teachers with immediate practical teaching demands. The situation is one in which the ideological debates centring on the ends and means of education can and do become too easily disconnected from the real-world concerns of practical educators.

There have been several attempts to characterise the different kinds or types of beliefs, assumptions and values in fundamental theorising about education. Some attempts refer to differences in theories and some to differences in philosophies or ideologies. Others refer to differences in assumptions about designing the curriculum. Whatever terms are used, the differences can be understood to refer to the ends and means of education: differences in values, beliefs and assumptions about society and the individual. Skilbeck (1984) has identified four distinct briefs for curriculum design. These involve curriculum:

1   as a structure of forms and fields of knowledge,
2   as a chart or map of the culture,
3   as a pattern of learning activities and
4   as a learning technology.

When approached as a *structure of forms and fields of knowledge*, the curriculum is considered as a corpus of knowledge which is to be assimilated by learners through a process of transmission from teachers. Though criticised by more progressive educationalists as irrelevant to modern technological and science-based societies, this traditionalist approach has been reaffirmed and renewed, as Skilbeck has argued. The main function of education in this approach is to foster the growth of the mind in a variety of distinct knowledge areas. By contrast, when approached as a *chart or map of the culture*, the curriculum is considered as a means of socially inducting people into the norms, values and belief systems of a people. Induction can be construed as a process of joining a pre-established culture, but also of projecting as yet unrealised values and aims into the future. Cultural induction is not construed simply as a transmission process, but is an active two-way collaborative process between teachers and learners. In this approach, selections from the culture have to be made from a number of sub-cultural systems, if a viable curriculum design is to be achieved. However, as in the more knowledge-focused approach, there are as many issues about analysing and schematising cultural systems as there are about knowledge systems.

When approached as a *pattern of learning activities*, the curriculum is considered in terms of experiences and activities rather than knowledge and facts to be acquired. The focus in this approach is on the learner's experience and needs, treating the learner as the active subject whose growth and development is the main function of education. This expresses a progressive vision which opposes the treatment of the learner as an object to be pushed, filled or acted upon. Identified as the approach which places value on ceding power to the learner, this learner-centred approach has defined itself mainly in terms of opposing the impositions of others, whether as prescribed cognitive curriculum sequences or as patterns of social norms. Skilbeck's fourth kind of curriculum design, *curriculum as a learning technology*, focuses less on the basis of what is worth learning or the control and selection of the content than on the appropriate means or techniques of promoting learning. Underlying this approach is the application of a rationalist problem-solving framework which has proved successful in other spheres of activity, such as industry. It is characterised by the adoption of a single model and method across the diversity of kinds of learning and learning areas. And its key method is to prescribe that intended learning outcomes be defined in specific measurable terms. Once learning objectives are defined, then the means of achieving these learner outcomes can be selected by empirical trial and error methods. It is an approach which is associated with training prespecified skills and has evoked both considerable criticism and support over its relevance to education.

In contrast to Skilbeck's four curriculum approaches, Lawton (1989) describes three basic educational ideologies: classical humanism, progressivism and reconstructionism. *Classical humanism* concentrates on the cultural heritage which education is to promote and reproduce. In value terms, classical humanism is conservative of what is good in literature, music and history. It is a broad set of values and beliefs which have been associated with the ruling classes or an elite whose function was seen to be guardians of what was good in cultural heritage. As an ideology it can be traced in various forms back to the times of Plato in the fourth century BC. By contrast *progressivism* can be traced back only a few hundred years to the growth of Enlightenment ideas in the eighteenth century. Progressivism represents a romantic rejection of traditional values and practices. As Lawton (1989, p. 5) puts it: 'The transmission of cultural heritage is abandoned in favour of the goal of the child discovering for himself and following his own impulses.'

Progressive values and ideas have been given concrete expression by educationalists such as Froebel and A.S. Neill. These have taken different forms, but where there is a planned curriculum it would be based on experiences and topics chosen by the learner, with discovery learning being the dominant teaching method. The third educational ideology, *reconstructionism*, has been portrayed by Lawton (1989) as the synthesis of the thesis of classical humanism and the antithesis of progressivism. Where classical humanism is knowledge-centred and progressivism is learner-centred, reconstructionism is society-centred. Developed by and associated with the US educationalist John Dewey, it is an ideology which aims to improve society and to promote individual growth. It tries to combine the active individualism of progressivism with the value placed on knowledge by classical humanism.

There are other ways of characterising the range of differing fundamental educational values and assumptions. Tanner and Tanner (1980), for example, distinguish between the *conservative*, the *progressive* and the *romantic* vision. The *conservative vision*, according to Tanner and Tanner, sees the curriculum as concentrating on the cultural inheritance and preserving the best from the past. The emphasis is on cultivating the intellect and this is best done through traditional studies. The Tanners' scheme is more refined than those discussed above in distinguishing between versions of these broad positions. Within the conservative position can be distinguished the *perennialist* view, which focuses on academic excellence in terms of cultivating humanity's rational powers through the study of the liberal arts and the great books in the Western tradition. The Tanners contrast this commitment to the perennial truths with a conservative vision which sees the cultural heritage being directed to contemporary needs through study of certain essential subjects, what they call *essentialism*. This is a more modern version of the conservative position which opposes a curriculum focus on personal and social needs rather than intellectual development. It is one which includes a range of subject disciplines, including science, as essential, but excludes subjects like vocational studies. The continuing influence of these conservative values and assumptions has been evident in the resurgence of the 'back to basics' moves in the UK and the USA since the 1970s, and in the development of the subject-based National Curriculum in the UK. What is interesting about this renewed interest, as the Tanners have remarked, is that some version of essentialism comes to be resurrected during periods of economic retrenchment and when conservative social influences become more dominant. Whatever the precise relationship between social and economic factors and interest in different educational values, these historical trends can be interpreted as showing that educational theory reflects and is shaped by wider factors and process. This also applies to the psychological assumptions about learning and learners built into these theories. This is an important point, relevant to the nature of psychology and its relationship to education, that will be discussed in more detail in chapter 3.

The *progressive vision*, according to the Tanners, can be identified in two main versions, one of which they call *experimentalism* and the other *reconstructionism*. Experimentalism, which is associated with John Dewey, represents an American position which reflects the growth of democratic ideas and a

Table 1 A typology of educational models

Skilbeck's curriculum models	Lawton's educational ideologies	Tanners' educational visions
structure of fields of knowledge	classical humanism	conservative – perennialist – essentialist
chart of culture	reconstructionism	progressivism – experimentalism – reconstructionism
pattern of learning activities	progressivism	Romanticism – romantic naturalism – existentialism
learning technology		

commitment to the testing of ideas through experience. It expresses the Enlightenment reaction to fixed traditional ideas and dogmas and the espousal of tentativeness and open-mindedness. Science, in its widest sense as a method of rational inquiry which is responsive to experience, is seen as providing the model for social problem-solving and democratic citizenship. Education, in this position, is strongly linked to certain forms of democratic government; educational values and assumptions are geared to wider social and political values. Reconstructionism is taken by the Tanners to express a progressive vision which is more committed to correcting social problems through educational reforms. This reflects a more direct linking between education and social renewal and reconstruction, often associated with social ideals and transformations. Reconstructionism in its more idealistic orientation can be seen to run the risk of prescribing beliefs and values rather than presenting the learner with problem areas in which she or he can find solutions. It is clear that the Tanners represent reconstructionism differently from Lawton, who sees it as a synthesis of progressivism and classical humanism. The difference is that the Tanners see reconstructionism as a version of progressivism, whereas Lawton distances it from progressivism, which he takes to be what the Tanners call Romanticism. This may be simply a question of semantics, but it may also represent the different value positions of those who portray the different educational ideologies. Table 1 shows the similarities and differences between the three typologies of educational models.

In distinguishing between the progressive and romantic visions, the Tanners are differentiating between two approaches which reject conservative classical humanism. The romantic vision is seen to focus more on the natural inclinations and powers of the individual learner than on the individual's part in the wider society. They identify two main strands in this romantic vision, which they call *romantic naturalism* and *existentialism*. Romantic naturalism expresses a thoroughgoing commitment to the individual learner's freedom to develop her or his potential without outside imposition and determination. The unfolding of natural potentials through spontaneity and the expression of felt needs is seen as central to genuine and effective learning. This emphasis on the feelings and interests of the learner has been seen historically as a reaction to authoritarian educational ideas and methods which denied opportunities for genuine learning experiences and achievements. Giving up outside direction of learning requires that the learner be seen as having the innate potential to become knowledgeable, wise and good. These ideas can be traced back to those of Rousseau in the eighteenth century, based on a belief in the child's ability to learn through discovery without outside guidance. They have had a resurgence at different times since then, most recently in the radical views about schooling in the 1960s and 1970s, associated with thinkers like Goodman (1964), Illich (1971), Freire (1973) and others. The existentialist strand of the romantic vision focuses more on the inner search for the meaning of existence and less on individual freedom to develop potential. It is oriented more towards reflections about one's existence and is opposed to what is seen as the cold mechanical rationalism of science. It is romantic in seeing the individual striving for meaning and commitment, unencumbered by outside direction. The Tanners explain that the existentialist version of the romantic vision shares much in common with the more naturalist version when it comes to curriculum matters.

The resurgence of interest in romantic educational ideas and values during certain historical periods can be understood to reflect wider social and economic conditions and trends. A renewed interest in romantic ideas about learner-centred education might represent a reaction to inflexible and authoritarian social practices. These are practices which exclude and deny inner experiences and do not take genuine account of the felt interests and needs of individuals, not only in education but in other areas of social life. Understanding the renewal of interest and the reformulations of basic educational assumptions and values in response to contemporary social and economic conditions is an important theme of this book. It has a strong bearing on the relationship between education and psychology.

Role and nature of ideology

In outlining different educational theories, mention has been made of differing conceptions as ideologies. The term ideology is often used in two distinct ways with different functions and implications. It refers sometimes to the influence of dominant social beliefs and values which distort perceptions of social and other realities. But it can also be used merely to refer to a system of social values and beliefs without any implication of a distorting influence. This is a more descriptive usage referring to different conceptions and values, and is the one I used in the previous section. It is a usage which does not presuppose some prior position about reality against which an ideology is compared to identify whether it is distorting or not. However, educational ideologies, in this descriptive sense, can be assumed to influence educational planning and practice. Alexander (1992) has presented an interesting model of the various influences on primary education practice, on what is called 'good practice'. It is a model which identifies five competing influences – value, pragmatic, conceptual, empirical and political considerations – and it can be applied more widely to other areas in education. *Value* considerations answer the question what practices do I most value and believe in? *Political* ones relate to what practices others approve or disapprove of; *conceptual* ones relate to what is practice and what are its essential elements; *pragmatic* ones relate to which practices work best or do not work for the teacher; and *empirical* ones relate to which practices can be shown to be most effective in promoting learning. This scheme provides a useful way of thinking about educational theory when understood as basic educational beliefs and value. What Alexander found in a large-scale evaluation of primary school practice in Leeds was that although teachers were concerned with practical matters, there were surprisingly few accounts of good practice which were concerned with the pragmatic – what worked – or with the empirical – what could be shown to be effective. For some teachers, ideas of good practice were found to be influenced only by pragmatic, value and political considerations. For others, when reference was made to empirical matters, this was often to dismiss them.

Alexander's approach is also interesting because he recognises that educational practice, whether primary or other, requires some compromise with and the reconciling of competing values, pressures and constraints:

> Primary practice – any educational practice – requires us to come to terms with and reconcile competing values, pressures and constraints. If this is so of practice in general, it must be the case, a fortiori, with practice we wish to define as 'good'. Far from being absolute, therefore, as it has been treated for decades, good primary practice requires us to compromise.
>
> (Alexander, 1992, p. 187)

He makes the distinction between *good practice* and *practice*, a distinction which can be seen to represent a model of the relationship between educational theory and its practice. Practice, in this model, is seen as the outcome of political and pragmatic considerations, of expectations and pressures within the teaching profession and beyond, and of the opportunities and constraints of particular situations. What distinguishes good practice from mere practice, for Alexander, is the value and empirical considerations. Education is centrally about vision and goals, it is about value positions which can be sustained and justified. Good educational practice has therefore to be viewed in terms of values, but not values alone. Values provide a basis for judging educational ends, but not for selecting the means. Only empirical considerations can provide knowledge of effective and viable means relevant to chosen ends and values.

The critical point of Alexander's model, which accords with my discussion above about educational theory, is that good practice depends jointly on value and empirical considerations. This is an important point because it questions current conceptions of the effectiveness of schools, teaching and learning (Hargreaves, 1996; White and Barber, 1997). Effectiveness cannot stand alone without relating it to the specific goals, vision and values which answer the critical question 'effective for what?'. But similarly, good practice cannot be based mainly on educational beliefs and values, on the false assumption that it is sufficient to enact beliefs and values and that evidence about means and consequences can be ignored.

Alexander's position is especially interesting as it focuses on the interplay of different ideas about good educational practice. His approach looks more at the links between theory and practice and less at the differing general theories outlined above. Yet, it is one which recognises the differing and competing values and beliefs about education, which could be elaborated by further thinking about the relationships between the differing educational ideologies discussed above. These different educational ideologies, in the descriptive sense of the word, are usually defined in distinct terms with an emphasis on their coherence and their simple competition with each other. The above account of different kinds of ideologies, whether one identifies two, three or four broad types, fits this pattern of positing either–or positions. However, there is another way of considering educational ideologies, proposed by Billig et al. (1988), which identifies several of their common features as the basis for proposing a different conception of their relationship to each other. Firstly, educational ideologies relate to wider value issues about the relationship between the individual and society, about the freedom of the individual versus the demands of authority and about conserving traditional ways from the past versus seeking change and progressive developments. The second common feature is that ideologies are often presented as opposites and alternatives, with the implication that they are formulated independently of each other.

The view of Billig et al. is that formalised ideologies are positions which are extracted from an argumentative dialogue about education. Each ideology is therefore not a separate self-contained conception but is formulated in response and contradiction to other positions which are part of the same scheme of discourse. The third common feature develops out of the second one: that these different positions, while being part of a dialogue, are not as mutually exclusive of each other as their self-contained and purist formulations might suggest. This dialogic perspective can be applied to the relationships between different educational ideologies. For example, proponents of learner-centred autonomy will rarely propose that learners should be taught nothing and should not acquire some ready-made knowledge, however this is achieved. If proponents wish to pursue a radically purist line, then they find that at some point they have to own up to asserting authority, if only to set the agenda as one of learner autonomy. One finds a similar pattern with proponents of traditional teacher-centred education. Rarely do they see learners as only passively receiving wisdom with no change in the reproduction of traditional knowledge and understanding. Radically purist versions of transmission views also have to own up to believing that when learners receive and carry forward traditional knowledge, they have to actively own their learning. Pure passive acquisition is not compatible with the conservative transmission goal.

The significant point in this analysis is that differing educational ideologies do not compete in a pure either–or way. Educationalists are presented with dilemmas about the balance between different and opposing elements: learner versus teacher-centred approaches and conservative transmission versus progressive construction assumptions. The dilemmas are construed as ideological because they face educationalists with hard choices which relate to the basic issues of freedom, authority and the connection between society and the individual. Billig et al.'s line is to illustrate this position by considering how and what teachers think in practice. They draw on the work of Edwards and Mercer (1987), who explored the thinking and practice of primary school 'progressive' teachers. This study showed that teachers tended to draw on elements of the opposing ideologies, at some times on a discourse of exploratory and experiential learning and at other times on a discourse which attributed failure to innate, personal and social factors, not to inappropriate teaching and learning conditions. There was also evidence that teachers themselves felt a dilemma in being aware of the competition between different educational ideologies and the need to find a resolution and balance between them. Edwards and Mercer also found that what teachers did to cope with this was to engage in a style of teaching in which solutions and answers appeared to be elicited, though on closer examination it could be seen that the required information or conclusions were cued by the teacher. They call this process *cued elicitation*, a term which resembles the allied notion of *guided discovery*. As both terms imply, the processes of teaching and learning involve as much 'putting in' as 'bringing out'. Edwards and Mercer outline a series of communicative devices which teachers use while overtly eliciting answers and solutions from pupils. These include the use of silence to mark non-acceptance of a contribution; side-tracking unwelcome suggestions; introducing 'new' knowledge as if it were already known; and summarising what has been done in a way that reconstructs and alters its meaning. The point which Billig et al. draw from work like this is that there are no clear-cut distinctions to be drawn from alternative educational ideologies. There are dilemmas about how to 'bring out' of learners what is not there to begin with, and how to ensure that they 'discover' what they are meant to. The point is that these oppositions are intrinsic to the educational process, and are interlinked and do not belong to separate and coherent systems of ideas.

This dialogic perspective on differences among educational ideologies is important in questioning the common and often unexamined assumption of radical proponents that positions are pure and coherent. It usually involves a denial that there are any elements of the opposing and criticised position in the favoured position. The dialogic perspective reveals a set of pretences about the nature of the favoured position which are not readily given up because this is seen as conceding to the opposition. This perspective will assume a central role in the argument developed in this book. It can be seen to reflect a view which questions the neat separation of and competition between different educational theories, and their underlying assumptions, beliefs and values about the development of individuals and society. It is a view which recognises differences and oppositions, but casts them within a struggle in which some balance is found, rather than the outright victory of one side and defeat and destruction of the other. This use of the language of battle, conflict and supremacy is relevant to the field of education and educational ideology, considering the continuing political contention in the field. The political debate about education in Great Britain has taken the form of wider political struggles of opposing positions which find it hard to concede some common ground to each other. The value of the dialogic and argumentative framework of analysis is that it places the wider political struggle over education ideologies into a historical perspective. Argumentative dialogue can be seen to move forward through periods of acute differences to periods of finding common ground. In this way the ideological debate can be seen to be more than the assimilation of difficult points to existing values and assumptions and the winning of argumentative points. It also involves some accommodation to empirical factors and some clarification of values.

Psychological assumptions required by ideological positions in education

It has been widely acknowledged that educational ideologies are related to psychological assumptions about the nature of the learner and the learning process. Often comments on this, like those of Lawton (1989), are accompanied by a reference to the relationship between educational ideologies and social and political assumptions. Sometimes this is discussed in the introduction to textbooks on learning theories, for example Bigge (1987). Reference is made to people's 'basic nature' or the image or models of humanity; and usually well-known figures in the history of some school of thought in psychology are quoted, for example:

> Theories of learning (like much else in psychology) rest on the investigator's conception of the nature of man. In other words, every learning theorist is a philosopher, though he may not know it. To put the matter more concretely, psychologists who investigate and theorise about

learning start with some preconceived view of the nature of human motivations.

(Allport, 1961, p. 84)

The critical battles between approaches to psychology . . . in our culture in the next decades, I propose, will be on the battleground of the image of man – that is to say, on the conception of man which underlies the empirical research.

(May, 1967, p. 90)

These remarks express the view that there are sometimes assumptions which are hidden from practitioner teachers and empirical psychologists. These assumptions are often taken as given in different approaches to education, although, as discussed in the second remark and in my previous section, they are at the root of the differences between different approaches. I will refer to these basic assumptions as the *meta-psychological* assumptions associated with educational theories or ideologies. The term 'meta' is used as in 'meta-physical', to refer to frameworks and assumptions which underlie or go beyond, but relate to, the domain of the psychological. Meta-psychological assumptions are therefore basic assumptions about the individual person and his or her functioning, development and relationship to the biological and social aspects of being. The point has also been made that teachers – whether they know it or not, or even like it or not – when thinking and acting in certain ways are reflecting certain basic meta-psychological assumptions about learning and learners. From this it can be concluded that it is better to be aware of such assumptions and to base professional practice on examined assumptions. This type of attitude to the implicit theoretical assumptions of practitioners in education is also found in other areas of social sciences. For example, the economist John Maynard Keynes (1936, p. 54) made similar comments about practical people in the business field: 'Practical men who believe themselves to be quite exempt from intellectual influences are usu-ally the slave of some defunct economist.'

The implication is that ideas matter; even though they work by gradual encroachment and take time to show through, they count.

There are two aspects of the relationship between meta-psychological assumptions and educational theories or ideologies which need to be consid-ered. The first aspect is about whether one starts with educational ideologies or with the psychological assumptions. The second aspect is the direction and nature of their influence on each other. The first aspect, where one starts, is important in revealing professional identity and interests. Educationalists or curriculum theorists would start by outlining different types of ideologies and their associated assumptions, irrespective of their social-science discip-linary links. These assumptions would cross disciplinary boundaries by linking to psychological assumptions about the learner and learning; to philosophical and ethical assumptions about values and knowledge; and to social assumptions about society, its maintenance and development. The educationalist starting point is an important one because of its focus on the integrity of different kinds of assumptions. It does not privilege any one set of assumptions, whether they be sociological, philosophical or psychological, as would the disciplinary specialist. The effect of this starting point is to put disciplinary considerations in the background and educational considerations in the foreground. Another effect of this starting point is that the distinct disciplinary perspective is treated as one amongst several perspectives which require co-ordination to bring about some integral educational ideology. This is a challenge for the disciplinary perspective, which has to be adjusted and co-ordinated with other perspectives within an educational framework. Starting from a disciplinary approach such as educational psychology, on the other hand, tends to put critical assumptions about individual or personal learning and development into focus. This enables in-depth analysis of the different meta-psychological assumptions or models in certain educational ideologies. However, it overlooks those aspects of educational ideologies which are concerned with other key aspects of the educational process, the aspects of values and the connection between education and social maintenance and development.

The second aspect of the relationship between meta-psychological assumptions and educational ideologies concerns the direction and the nature of their influence on each other. This would have been a less significant question before the growth of psychology as a distinct discipline with empirical scientific aspirations at the end of the nineteenth century. Psychological ideas and principles were studied for centuries prior to this relatively recent disciplinary development, though not with the same ideals of developing an authoritative empirical science and its promise and application to various spheres of human endeavour, such as education. They were studied as speculative ideas as part of either the philosophy of mind, educational philosophies or political theories. Meta-psychological assumptions therefore have historical connections to wider thinking about education, politics and philosophy which pre-date the emergence of psychology as a distinct scientific discipline. This historical perspective indicates that educational ideologies, with their long-standing importance, have been a primary influence on meta-psychological assumptions about learners and learning. The view that psychology has been relevant to education only since it became a distinct empirical science is therefore historically parochial as regards the critical role of meta-psychological assumptions at the very core of educational thinking over the centuries.

These points about the relationship between meta-psychological assumptions and educational theories or ideologies will be illustrated with a brief analysis of the connections between different educational ideologies and certain meta-psychological assumptions. The point of this analysis is to illustrate the significance of the two issues raised above: first, the implications of the starting point in the relationship between educational ideologies and meta-psychological assumptions, and secondly, the nature and direction of their influence on each other. It is also worth reminding ourselves that there is no one definitive classification of different types of educational ideologies or kinds of meta-psychological assumptions (see table 2, p. 44). If one starts with different educational ideologies and ideas about the curriculum, such as those of Skilbeck (1984) outlined above, then it is clear that psychological assumptions are not the only key ones involved in educational thinking. For the view of curriculum as a structure of forms and fields of knowledge, associated with the educational ideas of classical humanism, the main emphasis is on preserving and promoting the cultural heritage. The learner's role is secondary to the main social functions of transmission and reproduction of what is best in the heritage. Yet the learner is assumed to have intrinsic mental powers which need training. Education is not the mere transmission of the curriculum to passive learners but the exercising and training of the mind in the process. Similarly, for the view of the curriculum as a chart or map of the culture, education is about inducting people into various areas of a culture. Again, the emphasis in this type of educational theory is on the social question of which selections to make from the culture. This approach requires decisions about the balance between what to preserve from the past and what unrealised values to project into the future. It is associated with what Lawton and the Tanners call a reconstructionist approach to education, with its orientation to progressive social change. It is an approach which also has to make assumptions about the learner: whether the learner is passively inducted into the culture or plays some active part in constructing the culture. Certainly, in Dewey's version of the reconstructionist approach the learner is seen as an active developer of knowledge and values. But like the cultural-heritage approach to educational thinking, the meta-psychological assumptions in the reconstructionist approach are influenced by the primary focus on the social functions of education. However, with the reconstructionist approach the social functions are those of social induction and transformation.

For educational thinking about the curriculum as a pattern of learning activities (Skilbeck's third model), or as being 'progressive child-centred' as others like Lawton have put it, the shift is clearly to the needs and experiences of the individual person. Here the meta-psychological assumptions are central to the educational approach. The reason for this is that unlike the more socially oriented approaches to education, this one sees the primary function of education mainly in terms of promoting the growth and development of the individual. It opposes a view of the learner as an object to be shaped, filled or acted on. Put briefly, it is an educational approach which requires the meta-psychological assumption that the learner is actively and naturally promoting his or her own best development in socially harmonious ways. This kind of assumption can be found in Carl Rogers's descriptions of the fully functioning person, who is able to live fully in and with his or her feelings and reactions (Rogers, 1983). Full use can be made of her or his organic equipment to sense the existential situation; yet this person does recognise that his or her organism may be wiser than his or her awareness. An implication of this description of the fully functioning person is that basic human nature, when functioning freely, is constructive and trust-worthy. So when an individual is freed from defensiveness, and therefore open to a range of his or her own needs and external demands, reactions can be trusted to be 'positive, forward-looking and constructive'. According to Rogers:

> When he [the individual] is fully himself, he cannot help but be realis-tically socialised. We do not need to ask who will control his aggressive impulses, for when he is open to all of his own impulses, his need to be liked by others and his tendency to give affection are as strong as his impulses to strike out and seize for himself.
>
> (Rogers, 1983, p. 292)

It is clear that the meta-psychological assumptions of this humanistic or person-centred approach include inbuilt potentialities, which can be realised through the best of education or personal therapy so as to promote personal renewal and socialisation.

Insofar as psychology is seen to include a humanistic tradition of thought, it could be said that there are strong links between the psychological think-ing and practices in this tradition and a progressive child-centred educa-tional ideology. In the USA, this tradition of thought was seen as an alternative to the forces of behaviourism and psychodynamic thinking and practice (Rogers 1983). Much of humanistic psychology has been associated in this century with psychotherapeutic practice, and it is usually seen as different from educational practice, given the professional and service separation be-tween education and mental health or psychotherapy. A consequence of this separation might be to view this school of psychological thinking and prac-tice as an influence from education. But this would be to overlook the historical origins of person-centred views in philosophical and educational ideas which originated in the Enlightenment and have had a continuing and pervasive influence on social practices. Though there has undoubtedly been a recent influence on education of humanistic psychologies, such as those of Carl Rogers and George Kelly (Salmon, 1995), these psychologies can them-selves be traced back to the Enlightenment. Though humanistic psychology has been further developed and applied this century, its origins lie in En-lightenment philosophical and educational ideas. The relationship between educational and psychological ideas is therefore, from a historical perspec-tive, two-way. So the prevalent view in the twentieth century, that psychol-ogy is used in and applied to education, can too easily overlook the central place of meta-psychological assumptions built into educational ideologies. It can also ignore the historical origins of the basic assumptions of different schools of psychology in educational ideas and ideals.

The focus of educational thinking in Skilbeck's fourth kind of curriculum design, curriculum as technology, is less on what is worth learning than on the appropriate means or techniques for promoting learning. Underlying this approach is the application of a rational problem-solving framework which has proved successful in other spheres of activity, such as technology in industry and the armed forces. The meta-psychological assumptions are central to this educational approach. The educational focus is on finding specific and effective techniques to predict and control the educational process in order to achieve specific educational outcomes. This requires the assumption that learners follow identifiable patterns or mechanisms in their learning. It presumes that particular circumstances or conditions of learning inevitably result in certain learning effects or outcomes. The learner is cast in a reactive or passive mode, even when causal processes are internal to the person. A central part of this educational approach is the search for a mechanistic scientific basis from which to produce knowledge in the form of general procedural rules which can be used to enhance learning and its outcomes. Its origins, compared to those of the other educational ideologies discussed above, are fairly recent and strongly influenced by the growth of a mechanistic view of psychological science and its relationship with education over the last century.

This technological view of education arose after psychology had itself become a distinct humane science in the late nineteenth century. Its development can be understood as the outcome of the growth of scientific psychology and its application. There can be no doubt that many of the key figures in the development of behaviourist learning theories, such as Watson and Skinner, were interested in the educational applications of their ideas. From this perspective, the technological approach to education was influenced strongly by psychology. However, there is another view which regards both education (in its technological approach) and psychology (in its mechanistic forms) as expressions of a pervasive cultural mode of operating which gained ascendency in the nineteenth century. This is the systematic rational problem-solving mode, a technical rationality associated with technological practices. The technological approach to education focuses on learning objectives which are set in concrete observable terms. The emphasis is on effective and efficient methods of ensuring specific educational products. Planning works from the specific required products back towards the optimal means of attaining these products. Planning reflects a rational problem-solving stance or framework which began to be applied systematically and increasingly to a whole range of areas of social endeavour, including education, over the last century. As a rational problem-solving stance, the technological approach could be pursued in two ways. One sought practical solutions to problems through trial and error. In the case of education this meant defining the specific objectives of education and then finding the optimal practical means to achieve them. This represents the technological approach to curriculum design, discussed above. The other way of pursuing the same stance sought to increase knowledge about the nature of the problem and use that knowledge to provide solutions. This is found in the mechanistic scientific approach to the study of learning, best exemplified in the technologically driven approach to psychology, the radical behaviourism of Skinner. So, in the alternative perspective, psychology and education are both influenced by the growth of a common and pervasive technological mode of operation in Western societies. This common mode was reflected in both the explanatory orientation of psychology and the prescriptive orientation of education.

Meta-psychological assumptions and their links with educational ideologies

In the previous section, I started with educational approaches and then considered the meta-psychological assumptions required by those approaches. This discussion can be summarised in terms of educational ideologies requiring assumptions about the nature of learning and the learner. But it is also possible to consider the relationship between education and psychology from the other perspective, that of different meta-psychological assumptions. This is an important perspective, particularly for psychologists wishing to use and apply their psychology to education. It is the perspective which can show where different kinds of psychology do and do not fit with different educational ideologies.

Two distinct but related ways of understanding different basic psychological assumptions will be discussed. The first has more direct relevance to learning theories and therefore education, while the second one is more focused on different models of knowing in the human sciences and psychology in particular. The first scheme focuses on the basic moral and actional nature of human beings in their relationships with the environment (table 2). As Bigge (1987) put it, what would children and young people be like if they were left to themselves? This question is about the raw material or potential that carers and nurturers work with. Bigge identifies three possible assumptions about human moral and actional nature. The moral nature can be assumed to be either innately good, innately bad or neutral. Innateness refers to what is unlearned, what is inborn or built in. Assumptions of innate goodness imply that pro-social behaviours are built in and that little or no environmental intervention or nurturing is required to implant morally good behaviour. Assumptions of innate badness similarly imply that anti-social behaviours are built in and that major intervention or nurturing is required to correct innate tendencies and to instil moral behaviour. By contrast, assumptions of moral neutrality imply that there is no built-in moral tendency and that moral behaviour reflects intervention and nurturing. In a similar way, the actional nature can be assumed to be either active, passive or interactive. Assumptions of activity imply that underlying characteristics are inborn or built in. Psychological characteristics come from within the

Table 2 The relationship between human moral and actional nature, educational
theories and psychological traditions

Moral nature	Actional nature	Educational theory	Psychological tradition
bad	active	fundamental Christian	
good	active	romantic/ progressive	humanistic
neutral	active	classical humanism	gestalt
neutral	passive	technological	behaviourist
neutral	interactive	progressive	cognitive, constructivist

person; environments are only locations or triggers for their unfolding. Assumptions of passivity or reactivity imply that human characteristics are mainly the product of the environment, caused by outside forces. Assumptions of an interactive actional nature, by contrast, imply that psychological characteristics come from person-environment relationships. Characteristics are the outcome of what the person makes or constructs out of what the environment presents.

Bigge suggests that certain combinations of the different possibilities of learners' actional and moral natures underlie some of the key types of learning theory relevant to education. The *bad moral nature* and *active actional* combination represents a long-standing approach to education associated with the fundamental Christian idea that teaching aims to exercise the mind and to curb anti-social tendencies. Another well-known approach, associated with progressive education, combines assumptions of a *good moral nature* with an *active actional* one. Given these assumptions, teaching can be permissive and rely on an unfolding process of natural potentialities. The other three combinations hold neutral assumptions about moral nature, that is, they assume that people are innately neither inclined to good or bad behaviour, their behaviour reflecting their social experiences. The first of the three combinations is of *neutral moral nature* and *active actional nature*, one which also has a long history in education, associated with classical humanism as discussed above. It is an approach to education, which aims to train built-in mental powers which develop through exercise. The neutral–active combination also underlies the more recent gestalt approach to learning in which mental activity follows organisational principles. Teaching from this perspective is about promoting insightful learning.

The other combinations are historically more recent and relate to developments within the discipline of psychology. The fourth combination is of a *neutral moral nature* with a *passive actional* one. This combination underlies the tradition of behaviourist learning theories of classical and instrumental conditioning. Teaching on this neutral–passive assumption is directed at promoting the acquisition of stimulus–response connections and bringing about environmental changes so as to increase response probabilities. The fifth combination is of a *neutral moral nature* with an *interactive actional* one. This combination underlies a psychological tradition which incorporates the active causal participation of the individual and environment in learning, one which is associated with cognitive, constructivist and field psychologists. Teaching in terms of this neutral–interactive assumption is about assisting learners in their interactions with the environment in a reconstructing process.

From these five combinations of moral and actional natures, it is possible to identify three which link contemporary schools of psychology with different educational ideologies. These are the good–active, the neutral–passive and the neutral–interactive assumptions. The model of a good–active individual links humanistic psychologies, such as Rogers's client-centred and Kelly's personal-construct psychologies, with progressive or learner-centred approaches to education and teaching. The neutral–passive and neutral–interactive models both attribute greater causal influence to the environment than does the good–active model. The neutral–passive model goes the whole way by treating the individual as reactive, and so links behaviourist learning theories and methods with technological or objective-oriented approaches to education and teaching. The neutral–interactive model assumes a causal interplay between environment and individual, and is linked with various cognitive constructionist learning and developmental theories, such as those of Piaget, Bruner and Deci. Some of these psychologies have been linked with learner-centred approaches to education, despite their differences from psychologies based on a good–active model. Their function in relation to education has sometimes been to present learning theories which undermine and counter the assumptions which support objectives or technological approaches to education. However, the neutral–interactive model might be better linked to what the Tanners call the progressive rather than the romantic educational ideology, a distinction which was discussed in a previous section. The progressive ideology involves learner participation in which the active testing of ideas against experience is the basis of knowledge and learning. The interactive assumptions of the neutral–interactive model are more consistent with this than a romantic kind of educational ideology. A romantic educational ideology is more person- or learner-centred in its assumptions about natural inclinations and powers to develop without outside influence.

A second way of understanding psychological assumptions and how they link to educational ideologies is based on different models of knowing in psychology, namely different epistemologies. Different schemes have been proposed, but the one set out in Overton and Reese, 1973, and Overton, 1980 is well rooted in the philosophy of science as applied to psychology. Their analysis is of basic differences in theoretical models, which they take to be general world-views or paradigms, depending on which term is used.

These theoretical models underlie the generation, analysis and interpretation of empirical data, and as such influence both the content and methods of more concrete theories and explanations which have been current in psychology. Overton and Reese, basing their work on previous analyses such as that of Pepper (1943), identify two important theoretical models in psychology, the *mechanistic* and the *organismic*. The basic metaphor in the mechanistic model is the machine, and whether it is the pulley or the computer, the same fundamental categories and assumptions operate. These include the idea that causes are external and operate as chain-like sequences. Complete prediction is possible in principle, given knowledge of the forces and the initial state of the mechanism. When this is applied to psychology, individuals are regarded as *reactive organisms*. Human change, such as takes place in learning, is the result of outside causes. Complex human processes are regarded as reducible to simple elements which are regulated by prior causes. Novelty and qualitative change are reducible to quantitative change. By contrast, the organismic model is based on the metaphor of the living organism, in which the whole is more than the sum of its parts and therefore gives meaning to its parts. The whole is seen as being in continuous change from one state to another and in which purposes or functions are basic explanatory categories. A fully quantifiable and predictive world is not compatible with this theoretical model. Applying this to psychology, individuals are regarded as active organisms who are inherently and internally active, and so do not require external causes in order to change. Humans are regarded as organised wholes whose parts derive meaning and function from the whole. Behaviour comes to be understood, therefore, in terms of means–ends or structure–function relationships. The basic causes are purposive and change is given, though prior causes can inhibit or facilitate change. Change can be qualitatively different and not be reduced to previous forms.

The significance of the key distinction between the mechanistic and organismic models is that they are rival and incompatible approaches to psychology and therefore to the nature of learning and development. Mechanistic psychologies include the behaviourism of classical and instrumental learning theory, the social and cognitive learning theories and information-processing accounts. Despite their differences at more concrete theoretical levels, this family of theories shares common assumptions about the basic nature of human behaviour and what it is to know about human behaviour. Phenomena are reduced to their elements, whether stimuli and responses or bits of information. Explanations are sought in terms of antecedent and consequent factors, and change arises from accidental factors which could have turned out otherwise. Causal factors are identified as independent of each other and causation works from causes to effects. Organismic psychologies include those of structuralists like Piaget, Kelly, Allport and Kohlberg, and some humanistic, gestalt, ecological and ego-psychoanalytic psychologies, such as those of Erikson and Bronfenbrenner. Despite their differences, these psychologies can be seen to share assumptions about the significance of the

whole for understanding the parts, explaining behaviour in terms of underlying structures while relegating causal explanations to understanding the
rate of change and deviations in behaviour. Change is understood in terms of
the order of underlying organisational change and the introduction of qualitatively new characteristics. Causes and effects are treated as inseparable,
each affecting the other in reciprocal interaction.

Whether these rival general approaches, as conceptualised by Overton
and Reese, can be compared and evaluated against each other is a central
question about the scientific nature of psychology and its potential for
progressive development as an explanatory endeavour. But the issue will not
be considered further in this section, as we are focusing on how different
psychologies relate to different educational ideologies. I will return to it in
the next chapter. From the above brief account of the mechanistic and
organismic theoretical models, it is evident that there are clear links with
different educational ideologies. The mechanistic model implies that learning is predictably determined by external causes in an additive linear
sequence. This has been a clear influence on what Skilbeck called the technological approach to the curriculum, the approach which aims to prescribe
ways of controlling learning outcomes. But given the range of different
theories which draw on the theoretical assumptions of the mechanistic model,
the influence of psychology in this model on education will be diverse. This
can be illustrated by comparing the application of behaviourist concepts,
principles and methods, such as behavioural objectives (Ainscow and Tweddle,
1978) with that of cognitive social learning theory, such as vicarious learning and modelling (Bandura, 1977); or information-processing ideas, such
as self-instruction and strategy use (Pressley, Harris and Marks, 1992). The
more cognitively oriented theories are sometimes assumed to be inconsistent
with the reactive assumptions of the mechanistic model, because they deal
with internal mental processes which can be associated with inherent activity. But this does not follow, because many information-processing theories
treat processing in mechanistic terms of linear causation involving parts
and not the structured whole. There is a clear contrast between information
processing and the structural theories of Piaget, which, while dealing with
mental processes, does so in the organismic terms of structures underlying
function, the connectedness of qualitatively different stages of development
and the inherent activity of the child.

The organismic theoretical model also encompasses a wide range of specific theories, because of the generality of its assumptions. These include the
cognitive developmental theories of Piaget, the personal construct theory of
George Kelly and the ecological theory of Bronfenbrenner. These psychologies,
through their common assumptions, link with educational ideologies which
focus on the pattern of learning activities, as Skilbeck calls them. Education
from this perspective is about learners' experiences and their active part in
the learning process. Such an approach to education has drawn on psychological theories which recognise the significance of the whole, the interrelationship

rather than the separation between the parts, the activity of the person in bringing about change and explanations in terms of ends or functions. The best-known example of this was Piaget's theoretical ideas about learning and development in supporting and developing child-centred primary education practice.

However, this analysis of basic differences in psychology and their links to basic differences in education assumes only two traditional theoretical models in psychology. It overlooks a third way or metaphor of understanding in psychology: the personal metaphor (Sullivan, 1984). This theoretical model has a less clear counterpart in education as its origins are in current philosophical considerations about knowledge and ethics, though it has some links with progressive educational ideologies as described by the Tanners. In particular, it has links with what they call the reconstructionist version of the progressive approach, one which sees education as a means of correcting social problems of disadvantage and oppression through educational reform. What links this educational ideology with the personal model of psychology, as expressed by Sullivan, is the central role of an ethical commitment to emancipation, what is sometimes called a critical perspective.

The personal model assumes that humans are symbol-users in communication with each other. This immediately distinguishes it from the mechanistic and organismic models in that it takes the basic unit of analysis as the *relationship of dialogue*. Opting for this theoretical model is seen by its proponents as an ethical commitment in the sense that it rejects the assumption that human action is just the effect of some cause. Humans play a part in making themselves, and in this connection the choice of a model represents a moral choice about human potential and progress. The point of entry for this model is language in its role in the communication between people in relationships. It is not focused on personal subjectivity, like phenomenological and humanistic psychologies. The task of psychology is seen rather as one of systematic interpretation of human communicativeness. Set in these terms, psychology is seen as reflexive in applying the same principles to those interpreting as to those being interpreted. At the root of the model is the assumption that communicative actions and expressions are ambiguous and therefore in need of interpretation. It is in this sense that psychology takes on what is called a hermeneutic orientation.

This third model or metaphor represents a break from the view of a psychological science which separates the descriptive from the prescriptive. The mechanistic and organismic models discussed above represent a common approach to knowledge which separates the *is* from the *ought*, facts from values. They share a commitment to knowledge and science which is not biased by external values and norms. Yet those supporting the third model draw attention to the ways in which social values and interests affect what is claimed to be value-neutral psychological science. They question whether theory can be disconnected from practice and from what ought to be the case. They start from a fundamentally different entry point: the assumption that our cognition and knowledge arise and are formed by social and historical practices. Epistemology cannot therefore be separated from changing social interests and values. This model is in the Hegelian-Marxist tradition which gives precedence to socio-historical practices in understanding the development of psychological activities. It is opposed to empirical and individual constructivist epistemologies or knowledge bases in the human sciences, including psychological science.

The socio-historical tradition has been underpinned by Habermas (1978), who has challenged the idea that rationality and knowledge are value neutral. His analysis rests on basic 'knowledge-constitutive interests', the underlying interests which are seen to define and shape what counts as knowledge. These interests give rise to different forms of scientific inquiry, each with its own epistemological standards. There are three such interests: the technical, the practical and the emancipatory. The technical interest seeks to achieve mastery and control over nature and is constitutive of the empirical-analytic sciences associated with the mechanistic model discussed above. But humans also live in a culture, and therefore have a practical interest in seeking to understand cultural traditions. These practical interests give rise to the historical-hermeneutic sciences which produce interpretive knowledge. The third, emancipatory, interest derives from basic desires to be free of constraints which interfere with human self-determination and autonomy. This emancipatory interest gives rise to a critical human science, which is seen to enlighten people about the origins of their actions, thus empowering them to think and act in more autonomous ways.

The conception of psychology as a critically interpretative science of the person, as developed by Sullivan (1984) and others, is clearly influenced by the Hegelian-Marxist epistemological tradition which connects the descriptive with the prescriptive. It draws heavily on Habermas's views about different basic interests and values which give rise to different kinds of sciences and epistemologies. But it seems that the practical interest in the meaning of social traditions and personal actions, in Habermas's sense, merges into the emancipatory interest in empowerment and autonomy. So it is unclear whether an interpretive human science can be distinguished from a critically interpretive human science. This is relevant to the point that the third model of psychology, one based on humans as communicators and symbol-users, represents a range of approaches with differing commitments to an emancipatory interest. There is also the question of whether this third model can only be defined in opposition to the dominant model in psychological science, the mechanistic one. This can be seen, for example, in recent attempts to rethink psychology by presenting the third model as a new model by contrast to old models (Smith, Harre and Van Langehove, 1995). These authors present the old model of psychology as being concerned with measurement, prediction and causation, reduction to numbers, atomism, universals, context-freedom and objectivity. By contrast, the new model is presented as being concerned with understanding, meaning, interpretation, language, discourse, holisticity, particularities, cultural context and subjectivity. There is no reference in this set of dichotomies to a critical emancipatory psychology. Yet some psychologists working within this model from the feminist perspective (Nicolson, 1995), would present their contribution as being concerned with emancipatory interests. Like the other two models, it is clear that the third one includes a range of differing theoretical approaches and value orientations.

The influence of this third model can be found in the recently developed critique of progressive and child-centred pedagogy. Reference was made above to the dilemmas associated with a child-centred pedagogy (Billig et al., 1988). These concern the conflicts experienced by child-centred teachers over their commitment to non-interference and to promoting autonomy while having institutional responsibility for learning outcomes. Walkerdine (1981), for example, has illustrated the guilt and helplessness of teachers who espouse such positions. Child-centred approaches have also been interpreted as perpetuating unequal treatment of children from different social backgrounds (Sharp and Green, 1975). This is seen to arise from the uncertain use of concepts like readiness, which are applied more to middle class than to working class pupils. The critique also extends to a denial of the real power relations existing between teacher and learner (Burman, 1994). This position contends that despite the rhetoric of emancipation and empowerment, child-centred approaches are preoccupied with social control and regulation. The child-centred focus on self-regulation is revealed to be a more effective form of coercion than overt control, because it gives the illusion of freedom and choice. These examples illustrate how a critical version of an interpretivist model, the third model outlined above, relates psychology and education.

Teaching: art or applied science?

It goes without saying that teaching and learning are basic to the educational endeavour. But as interrelated processes they can be regarded in different ways depending on the assumed aims of education. The ends of education are generally considered to be about the learning and development of individuals, groups or societies. As I have argued above, the balance between these individual and collective ends of education is critical to the role of education in the maintenance and development of society and the nation state. In this section I will focus on the nature of teaching, which needs to be seen in terms of the balancing of different educational ends.

Giving priority to learning in education implies that teaching is either part of the means to educational ends or a dispensable part of the educational endeavour. Teaching is an intentional activity undertaken by one person towards another. It can be a dispensable part of education if learning is regarded as something which people can do for themselves. This idea represents what some see as the ultimate goal of education; self-regulated autonomous learning with the person able to undertake learning in independent ways. It is also represented in the phrase describing someone as 'self-taught'. The alternative and more conventional conception is that teaching is the intentional promotion and enabling of learning by more knowledgeable and 'expert' others. Teaching in this wider sense relates to various roles in society, including parenting, and not just to teaching in educational institutions such as schools or colleges. The importance of the wider conception of teaching is that it locates school teaching and education within a broader conception of the aims of education. It also directs attention to the similarities and differences between kinds of teaching which take place in different institutional settings and with different age groups. It places teaching within the broader context of learning and development throughout the life-span and across the range of social contexts and institutions.

Those who are responsible for teaching, whether parents, school teachers, lecturers, professional trainers, religious or political leaders, operate with theory in the sense that they deal with ideas and assumptions about education. This is neatly expressed in the following quote from the US educationalist Eisner:

> All teachers, whether they are aware of it or not, use theories in their work. Tacit beliefs about the nature of human intelligence, about the factors which motivate children, and about the conditions that foster learning influence the teacher's actions in the classrooms. These ideas not only influence their actions, they also influence what they attend to in the classrooms: that is, the concepts that are salient in theories concerning pedagogical matters also tend to guide perception.
>
> (Eisner, 1979, p. 156)

Claims about the inevitability of theory in teaching refer only to theory in the general sense of ideas used to make sense of teaching and learning. Theory in this wider sense does not necessarily imply scientific or formal theories of learning based on empirical research. This is an important point as it does not presume that the only acceptable type of theory is the dominant and authoritative mode of theorising: that is, scientific theory. This point also has significance because psychology as an empirical science has been commonly presented as providing *the* authoritative and dependable theory underlying teaching and learning. However, the intention in arguing for a broad notion of theory is not to exclude empirical generalisations as relevant theory for education. It is rather to preserve a place for more general ideas, principles and values in what counts as relevant theory.

Much theory and research in educational psychology has been based on the assumption that teaching implies an achievement of learning. In this sense an activity can be considered as teaching only when learning has occurred. John Dewey underlined this point when he likened the concept of teaching to that of selling (Dewey, 1934). Someone can be said to have sold something if someone else has bought it. Similarly with teaching, someone has taught something if someone else has learned it. However, there is another sense of teaching which does not relate to the achievement of learning. This relates directly to teaching activities guided by intentions to *foster* learning. The difference between these two senses is that between the achievement of learning and the intention to foster learning. As Eisner (1979) argues, neither concept of teaching is wholly correct or wholly false. We have to work with both concepts: teaching as an achievement and as a task concept.

This duality is critical to different approaches to practice and the relationship between psychology and education. There is a well-established practice associated with technological approaches to the curriculum, which defines teaching exclusively in terms of learning achievement. In this sense teaching is about achieving predetermined learning outcomes or objectives. This is the basic assumption underlying behavioural and other instructional psychology approaches to teaching. This is the sense of teaching connected to the concept of training. This notion of teaching as instruction, or training to pre-specified ends, is an important and valid approach if it is not seen as the only framework. There is, unfortunately, a tendency to exclusiveness in adopting frameworks of teaching: teaching only as achieving pre-specified learning outcomes or only as the open-ended task of fostering learning. Both sides are prone to this exclusiveness, finding it hard to encompass the two frameworks and relate them to each other. Those favouring the task framework of teaching criticise the achievement one for being narrow, mechanical and controlling. Such criticisms draw attention to how the technological focus on optimal methods and sequences to achieve pre-set outcomes diminishes and restricts the broader aims of education. The technological approach, which draws on the techniques of applied science, reduces aims to measurable objectives. In so doing, as the critics have pointed out, what cannot be measured can become relegated to the category of what is not worth pursuing (MacDonald Ross, 1975).

Criticisms of the achievement or objectives framework of teaching have been extended to its impact on our conceptions of intentionality and rationality. Eisner (1979), for example, has argued that to require all aims to be specific, to be capable of linguistic formulation and measurable, is narrow and coercive. He reminds us that some aims are held as images and not as propositions and that not everything that is valued can be translated into discourse. There is no justification either, he argues, for requiring that intentions always precede action. Actions sometimes breed intentions; aims sometimes emerge through actions, producing a novel outcome not designed in advance. This argument then raises the question Eisner asks: why is the objectives/achievement framework so dominant? His answer, which echoes that of many other critics, is that the idea of rationality which came to the fore in the nineteenth and twentieth century in Western societies exerts a strong influence on educational thinking. This is the technical rationality with its focus on productivity, standardisation, routine and efficiency. It is a form of rationality in this century which has also influenced psychology and its relationship with education. Psychology has been one of the routes through which this kind of rationality has entered education. But this has not been the only route of influence on education. Both psychology and education develop within wider cultural influences and are likely to be influenced directly by dominant types of rationality.

It is clear from the above discussion that the achievement/objectives framework relates to teaching as an applied science (in the sense of a mechanistic science), while the task framework relates to teaching as an art. When it is said that teaching is an art, what is meant is that it is a practical art or craft (Marland, 1976), not a fine art like painting. Much has been written and said about education as an art or applied science. Those who have promoted ideas about teaching as an art are usually careful to explain what this means, which is especially important at a time when others have looked to science to develop and improve teaching. There is a presumption (not shared by all, however) that to call teaching an art represents it as being in an undeveloped state: in time it will be better understood and improved as it becomes more of an applied science. The risk here is to perpetuate the exclusive dichotomy of teaching as either nothing but an art or nothing but an applied science. In thinking like this, the definitions of art and science can become categorically sealed from each other in a way which might seem to protect favoured positions, but actually devalues them.

When teaching is considered as an art, it is assumed that its complexity prevents it from being reduced to systematic formulae or procedures. Being artistic in this sense means that teaching can be spontaneous, unpredictable, idiosyncratic and creative. What underlies an exclusively artistic approach is a rejection of the aims and methods of science as applied to teaching. Science is characterised in terms which are antithetical to what are considered to be the essentially creative and human aspects of teaching; as mechanical and reductive of individuality to statistical generalities. Eisner (1979) identified four senses in which teaching could be considered an art. The first sense relates to the performance of teaching with such skill and virtuosity that the experience can be described as aesthetic. In this sense teaching can be a form of artistic expression. In the second sense, teaching is an art because it involves judgements that unfold or emerge during the course of action. In the third sense, teaching is an art because it is the outcome of the tension between automaticity and inventiveness. Teaching at its best, in this sense, is not an activity dominated by routines known in advance. This does not imply that there are no routines or prescriptions in teaching, for without them teaching would be hindered. But if that was all there was to teaching, then there would be no inventiveness. In Eisner's fourth sense, teaching is an art because the ends it achieves are often created in the teaching process. In this sense, the ends which teaching seeks are emergent in the teaching process.

However, what is most interesting about Eisner's view of teaching as an art is that it does not deny that teaching also depends on routines and prescriptions. It does recognise that its inventiveness depends on routines and that sometimes there are preconceived ends or objectives in teaching. To quote Eisner (1979, p. 153): 'It is my thesis that teaching is an art guided by educational values, personal needs, and by a variety of beliefs and generalisations that the teacher holds true.'

Eisner in his earlier work had distinguished between two concerns of education, one being to promote mastery of the cultural tools already available, and the other to make possible creative responses which go beyond what is available. From this arose his well-known distinction between instructional and expressive objectives. Instructional objectives are outcome-based objectives in which teaching is directed to preconceived learning outcomes. Expressive objectives, however, do not specify learning outcomes in advance, they describe *educational encounters*, problems to confront and tasks to cope with. Expressive objectives invite personal interpretation and exploration, with diverse outcomes between learners, while being unique and personal to each learner.

The use of the term 'objectives' in Eisner's notion of expressive objectives has been criticised as having too many associations with instructional objectives (Stenhouse, 1975). Stenhouse also pointed out that Eisner linked the applicability of expressive objectives too closely to his own area of interest, that of the arts. However, it is not important that the term 'objectives' evokes negative connotations through its association with behavioural or instructional objectives. What is important is the breadth of Eisner's dual conception of teaching, which the single term 'objectives' could be seen to unify. Eisner's position is also reminiscent of Dewey's earlier view of the relation between science and artistic modes in education and teaching (Dewey, 1929). Dewey believed that there was no opposition between science and art in education, though he recognised the distinction between the modes. He compared education with engineering, considering both as arts in their practice and their focus on originality, and both as incorporating science to further their ends. He was not implying in this comparison that education could draw on science to the same extent that engineering has successfully done. His concern in the 1920s was that scientific approaches to teaching and education might undermine education as an art. This arose, he believed, because teachers tended to want to learn about how to do things: they wanted techniques, or recipes, to use his word. As the comment below illustrates, Dewey's main concern was the false use of science in education, that:

> science is prized for its prestige value rather than as an organ of personal illumination and liberation. It is prized because it is thought to give unquestionable authenticity and authority to specific procedures to be carried out in the school room.
>
> (Dewey, 1929, p. 15)

It is interesting that the above discussion of the relation and compatibility between artistic and scientific modes in education draws on the views of US educationalists. There are fewer UK educationalists who propose similar views. Perhaps the gulf between the artistic and scientific modes of thinking is more pronounced in Britain. C.P. Snow, the originator of the phrase 'the Two Cultures' to describe this gulf, considered it more bridgeable in the USA than in Britain (Snow, 1969). One well-known British educationalist, Stenhouse, though a strong opponent of the universal application of the objectives model of teaching, did identify several distinct processes which implied that education and teaching were in some situations compatible with applying scientific methods. Stenhouse called these four processes training, instruction, initiation and induction. Training was concerned in his scheme with acquiring skills, with success identified through performance capabilities. Instruction was concerned with learning information, with achievement expressed in terms of retention. Initiation, according to Stenhouse, is concerned with becoming familiar with social values and norms and could be expressed in objectives terms. In practice, initiation comes about from living in a community and it is often part of the hidden curriculum of the school.

As discussed above, training and instruction as activities are sometimes denied the status of teaching and what teachers do. This is understandable if teaching is confined to training and instruction. But to pre-empt the definition of teaching and construe it only as induction weakens the breadth and complexity of teaching. For Stenhouse, induction is about introduction into the knowledge systems of the culture. Successful induction leads to understanding, which involves the grasping and the making of judgements and relationships. Knowledge in this scheme is not mere information which can be categorised and retained, but is indeterminate and the raw material for thinking. To quote Stenhouse:

> This is the nature of knowledge – as distinct from information – that it is a structure to sustain creative thought and provide frameworks for judgement. Education as induction into knowledge is successful to the extent that it makes the behavioural outcomes of the student unpredictable.
>
> (Stenhouse, 1975, p. 82)

So, though Stenhouse stresses the inductive aspects of teaching, his concept of teaching is broad enough to find a place for the objectives approach which can draw on applying science. Like others discussed above, he considers that there are difficulties in identifying easy recipes or rules for action as there are too many variables to allow generalisations. Yet, he does consider the psychology of learning, child development, social psychology and sociology of learning, with the logic of the subject and accumulated practical experience as the principal sources of information and grounds for judgement in devising teaching strategies or methods. Stenhouse was aware that psychology had had a poor reception from curriculum workers, which he attributed to misplaced attempts to derive curricula from psychology. The mistake, as he saw it, was to see the classroom as the place to apply research findings, rather than as the place to refute or confirm them. There are similarities in this view to the earlier one expressed by Dewey (1929). Dewey believed that the tendency to convert the results of research studies into teaching rules arose from the pressure for immediate results and instant usefulness. No scientific conclusions, argued Dewey, can be converted into immediate rules of educational art. Yet he maintained that scientific findings were useful and he warned against 'disparaging the value of science in the art of education' (p. 19).

A more recent exposition of the interrelated nature of science and art in teaching is by Gage in his notion of the *scientific basis for the art of teaching* (Gage, 1985). Gage has over many years in the USA promoted a compatibility between teaching as an art and as an activity which can draw usefully on scientific methods and findings. Gage sees teaching as a process which calls for intuition, creativity and improvisation; one that is not confined to rules and formulas, what he calls artistry. He identifies the scientific basis as consisting of statistical relationships between teaching practices and various student outcomes. Making use of these relationships relies, he asserts, on teacher artistry and it allows teachers to base their artistry on something more than unaided insight or raw experience. Gage's position is highly relevant to some of the key arguments in this book. As a proponent of a scientific basis for the art of teaching, Gage has addressed and debated many key points and criticisms. These include questions such as the relationship between the nomothetic nature of much social science (i.e. it involves generalisations) and the idiographic problems of teaching (it involves particular situations); the assumed obviousness of social science research findings, the complexity of interactions between variables in the field; the weak relationships usually found; and the doubts about whether empirical generalisations can even be considered as scientific. Some of these issues, which are about the nature of the social sciences, will be discussed further in the next chapter on psychology, but will be considered here too, because they are central to questions about the nature of theory in education.

Can teaching have a scientific basis?

> Teaching is not, and never will be, an exact science. People don't conform to grand designs. The successful teaching of literacy skills relies on professional decisions made on a day-to-day basis by an individual teacher in a particular classroom.
>
> (Palmer, 1997, p. 4)

One of the key arguments against the applicability of scientific generalisations to the art of teaching is one generally applied to allied activities such as psychotherapy, social work, parenting and so on. It is that these practices are concerned with individuals who are unique in their characteristics and about whom generalisations cannot be made: they are idiographic in nature. It is this idiographic characteristic which prevents these practices from fitting with the generalisations about individuals which are the stock-in-trade of science. Behind these questions are important philosophical issues concerning the nature of the social sciences and whether the same methods and assumptions can be applied to the natural and social sciences: the debate about positivism in the social and psychological sciences. When these issues are considered in education, they take the form of questioning whether educational phenomena are socially constructed, or human-made, in which case they can be changed by social action. However, to recognise this important point does not imply, as Gage has argued, that there is no worthwhile place for empirically based general relationships in education. Relationships may be context specific and can change over time, but this does not mean that all relationships change across context and over time. At least some relationships may remain constant over certain periods of time and across some settings. For this reason, empirical generalisations can have some wider applicability. The point is that people who develop and apply generalisations need to understand the nature of the phenomena they are working with, and what this nature means for the generalisations they develop and then apply.

Gage has also addressed the criticism that the relationships in the social and psychological sciences relevant to education are complicated by interaction effects: i.e. simple two-variable relationships do not operate when a third and further variables are brought into the analysis. His approach is not to deny the presence of interactive effects, but to interpret them as improving knowledge and to recognise that they have not been found to be consistently higher than the primary main effects. Here the point is that attitudes to interactive effects can be either welcoming or critical. Gage's position is to welcome them and continue to find ways of exploring them, in contrast to many critics of a science of education, who conclude that the complexity of the individual phenomena and their causal interactions defies generalisations. A radical idiographic position can dismiss generalisations by easy caricature as timeless absolute laws. A nomothetic position is, however, not necessarily an absolutist one. It can be interpreted instead as one where empirical generalisations are treated as tentative, historically and culturally located and open to change. A key difference between this nomothetic and the radical idiographic position is the status of the particular or individual case. The radical idiographic position asserts the basic difference of each individual case from any other similar case. It is reluctant to recognise that the individual case can retain some difference while still embodying something which is general across cases. It is a position which rejects the assumption that individual cases can be subsumed fully within the generality. This is an assertion of the richness and distinctness of each particular case, a view which could be defended were it not presented as also denying something of the general in the particular. The weakness of the radical idiographic position is that unless we assume something general which links and subsumes particular cases, there is no conceptual basis for comparing particular practices with other cases. The effect is to leave education subject to unquestioned local practices, to pressures from those in powerful positions and to uncritical imitation.

It is possible to acknowledge the richness and complexity of the individual case while still looking for and recognising similarities and differences between individual cases. This position calls for a nomothetic position which does not presume that definitive generalisations are applicable across historical and social settings. It requires a recognition that the search for generalities necessarily involves losing some of the particular richness of the individual case. In this sense, a non-radical idiographic position can be seen to be compatible with a nomothetic interest in generality. This compatibility position recognises the difference between the focuses of an idiographic and a nomothetic approach, but does not lose sight of the interrelatedness of their aims. The nomothetic stance is primarily focused on looking for generalities and so has to accept some loss of the complexity of the individual cases. The idiographic stance explores primarily the individual case and so filters out what is general. Adopting a compatibility position means that the choice of stance becomes a matter of clarifying the research purpose and applying a suitable stance or sequence of stances. Different stances might be chosen in a sequence either starting with the idiographic and then going on to the nomothetic or the other way round. What has to be given up in a compatibility position is a radical perspective which disconnects idiographic and nomothetic stances. It means abandoning the idiographic stance which focuses and fixes solely on the uniqueness of instances of teaching and learning. It also means abandoning a nomothetic stance that fixes on generalisations as timeless and definitive knowledge, while ignoring their contingencies and the loss of complexity and richness of the individual case in the process of abstraction.

Much of the criticism of the notion that teaching has a scientific basis comes from a critique of what is called the positivist paradigm or model of science. Put briefly, this model assumes that the assumptions and methods used in the natural sciences are applicable to the social and psychological sciences, and therefore to educational research. Positivism in education is usually associated with research aims of objectivity, explanation, prediction, control and quantification. This is the classic Enlightenment ideal of authoritative knowledge of an external world with the scientist avoiding the biases and local influences of others. Much of the current scepticism about positivist science, especially when applied to the human and social spheres, derives from doubts about whether positivist methods can escape from the social and historical conditions which affect theorising. This emphasis on the social and historical context has been developed into an influential view of the socio-political nature of science, what is called *social constructionism*

(Handy, 1987). The position denies that the social and psychological sciences discover timeless objective knowledge of some external reality. These sciences are seen instead as social and political constructions reflecting the contemporary concerns and values of professional social scientists and their institutions, often associated with particular ethnic, class and gender interests.

Part of the social constructionist position is that generalisations produced by social scientists become invalid over time, as they apply to particular cultural and historical periods. One argument is that once people hear about these generalisations, they can act to invalidate them, especially if they imply some negative consequences for themselves. However, the problem with this argument is its assumption that this possibility invariably becomes an actuality. Those who treat this possibility as actually happening need to provide evidence, as knowledge of such generalisations is not enough for people to invalidate them through deliberate action. Empirical studies, for example, indicate that even when a sample of people knew about a generalisation relating to their behaviour and were capable of acting or not acting in line with it, they still did act in accordance with it (Gage, 1996). Underlying this critique of the role of generalisations in human affairs is the assumption that people are threatened by the idea that they apply to them as individuals. The problem with a critique based on this assumption is that it is self-contradictory. One generalisation about people feeling threatened and therefore subverting generalisations is used to deny the applicability of generalisations in general. This is the same kind of contradiction found in assertions of the cultural and historical relativity of knowledge: a non-relative position is being used to assert a general relativist position. This particular issue of relativism will be discussed further in the next chapter.

As in the discussion of nomothetic versus idiographic stances in the social and psychological sciences, the positioning of positivism versus social constructionism reflects a radicalism and purism which are unsustainable. The idea of a scientific basis to education and teaching does not have to be forced into radical versions of objectivism on one hand, or subjectivism, whether of a social or individual kind, on the other hand. Hammersley (1993) has argued that a simple characterisation of a quantitative–qualitative research divide is unhelpful because it obscures the variety of research methods and ignores the looseness of the connection between research aims and adopted methods. As Hammersley points out, positivism has been associated with a realist view of knowledge – that there is something to find out or delve into – and has logical connections with quantitative methods. However, there is a tradition of naturalistic qualitative research which also shares realistic assumptions about research aims (Hammersley, 1989). What is at issue is the relationship between the social and the natural influences on knowledge (Phillips, 1996). The radical versions of both social-constructivist and positivist perspectives try to extract pure positions by embracing either relativist or absolutist approaches to the nature of knowledge. By contrast, the position adopted in this book is one which recognises the tensions between these positions, but acknowledges their interconnection. A science of teaching and education cannot be based on simple observation of the 'given' phenomena: it requires conceptual and theoretical constructions by individuals and groups of researchers situated in a social and institutional context. These constructions are open to social and other influences. Similarly, a science of teaching and education cannot just consist of the rich, thick and elaborate interpretations of particular instances of the educational realm. These interpretations are sometimes intended to reveal the underlying nature of the phenomena and at other times to provide knowledge applicable to other situations. Being positive about the prospects of knowing and understanding the processes of teaching, learning and education does not mean searching for absolute knowledge detached from the social and personal situations of its construction. It does not mean that generalisations are sought which tolerate no contingencies or exceptions. If that is what is understood by many critics as positivism, then they may find that positivism in this sense is adopted by neither physical and biological scientists nor philosophers of science (Popper, 1963). Following this line of argument, it is possible to be positive or affirmative about the possibility of a scientific basis for education by avoiding the purism of objectivism or subjectivism, and by recognising the interrelationships between the particular and the general, between what is humanly constructed and what is 'given'.

Another criticism of the scientific basis of teaching and education is that the fruits of this endeavour are obvious in the sense that any thoughtful educationalist could predict the empirical generalisations. Sometimes criticism is expressed in assertions that the social sciences are trivially true when they state what is contained in the meaning of the concepts used (Smedslund, 1995). This critical attitude is important because it reveals something about the nature of any science relevant to education: that it concerns phenomena about which people already have ideas, principles and generalisations. The social sciences tend in general to have as their field of study what is already familiar to people. This is unlike much in the physical and biological sciences whose fields, whether at the planetary, atomic or biochemical levels of analysis, are not easily accessible to everyday experience and analysis. It is also worth noting that the working beliefs and assumptions of teachers and teacher trainers may have been influenced by social and psychological science, and that many may not be fully aware of the wider theoretical origins of their perspectives. These perspectives may also have been formed out of the professional experience and reflective analysis of individuals and groups.

Given the nature of the fields covered in the social sciences it would be expected that some theories and conclusions would contain principles and generalisations which educationalists would consider true by the meaning of the terms. For example, Phillips (1985) has asked, in relation to the research on instructional time and educational attainments, what kind of world would it be if children made greater learning progress the less time they spent on learning? The implication is that our concept of learning includes the idea that it depends on the amount of time applied to it. If the truth of general-isations can be arrived at merely through analysis and explication of the meaning of concepts relating to a field, then there will be some doubt about the value of seeking empirical relationships. But the logical connections between concepts involved in some theoretical and empirical generalisations do not constitute the full account. A scientific approach can go further than asserting generalisations. It explores the degree of the relationships which operate in different conditions and for different domains of activity: for example, the relationship between instructional time and attainments in different domains of learning using different instructional methods. Sec-ondly, logical analysis might reveal implicit relationships in everyday con-cepts of learning – for example, between self-confidence and persistence in learning – but such concepts are general and open-ended in their meaning. Psychological theorising specifies the meaning of related constructs, such as self-efficacy, and through empirical exploration and testing can examine more complex relationships and contingencies (Schunk, 1990). The out-comes of empirical testing then reflect back on the nature of the constructs in terms of their specificity or generality. In this way there is a two-way interaction between conceptualisation and empirical applications.

Thirdly, though some social science generalisations can be linked to logi-cal relationships in everyday concepts, others cannot. In these cases, gener-alisations may have an air of familiarity and obviousness once they have been encountered. A common response is to ask the social scientist to say some-thing new and non-obvious. This tendency for generalisations to be judged as obvious, whether they are research-based or not, is a feature of a wide-spread scepticism about the value of a scientific approach to the social and psychological sciences in general and to a scientific approach to educational matters in particular. Yet it is interesting that several studies have shown that research-based sets of generalisations and their opposites, when pre-sented to even well-informed people, have been judged as equally predict-able (Gage, 1991). Obviousness can be seen therefore as an expression of familiarity with the field, a sense of the plausibility of generalisations which relate to educational matters. But the obviousness of generalisations can leave potential research users thinking that contradictory generalisations are equally plausible. This is an untenable position for them, which they need to resolve by finding a way of selecting between possible generalisations.

There have been continuing doubts about the prospect of teaching and education having a scientific basis. The felt need amongst professional edu-cators and policy makers has been expressed over a long period. For instance, a hundred years ago William James recognised the desire of school teachers for professional training based on fundamental principles (James, 1899). James was keen to dispel what he considered to be the 'mystification' that there was some new psychology which could be of direct use in classrooms:

I say moreover that you make a great, a very great mistake, if you think that psychology, being the science of the mind's law, is something from which you can deduce definite programmes and schemes and methods of instruction for immediate schoolroom use. Psychology is a science, and teaching is an art; and sciences never generate arts directly out of themselves. An intermediary inventive mind must make the application by using its originality.

(James, 1899, p. 3)

James, like some others referred to in this chapter, believed that 'a science only lays down lines within which the rules of the art must fall' (p. 3), that what the teacher does is not set out by science and that there are different ways of working within the lines. However, there is a position that goes even further and questions the idea of an educational science that generates knowledge in the form of empirically based generalisations which can be applied to the improvement of education. This is a critique of 'technical rationality' in education in which reason is held to have been diminished by the search for techniques to better achieve pre-defined goals. It is a position which places reason in an open-ended dialogue about the nature and goals of education among those practically involved (Carr, 1989). This is a critique which draws on the ideas of Habermas, referred to above, in particular that the accomplishments of the natural sciences in the control of the natural world have led to the belief that similar methods can be used to extend control over the social and human world. Habermas called this belief – that knowledge of the social world should be identified with science in the technical rational sense – *scientism*. For him and others, scientism undermines our understanding of the nature and role of the human and social sciences. It weakens human confidence in our abilities to determine the purposes of our actions.

This critique raises important questions about what is meant by the term 'science' and how it is used. The growth and successes of the natural sciences has given great authority to the human endeavour to construct general explanations which are predictive and thus provide the basis for control of the natural world. Science has consequently come to be identified commonly with assumptions and procedures adopted in the natural sciences: for example, that there are patterns in the natural world which are definable, measurable and predictable in general terms. An endeavour to understand and interpret the personal and social world from different perspectives and in the richness of particular situations would not therefore count as a science in this strict sense of the term. This can result in a confusion which needs to be clarified by reference to the underlying assumptions and aims of knowledge-seeking, what Habermas called 'knowledge-constitutive interests'. The wish to extend the term 'science', therefore, to endeavours which are concerned with practitioners refining the rationality of their practice for themselves, as expressed by Carr (1989), needs to be understood in terms of these underlying interests. To call 'scientific' an activity which 'generates reflective self-knowledge and defends the criteria of rational evaluation' is to use the term in a distinctive way. It is an attempt to prevent the reduction of all forms of knowing in education to the technical rational form.

A science of education and professional knowledge

Whether there can be a scientific basis to teaching and education is a central question for what counts as the required professional knowledge of educators. Schon (1983) has been associated with a strong critique of the dominant technical rationality model of professional knowledge based on positivist assumptions. Schon eloquently describes the artistry of professional practitioners and supports an epistemology based on *reflection-in-action* to counter the weaknesses of technical rationality. These he sees in terms of the complexities of the real world, which do not lend themselves to the simplifications required by a positivist model. He also argues that technical rationality fails to take into account how professionals work to achieve their goals. But, as Eraut (1995) points out, there is uncertainty about whether Schon is offering an alternative epistemology to replace technical rationality or something to complement it. In the latter interpretation, his work can be understood as a challenge to the over-inflated position of research-based professional knowledge. Schon's position could alternatively be taken to imply a dichotomy between technical rationality versus reflection-in-action. As Shulman (1988) has argued, such dichotomous thinking is a powerful rhetorical device for capturing our attention. But it portrays technical rationality as necessarily exclusive, tolerating no practitioner reflection or artistry. Shulman rejects this characterisation of practitioner reflection as opposed to technical applications, seeing many teachers as capable of combining the technical and the reflective, the theoretical and the practical, the universal and the concrete. In doing so, he questions the idea, at the heart of Schon's thinking, that teachers should be mainly concerned with treating the learner's own thoughts and judgements as worthy of serious consideration. Shulman's position is to accept that the learner's responses are to be treated with respect, but to question whether teaching responsibilities can be expressed simply in that way. He argues that professional responsibility involves marrying the learner's reasons with what is considered reasonable, bringing together the traditions of technical rationality and reflection-in-action. Shulman is drawing attention to the view that personal reasons and perspectives are not our only concern: there exists a world which operates according to certain principles whether people choose or not to believe in them.

Professional knowledge and learning involve an interaction between learning principles and the experience of cases. This position reflects the views of Dewey referred to above and the question of how social and psychological sciences find their way into the thinking and practice of teachers. One useful approach to this question derives from the work of Fenstermacher (1988), who has examined the idea of the *practical argument* as a concept for relating technical rationality to reflection-in-action. By practical argument he means 'a reasonably coherent chain of reasoning leading from the expression of some desired end state, through various types of premises to an intention to act in a particular way' (Fenstermacher, 1988, p. 41).

For Fenstermacher there are two types of premises, the situational and the empirical. Situational premises are about the specific circumstances and setting of the teacher. Empirical premises express testable claims that teachers make about students, how they learn, what they are capable of learning, how to identify difficulties in learning and other similar conceptions that could be or have been subjected to systematic empirical scrutiny. It is through the empirical premises that research connects to practice when its generalisations are used to alter the existing empirical premises or introduce new empirical premises into the practical arguments in teachers' minds. A concept like practical argument is therefore useful in forging a link between research, theory and practice. It enables a wide range of research conclusions to influence teaching practice, and it is based on a conception of the teacher as a complex thinking agent rather than as a simple technician who translates research into practice. Treating the teacher as actively engaged in formulating practical arguments is also consistent with deliberations about the different aims of education and the interplay of ends and means.

In arguing against the false dichotomy of knowledge-in-action versus technical rationality and for an approach to professional knowledge which combines the two, it is also important to consider the differences and relationships between them. As with the term 'science', there is the risk that reference to the term 'knowledge' comes to be used to invoke authority for one or other position and to deny it to the other. So claims from Schon and others that teachers can produce knowledge in the course of their practice have to be examined closely. Such knowledge-in-action is clearly not like the knowledge deriving from systematic empirical inquiries with either a nomothetic or idiographic focus. This knowledge-in-action may reach what Schon calls the 'swampy lowland where situations are confusing messes incapable of technical solutions' (p. 42), but such areas of professional practice are not in principle closed off from more systematic empirical inquiry. Judgements about areas incapable of technical solutions are, however, not based on logical grounds and therefore experience will tell what is open to systematic inquiry. The point is that teachers' personal professional accounts of teaching and learning are a vital part of professional practice, of their knowledge-in-action. But so could be (and in many cases are) the knowledge and understanding from systematic empirical inquiry.

Concluding comments

In this chapter I have examined issues to do with the theoretical needs of education and teaching. Education as a practical activity has often been understood in terms of the practical knowledge and skill required by educators and teachers. The significance of the 'practicality ethic' in teaching has been a key reference point for discussing educational theory in this chapter. I have also pointed out that theorising about education has sometimes been interpreted, in the dominant theoretical conceptions of the twentieth century, in terms of the theoretical knowledge deriving from the sciences, in this case from the social and psychological sciences. One of the key points has been the difference between the practical knowledge required by educational theory and the theoretical knowledge developed in the contributory disciplines of psychology and sociology. Educational theory, as I have explained, has focused on what is taught and why, how and when it is taught and why, and the expected outcomes. It is therefore prescriptive by contrast with the explanatory or interpretive knowledge from the social sciences. I have also argued that the practical knowledge needed in education can be developed and applied without the underpinning of theoretical knowledge. Education theory is therefore not subservient to the contributory disciplines of psychology, sociology and philosophy. They are not foundation disciplines, as previously assumed, but are in a two-way relationship with education theory. The role of the social sciences, it has been argued, is as a critical resource and guide for educational theory. This position implies that explanatory and theoretical knowledge can contribute and be applied to education only in the context of educational theory. This means that pressures to apply the results of social science research as practical principles, without the critical input from educational theory and the interpretive participation of teachers, has to be resisted. It has been a long-standing problem in the relationship between psychology and education. It continues as a contemporary problem in the current pressures to make education an evidence-based profession, with effectiveness research supposed to have a direct bearing on practice (Hargreaves, 1996). I will discuss these contemporary issues in the final chapter.

I have also examined in this chapter how the relationship between education and psychology is complicated by diverse and conflicting kinds of basic educational theories or ideologies. Different analyses of these different models were outlined to show differing foci – on the content of learning, on the social aims of education, on the personal aims of education and on the techniques of teaching. These theories were also shown to represent different values related to wider social and political ideologies. I then presented the perspective which questioned the coherence and purity of these different educational theories. This is based on the argument that different theories cannot be presented without incorporating aspects of other theories: that, for example, there are elements of teacher-centred assumptions in child-centred theories and vice versa. There are differences and oppositions between different educational theories which present dilemmas for educators. Different responses to these dilemmas represent the different theories about the balance between individual and society, and between freedom and control.

From this perspective educational theories are formulated, and change, as part of a dialogic and argumentative process within a wider historical struggle over political and social values. In their formulation educationalists make assumptions about what is to be learnt, how society works and how people learn. I noted that only some education theories are linked to specific psychological assumptions: those concerned with person-centred and teaching technology models. These assumptions were called 'meta-psychological' as they include basic beliefs about the nature of the individual person and are connected to different theoretical models in psychology. In the middle part of the chapter I outlined some correspondences and connections between the different educational models or ideologies and the different psychological frameworks. These links were in terms of the active–reactive, the reductionist–holistic and the individual–social nature of the individual person.

Following this philosophical and conceptual analysis, I then considered the nature of teaching as an art or an applied science. The distinct concepts of teaching as a task and as an achievement were linked to ideas about educational objectives being about mastery (teaching as an applied science) and expressiveness (teaching as an art). The tendency to adopt exclusive positions was criticised for excessive polarisation and the unjustified dominance of one or other conception. By recognising the diverse nature of teaching, I argued for a broad and encompassing model of teaching which retained the possibility of a scientific basis while preserving the inventive and spontaneous or artistic aspects of teaching.

I then examined more specifically questions about whether education and teaching could have a scientific basis. Several criticisms of a scientific basis were critically analysed, with reservations about the possibility of generalisations and the inevitability of social and historical influences on the social sciences. It was argued that as in the dialogues and debates about different educational models, the tendency to exclusiveness and purism needs to be resisted. I suggested that a focus on the individual case and a focus on the general, though different, were compatible if the two approaches were respected and connected. Similarly, methodological efforts to generate generalisations applicable across contexts are compatible with efforts to illustrate interpretive perspectives, if the scientific endeavour is not equated with establishing absolute and final explanations. It is possible to be positive about a scientific basis for education by avoiding the purism of objectivism and subjectivism and by recognising the interconnections between the particular and the general, and between what is humanly constructed and what is given. I illustrated this position towards the end of the chapter by resisting the exclusive dichotomy between technical rationality and reflection-in-action in understanding the nature of professional knowledge for educators. The concept of a *practical argument* was recommended as a useful way for representing teaching as a series of reflective and deliberative actions which connect direct and intuitive beliefs with ideas and generalisations from empirical research.

I have argued overall in this chapter for a position which is opposed to the exclusive dominance of any particular approach. Dichotomies such as those between practical and theoretical knowledge, education theory as teacher- or as learner-centred, teaching as a task or an achievement or models of the social science as idiographic or nomothetic are recognised as useful in drawing attention to significant differences. But when there is positioning for one which excludes the other alternative, then the value of and connections between different approaches are ignored and unresolvable contradictions and tensions are generated. The conclusion is that education has a need for theory which includes evaluative, conceptual and empirical elements. It is not exclusively for knowledge from one contributory discipline, nor for practical or professional knowledge derived only from practitioners or social scientists. Psychology's contribution to education theory and practice, though critical, is therefore one of many, with the 'many' including understanding and knowledge from allied disciplines, educational and curriculum theorists, educational researchers and practitioners.

3 Psychology: study of humanity or science?

Psychology is a vast and ramified discipline. It contains many mansions. But this does not prevent it from being intellectually divided against itself.

Taylor (1985, p. 117)

Introduction

I concluded in the last chapter that educational theories are diverse and focus on different aspects of the educational field: what is to be learned, the social and personal aims of learning and the techniques of learning. The latter two aspects relate directly to basic beliefs about the nature of the person and learning, what I called meta-psychological assumptions. When educationalists explore these assumptions conceptually and empirically they begin to ask psychological questions and become involved in problems and questions covered by the field of psychology. This connection also relates to the historical development of psychology by scholars and practitioners involved in education. Education therefore needs psychology as a theoretical and technical resource and guide, as what can be called a contributory discipline. There is the risk, however, that psychology, particularly in its causal scientific version, comes to be applied without the critical role of educational theory and the interpretive participation of teachers. Psychology then assumes the dominant role in the relationship. This raises the question of whether education also contributes to psychology. How much does psychology need practical problems and questions from a field like education? To answer these questions calls for an examination of the contemporary issues and agendas in psychology, which is the focus of this chapter.

Psychology is an alluring, puzzling and even a mysterious field. It can be seen to contain crucial knowledge and understanding about the mind and human behaviour which can answer many of the questions about human nature which concern us all. Such answers can hold out the promise of solutions to human problems, something which is particularly relevant in a secular age when the traditional answers from religion have become less plausible and acceptable. It is seen (witness the images projected by the media) as offering those who are familiar with its secrets the potential, if not the actual power, to control and perhaps manipulate others. Psychology, focusing on the mind or the psyche, also has associations with what is not physical and material, with ghostly processes which lurk in some immaterial realm. Though there has been a significant growth of a scientific approach to psychology over the last century, and that is now the dominant mode of study, this development has not been welcomed consistently. Put briefly and simply, a scientific mode offers the authority and power associated with science in other fields where it has achieved considerable successes, such as in physics and biology. This arises from an agenda which aims to identify causal mechanisms which can be applied to the control of psychological outcomes. But this very process can also be seen to be dehumanising in denying the role of human meaning and agency. Despite this, psychology has over the last century attracted many hopes and expectations. This was recognised by William James as regards teachers and teaching, as noted in the last chapter. Currently psychology is attracting many students in Higher Education. Figures quoted by Gale (1997), for example, indicate that in the USA psychology produces the second largest number of major graduates, after business administration and management. A world-wide survey indicates a doubling of the number of qualified psychologists between 1982 and 1992. There has been a similar growth in Higher Education psychology places in the UK.

Modern psychology is sometimes portrayed as a robust, if young, science which contains some explanations of key psychological phenomena and at least has the methods which have the promise to develop further and more powerful explanations and techniques. For example, Grey (1981) argued that psychology is much younger than other sciences, and that it is only a matter of time before it catches up. This commitment to a scientific approach to the study of humanity has been justified by its contribution to understanding and resolving some of our urgent and immediate problems. Science can be seen, argued Eysenck, as

> the expression of reason in its highest form and science therefore is our one and only hope for survival.
>
> (Eysenck, 1972, p. xvi)

> Science is the tool and creation of human reason; now is the time to introduce it into human affairs as well, and base our conduct on scientific facts.
>
> (p. 323)

Yet despite these confident assertions, there have been over the last half century continuing doubts about psychology's outcomes. For example, in the 1950s the philosopher Wittgenstein, who was interested in exploring the nature of psychological concepts and attributions, stated:

> The confusion and barrenness of psychology is not to be explained by calling it a 'young science'; its state is not comparable with that of physics, for instance, in its beginnings. For in psychology there are experimental methods and conceptual confusion. The existence of experimental method makes us think we have the means of solving the problems which trouble us; though problem and method pass one another by.
>
> (Wittgenstein, 1953, p. 232)

Other philosophers have expressed related reservations in other terms. For example, Charles Taylor, who questioned the viability of behaviourist learning theories in the 1960s (Taylor, 1964), has continued to reflect on the uncertain nature of psychology, as illustrated in the epigraph to this chapter. These concerns about psychology as a natural science have persisted into the 1980s with doubts being raised about its potential to grow into a mature science:

> Scientific psychology is not an infant discipline which will develop into a mature science. It is a combination of false starts involving quite complex intellectual muddles, not the least of which is the tendency to a special jargon we have called scientism.
>
> (Harre et al., 1985, p. 19)

The growth of more interpretive, social and critical kinds of psychological inquiry through the 1980s and into the 1990s, has brought about increasing fragmentation. As Fraser Watts identified in a Presidential Address to the British Psychological Society, psychology does not hang together: there are distinct lines of fragmentation (Watts, 1992). The continued growth of separate divisions and sections within both the US and British Psychological Institutions, the American Psychological Association (APA) and the British Psychological Society (BPS), illustrates this point. And, as Bruner (1987, p. 167) has bemoaned: 'Psychology, alas, seems to have lost its centre and its great integrating questions. I think it has given up prematurely.'

In this chapter I will examine and analyse some key issues in contemporary psychology. This analysis will centre around general questions about the relationships between a mechanistic science and a humanities-oriented interpretivist approach. It will illustrate the place of core values associated with psychological study, which will lead to a consideration of the ideological nature of psychology and how different psychologies arise from differing attitudes to these values. It will consider the differences between psychologies which arise in university as compared with service-practitioner settings, and show the importance of locating psychology within a historical and social context. There will be some analysis of concepts of science which are applicable to psychology, and an evaluation of some recent critiques of scientific psychology from a social-constructionist perspective. The chapter continues with a critical discussion of the relationship between common-sense and scientific conceptions of psychology. This leads to an outline of changing ideas in the philosophy of science which are then applied to psychology. The significance of a pragmatist philosophical position is explained, as a way of avoiding the 'anything goes' implications of relativism. This position is consistent with an evolutionary perspective on the place of mind in nature, which is explored in the penultimate section. The chapter concludes with an account of various attempts to promote co-existence and interconnections between different versions of psychology within a multi-disciplinary approach to seeking understanding in the wider social and human sciences.

Humanity versus science

What has been called fragmentation in psychology can also be seen as the flourishing of diverse lines of theory, inquiry and practice. Accusations of conceptual muddle (sometimes led by philosophers with an interest in psychology and the human sciences, like Taylor and Harre) support attempts to build up alternatives based on suppressed epistemological traditions and practices into viable and warranted schools of psychology. In undertaking such a project there is a tendency to portray the new in opposition to the old or established positions. For example, Smith et al. (1995) set out the dichotomy between an old and new paradigm in psychology in these terms. Understanding, meaning, interpretation, language, discourse, holism, cultural context and subjectivity represent the new paradigm. Measuring, predicting, causation, statistical analysis, atomism, universals, context-freedom and objectivity represent the old paradigm. The old paradigm comes to be criticised, often on a basis of changing ideas from the philosophy of science, for making false claims about scientific objectivity as providing absolute knowledge and understanding. This has also been identified as a form of *scientism* in psychology which is taken to be a false adoption of the language and methods of the natural sciences (Koch, 1959; Harre et al., 1985). Koch is a quoted example of a mainstream US psychologist who came to believe that the 'methods [of psychology] preceded its problems' (Koch, 1959, vol. 3, p. 783). He also appreciated that this conception of science arose from psychology's early days: 'man's stipulation that psychology be adequate to science outweighed his commitment that it be adequate to man' (p. 783).

Harre et al.'s more recent critique of scientism in psychology is based partly on the mainstream disregard for the subtleties of everyday psychological concepts as being itself a source of psychological theories. These implicit theories can be seen to include assumptions about personal habits when agency is at a minimum; distinctions between what is voluntary and what is out of control (as in obsessional behaviour); and explanations in terms of intentions which assume reasoning and judgement. Our everyday, common-sense or folk psychology, as it is called, has come to stand in opposition to a mechanistic scientific version of psychology. Accusations of scientism levelled against mainstream academic psychology, such as Harre et al.'s, pose a science of the person whose acts are based on beliefs and intentions, against a science of behaviour caused by stimuli. This can be cast as a science of agency versus one of automata. Harre et al. (1985, p. 11) summarise this difference in these terms: 'The old psychology tried to study human action within a causal order, while the new psychology tried to reach a scientific understanding of human life within a moral order or orders.'

Seeing actions as 'typically performed *in accordance with rules* rather than *determined by causes*' (p. 10, my italics) represents a fundamental commitment to accepting some personal agency outside a strict causal deterministic order. This can be brought out by distinguishing between action *which is governed by rules* and action *performed in accordance with rules*. The latter suggests that the person could deliberate and act differently, there being some voluntariness about it. The former suggests a stricter form of determination; with no scope for alternatives without a rule change.

Automata are systems which are strictly determined by causes or governed by rules. The fundamental question about the image we hold of ourselves as human beings and the kind of psychology we adopt is whether we see ourselves as automata. Criticisms of behaviourist and neo-behaviourist psychology have been supported by a gut rejection of this image of humanity. Negative reactions to Skinner's behaviourist philosophy and behavioural analyses in humanistic education circles illustrate this point. However, as our images of automata change and develop with the construction of computational machines of great power and complexity we may come to find the image of automata less demeaning. Academic psychology has undergone what has been called the cognitive revolution, with its rediscovery of the mind, although in a computational form. This computational psychology takes well-formed information as its given – information which is unambiguous and is related to states of the world. But the computational model assumes that all systems, whether human or artificial intelligence machines, are governed by specifiable rules or procedures. Unless regarded in this way, these systems cannot produce systematic and foreseeable outcomes. This model of psychology assumes, therefore, that if psychology as a science aims to explain and predict mental phenomena, it has to adopt these computational principles. By contrast, an agency model of humanity is concerned with the construction or making of meaning by active agents in a cultural context. These meanings are not seen as exclusively private entities, but as arising from human communication in socially constructed institutions. The interpretivist or agency model denies the well-formed and explicit starting points about meaning in the more objectivist computational model. Ambiguity, perspective and sensitivity to the situation are the hall-marks of the agency model of meaning.

The differences between the computational and the interpretivist models can be confused by assertions about the scientific nature of their respective assumptions. Whether the interpretivist model represents a science of the subjective or a cultural or hermeneutic science depends on why we call an approach 'scientific'. Is 'scientific' used to indicate a systematic field of inquiry? Does it apply to general explanatory theory based on quantification and experimental methods? Or is its function perhaps rhetorical, to connect the field of study with the authority and prestige of the natural sciences and technology? This issue relates to broader questions about whether psychology is a natural science like biology or whether it is a cultural science having more in common with the humanities, philosophy and the arts. These are issues to be dealt with more fully in this chapter.

As discussed in the previous chapter, these different conceptions and models of psychology are associated with different philosophical positions about the nature of the knowledge of human actions and individual persons. Overton (1980), amongst others, has identified two basic explanatory models or paradigms, the *mechanistic* and *organismic models*, seeing them as incompatible, with no common set of criteria against which they can be compared and judged; they are incommensurable. The mechanistic model encompasses a range of explanatory theories, including the behaviourist and the information-processing computational theory. They exemplify reductionist assumptions about explaining through analysing phenomena into parts and identifying prior causes through empirical and especially experimental methodologies.

The organismic model encompasses a wider and more disparate family of theories which have in common their concern with the integrity of the whole as being more than the sum of its parts. Change is seen as inherent in assumptions of basic needs or functions, with the direction of development being affected by structures and qualitatively different stages. These assumptions are found in the developmental and other aspects of psychodynamic theories and the structuralist theories of Piaget. They are also found in aspects of George Kelly's 'personal construct' psychology, in particular the holistic nature of construct systems. Piaget's developmental theories of mind and Kelly's construct systems share a constructivist assumption about individuals' active involvement in making sense of their worlds which is not so evident in classical psychodynamic theories. Psychodynamic theories focus on internal conflicts and unconscious processes which leave individuals out of touch with the meaning of their actions. There are, however, more interpretivist versions of psychodynamic theory which see the role of psychoanalysis as actively extending personal meaning-making to include hidden and repressed processes (Rycroft and Gorer, 1968).

But if the organismic model relates to wholes, systems, developmental stages and interpretations, it also focuses on the individual as distinct from his or her social context. This can be said of the three exemplars of organismic type theory mentioned above. Piaget's individual constructivist theory has been contrasted with theory informed by Vygotskian ideas, which understands the development of the mind in a socio-historical context as a process of internalising social interactions. This contrast between a more individual versus a more social-constructivist model is also evident in the posing of a Meadian symbolic interactionism against a Kellian personal construct psychology. Though both theoretical approaches are concerned with meaning, symbolic interactionist ideas, following George Herbert Mead's social orientation, are more focused on the social and interpersonal origins of meaning. It is no accident that parallels have been identified between Meadian symbolic interactionism and neo-Vygotskian mediational theories (Farr, 1987; Burkitt, 1991).

Some of the underlying theoretical differences discussed above can be captured in terms of these distinctions:

1   reductionist–holist
2   natural causal order–human moral order
3   objectivist–constructivist
4   individual focus–social focus.

These dimensions are not meant to be fixed dichotomies, with the terms on the left representing the old paradigm and those on the right the new paradigm, as depicted by Smith et al. (1995). One of the aims of this chapter is to explore the issues and relationships between the different positions expressed in these distinctions. So far, the argument has been that theories expressing mechanistic scientific assumptions, which include reductionist, objectivist and individualist principles, are not simply distinguishable from another set of coherent theories. Some alternatives to the mechanistic-scientific are constructivist and holistic while adopting individualist assumptions (Piagetian and Kellian). Other alternatives focus more on constructivist and social assumptions (Vygotskian and Meadian). This is an important point because it illustrates that there is no place for simple dichotomies in understanding the nature of psychology as a field of study.

Ideology and psychology

Differences within psychology reflect fundamental assumptions about how much humanity is part of the natural causal order and can be studied like other, non-human parts of that causal order. To accept this interpretation of differences within psychology is to recognise psychology's inherent connection to philosophical positioning. This can be taken further in assuming that ideology is inextricably connected with psychology. 'Ideology' is taken here to refer to basic social beliefs and values, which have a function in the exercising and contesting of social power and in maintaining or changing the social order. I will argue that this is an important perspective on the nature of psychology, its development and social and political uses.

Social movements have differing aims and hold differing power positions. One movement, which became established in the nineteenth century, worked on the assumption that scientific reason could be used to develop knowledge and techniques with the potential of improving social and human conditions generally. It also made psychological assumptions about the relevance and applicability of general concepts to the diversity of human characteristics and functioning. It assumed that causes are identifiable and have systematic effects that are alterable. This is the approach usually associated with the positivist movement. In its ideologically progressive form it has sought to identify environmental causal factors and intervene by altering them to alleviate suffering and promote human development and well-being. Empirical psychology in general (Broadbent, 1973), and behavioural and cognitive-behavioural theories and techniques more specifically, are examples of this kind of psychology. However, there has been a tradition of psychological explanations which has identified unalterable causes of a genetic nature, which have been used to justify limited social and educational opportunities. The well-known example is the mainly genetic explanations of IQ differences between people from different ethnic and social groups. This is the ideological context in which the perennial nature-versus-nurture debate continues to be conducted in connection with psychological differences between social, ethnic and gender groups.

The use of general psychological concepts across different historical and cultural contexts has been disputed from a critical perspective. This perspective questions the applicability of psychological constructs deriving from Western white male and economically advantaged groups and contexts to other groups and contexts. The empirical research base is exposed to criticism in terms of its sampling and assessment validity to reveal methodological errors and over-generalised conclusions. The point of these critiques is to show that certain disadvantaged groups have been inaccurately characterised, and unfairly treated as a consequence. The ideological orientation of this critical perspective is therefore progressive. It often adopts a stance opposed to mechanistic science and the validity of comparisons across cultural groups. An interpretivist mode is preferred to the objective attribution of characteristics, and quantitative analyses of outcomes are not seen as viable.

Recognising that ideology infuses much of psychology means accepting that questions of value are at the foundation of the field. Psychological knowledge and understanding will therefore reflect the balance between these different value commitments. We can think of these broad values as of two kinds: *epistemological values* and *well-being values*. Epistemological values are about what kind of understanding is worth having: whether of causal mechanisms, from a spectator perspective, or of meanings, purposes and reasons, from a participant perspective. This distinction is about the respective values of adopting outsider or insider views. It has been noted that this value question does not arise in the natural sciences, where the object of study does not itself have an insider perspective. But in a human field of study, like psychology, this is inevitably an issue. When natural science methods are applied in an uncritical way to ourselves as human beings, it is hardly surprising that we face the issue of science versus our humanity. The adoption of an exclusively spectator view is therefore likely to engender a splitting between the spectator and participant perspectives and the emergence of rival epistemological values concerned with meaning, interpretation and active agency.

Most statements about the purposes of psychology include something about seeking to enhance human welfare and well-being (for example, Gale, 1997). This connects psychology inextricably with wider values of human welfare and well-being. Thus differences within psychology reflect not only epistemological positions and values, but also values relating to human well-being. These are philosophical questions about what counts as a worthwhile life for individuals, and about their place and relationships to others in society. These are the same value questions which educationalists deal with, as was discussed in the last chapter: autonomy and self-determination; the prospects for and limitations on satisfying human desires. An ideologically conservative position is inclined to the values of social duty, compliance and resignation. These values derive from assumptions that human desires can threaten the social order, and that there are human and other limitations on satisfying basic desires. An ideologically more progressive position is, by contrast, inclined more to the values of entitlement, self-assertion and challenging limits. Likewise, these derive from assumptions that society involves a contract between equal and self-determining individuals and that there is scope for releasing suppressed and unrecognised human potential.

This analysis of epistemological and well-being value orientations can help us understand some of the differences within the field of psychology. If the spectator-epistemological perspective is taken to assume that all human action is subject to causal mechanisms, then there is no space for autonomy and creative human agency. A strictly mechanistic, scientific approach would therefore be incompatible with progressive values and ideas about human well-being. This point also shows how epistemological values are connected to well-being values. However, it is possible to adopt a more conditional spectator perspective which sees the applicability of causal assumptions as depending on empirical evidence. It can be seen as an empirical matter of how far such a mechanistic stance can be applied in practice: it is not to be presumed in advance, a position advocated by Eysenck (1972). This leaves space for differing views about the value of the participant-epistemological perspective. There are those who are impressed by the achievements of science and its technological potential and wish to pursue a strong scientific line. For them the participant perspective is of minor significance and at best a possible source of hypotheses for formal testing. But there is another view which sees interconnections between and supports a co-existence between epistemological perspectives (Bruner, 1997). This is the position supported in this chapter and the book overall.

This analysis of values in psychology also illustrates how different well-being values relate to the adoption of epistemological positions in the field. The history of psychology can be characterised in terms of the impact of different well-being values on methodological approaches and theoretical explanations. This has been evident in the IQ field, where it has been shown that there was an association between psychologists' ideological positions and their views about nature-versus-nurture explanations (Pastore, 1949). It is also evident in more recent debates about ethnicity, class and the genetics of intelligence (Hernstein and Murray, 1994). Some psychologists of a more progressive orientation react to this perceived association between a scientific-spectator perspective and conservative values by rejecting the spectator perspective altogether. Consequently they adopt the participant perspective as the more humanist and progressive stance. In doing so, they portray interpretivist methodological assumptions as more progressive. However, a spectator perspective can, but need not, imply conservative values. As mentioned above, identifying causal mechanisms can provide us with knowledge and techniques to intervene and improve human conditions. The scientific-spectator perspective has been adopted by psychologists with progressive values, though they tend to focus, as we might expect, on mechanisms where there are alterable factors.

Professional versus academic psychologies

There are different accounts of types of psychology. They vary depending on whether they come from textbooks, which tend to provide overviews for students on courses, or from proponents of particular strands or schools of thought. One view which was current in the middle of this century was that there were three broad positions: the behaviourist, the psychodynamic and the humanist. The behaviourist position represented the mechanistic scientific approach, which regulated its study by the disciplines of experimental and systematic empirical methodologies. The psychodynamic represented that family of approaches which assumed the central place of unconscious motivation and processes in human behaviour. The humanistic represented a family of approaches which assumed the active self-determining and interpretive nature of human behaviour. Over the last 20 years, since what has been called the 'cognitive revolution' (Bruner, 1997), information-processing assumptions have become dominant over classic behaviourist ones. However, some theorists would see a continuity between behavioural and cognitive principles and a unity in the adoption of experimental and empirical methodologies (Bandura, 1977).

A key difference between the psychodynamic and humanistic traditions was in their attitude to conscious human agency. The original psycho-analytic theories associated with Freud recognised the determining role of instinctual and unconscious processes, whereas humanistic theories, such as those of Carl Rogers and George Kelly, stressed the active, conscious and reflective aspects of functioning. However, it is possible to see continuities between instinctually based psychodynamic and humanistic psychologies. This is evident in the reaction to Freudian ideas by post-Freudian theorists (e.g. Fromm, 1956) and more recent ego-oriented theorists (e.g. Kohut, 1978). It is also possible to see some versions of personal construct psychology integrated with analytic ideas and assumptions (Ryle, 1990). That there is no clear distinction between dynamic and humanistic psychologies can also be understood in terms of their shared origin in the practice of psychotherapy and counselling. What theoretical differences there are could be attributed to professional and institutional differences. Psychodynamic ideas of a psychoanalytic orientation were strongly regulated by the original psychoanalytic movement. Theorists who propounded variations were excluded, with the result that rival factions and traditions emerged. The original psychoanalytic ideas also derived from Europe and were more in tune with conservative values. Their adoption in the US increased stress on ego orientation and the emergence of humanistic traditions. The growth of counselling as a form of psychotherapy and as an alternative to the analytic version also led to the development of more humanistic theories. Counselling had a base which extended outside the treatment of people with serious mental health and illness problems. The emphasis was more on promoting personal development and well-being.

Another thing that psychodynamic and humanistic psychologies have in common is a difference from academic psychologies in institutional origins. This is a difference in terms of theoretical development and use. Behaviourist and later cognitive psychologies originated amongst academically based psychologists involved in establishing psychology as an academic discipline in universities over the last century. The academic interest was in the development of a scientific discipline of psychology and the gaining of academic credentials for the field in the eyes of other scientific disciplines. Questions were derived from psychological issues in philosophy, other related fields such as anthropology and biology, and also partly from contemporary policy problems which were given a scientific treatment. Explanations and understanding were to be sought through experimental and systematic empirical methodologies. By contrast, psychodynamic and humanistic psychologies originated as part of professional practice which aimed to alleviate emotional suffering and promote personal well-being. Professional practice required techniques and procedures which needed to be based on relevant psychological assumptions and principles. These were derived directly from practitioners theorising from and about their experience in clinical and other service settings.

What this discussion shows is that different psychologies are associated with different institutional settings: university compared to service and practice. Methods for generating, and criteria for accepting, theory also differed in these settings. In academic settings psychological theory has mostly come from controlled and systematic methodologies; in service settings theory has come from and is for practice. This difference can be seen in the way in which psychodynamic and humanistic psychologies have been developed as the preserve of particular professional bodies which have their own training courses and professional journals. These psychological concepts and principles form the basis for the practice of professionals, such as counsellors, psychotherapists and psychoanalysts, who are not called 'psychologists'.

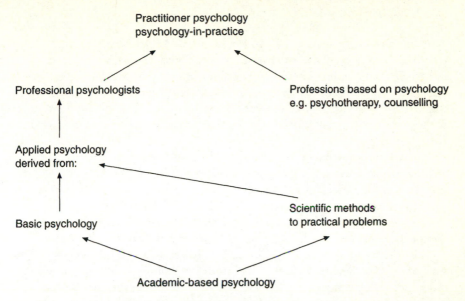

Figure 1 The relationship between different kinds of psychology

The distinction between academic and practitioner psychologies is also important because it underlies a distinction which can be made between *applied psychology* and *psychology-in-practice*. Applied psychology is usually contrasted with *pure* or *basic psychology*. The pure-versus-applied distinction depends on a basic science-into-technology model of psychology. According to this model, pure or basic psychology, in the form of general theoretical knowledge derived from systematic and controlled empirical study, can be applied to particular practical problems. But applied psychology can also be seen to derive from the application of scientific methods directly to practical problems from an academic base. So professional psychologists are represented as drawing on two kinds of applied psychology. But they also develop psychological knowledge and understanding in the context of their practice. This analysis is represented in figure 1. Also shown are other professions, such as counselling and psychotherapy, which develop psychologies in the context of their practice, but do not explicitly draw on academic psychologies.

Schonpflug (1993) has identified two strands of applied psychology. He identifies one strand within the academic discipline of psychology and the second as a trans-disciplinary approach which involves a psychological component to various fields such as medicine and education. His position is that applied psychology does not fit the scientific innovations model according to which technology is rooted in basic psychological science. It is a view based on a historical analysis of the field of psychology which will be discussed briefly in the next section.

Historical aspects

Histories are often written by those who are seeking interpretations of the past which give credence to current conceptions. The same can be said of historical accounts of psychology as a field of study and its emergence as a science. This is apparent in accounts which have been given by those wishing to present conceptions from various perspectives: applied psychological, socially oriented, gender based or critical. Some of these will be discussed in this section.

In the long tradition of Western thought, psychology was part of the field of philosophy. A common twentieth-century account is that psychology progressed from a pre-scientific to a scientific discipline towards the end of the nineteenth century in Germany with Wundt's establishment of the first psychological laboratory (Farr, 1987). This is the position of academic psychologists working in the scientific tradition who portray Wundt as the founder of scientific psychology. But as Farr has shown, it has been less widely recognised that Wundt wished to maintain psychology as part of philosophy. And more significantly, he recognised the limitations of an experimental approach based on introspection. His response to these limitations was his social psychology (*Völkerpsychologie*) which focused on collective phenomena related to the study of higher cognitive processes, language, customs and myths. This distinction between an experimental science of the mind and a social psychology was one between two different levels within psychology. Farr also shows that these misconceptions can be attributed to Titchener, an Englishman, who having studied under Wundt in Germany then worked in the US. Titchener's reading of the origins of experimental psychology came to influence the classic historical account of experimental psychology by Boring, who was one of his doctoral students.

Farr's account has considerable significance for our current understanding of the nature of psychology. His view is that psychology has been either the science of the mind, as in the early introspectionist studies or more recent cognitive studies, or the science of behaviour. But it has not been both at the same time. Its weaknesses as a science of the mind or of behaviour, he contends, have derived from overlooking the social nature of mind and behaviour. His historical account can therefore be seen to support his wider views that psychology as a science of mind and behaviour must be a form of social psychology. I will return to this view later in the chapter.

The common account is that psychology moved from a pre-scientific to a scientific stage and then moved on to the next stage, applications and professional services: what is called the two-stage model. The model reflects the fact that professional psychologists from the second half of this century have outnumbered academics. However, as mentioned above, there is an alternative historical account which reveals two separate traditions of applied psychology (Schonpflug, 1993). Schonpflug offers a critique of the two-stage developmental model of applied psychology: that applications and technologies are not based on basic theories. He argues that applied and basic approaches in the same areas tend to be largely independent of each other. For example, intelligence testing arose from the practical sphere without the benefit of theoretical models. He notes that when subsequent theoretical work in the intelligence area became available it had little impact on the design of intelligence testing (cf. Hunt, 1987).

Further support for his case comes from doubts about whether behavioural techniques have been derived originally from basic psychological theory and research, despite their presentation as such (Allyon and Azrin, 1968). His claim is that the basic principles of behavioural techniques, habit formation and rewards are not outcomes of basic research, but derive from practical knowledge with origins well before the development of more recent learning theories. Practices associated with habit formation and reward have a long history as educational techniques. So it could be argued that learning theories drew on these pre-existing principles and were the result of applying the precision of experimental methods to their testing and development. Their modern scientific formulation can be seen to have lent recognition to these historic principles and promoted their wider and more systematic use.

Schonpflug attributes this separation between basic and applied psychology to two distinct traditions in Western thought, which he calls the ontological and the pragmatic. The ontological tradition is concerned with essences and things beyond the physical. This has its origins in Greek philosophy which distinguished between mind and body: the mind concerned with ideas and essences, the subject matter of philosophy, and the body concerned with practical matters. This can be seen to reflect the difference between truth and utility. With basic psychology having its origins in philosophy, we would expect a continuing influence of the ontological tradition. This is to be found in basic psychology's focus on essential features and single human functions, such as attention, without connections to other psychological functions or to the social and technical environment. By contrast, the pragmatic tradition is concerned with principles for efficient practice in pursuit of improvement and the advancement of social life. The traditions of practical thinking, in the form of politics and economics, also go back to ancient Greece. Subsequently these pragmatic disciplines opened out into diverse practical disciplines which touched on matters of psychological concern like training, communication, selection and placement. These psychological matters were treated as part of disciplines such as medicine and education. Schonpflug calls the parts of practical disciplines concerned with psychological matters *trans-disciplinary* psychology, a psychology which was found in the training of practical disciplines such as teacher training. Schwieso (1993) and Thomas (1996) present evidence for this historical interpretation from the development of British teacher training. Training colleges in the mid-nineteenth century gave lectures on the philosophy of mind as applicable to education, and on attention, memory, rewards and punishments. From the mid-1880s there were textbooks on psychology for teachers. Hearnshaw

(1987), in his history of psychology in this country, notes that applied psychology as a discipline began in the field of education, arising from the needs of the expanding school system. From examples like this, Schonpflug identifies applied psychology as having grown out of the psychological components of domain specific work.

Schonpflug's use of the word 'applied' in 'applied psychology' is, however, confusing, as *applied* usually goes with *basic* in the sense of applying basic psychology. He identifies applied psychology as the newcomer compared with the longer tradition of trans-disciplinary psychology. His point is that within university-based academic psychology, what came to be called applied psychology was designed to complement basic psychology and was presented as a new discipline. This so-called applied psychology was, however, reviving the historical pragmatic tradition, whether its proponents were aware of the fact or not. These historical considerations are important for understanding contemporary issues about the nature of educational psychology. They concern different versions of educational psychology: as a service discipline (a professional psychology); as applying psychological knowledge and understanding from basic academic research to service issues; or as using systematic empirical and experimental research methods in service situations. They will be dealt with in the next chapter.

Much has been written about the development of psychology as a profession during the twentieth century (Woodward, 1987). A common theme has been to show how psychologists have been creatures of their cultural and political times. Psychology, as a discipline independent of philosophy, has been presented as coming of age with the social and political utility of mental testing (Ingleby, 1985; Burman, 1994). These views are compatible with Schonpflug's historical account of the ontological and pragmatic traditions. Late nineteenth-century psychology sought answers to questions arising from anthropology, evolution theory and philosophy. But psychology was also concerned with the classification and monitoring of large populations. This was in the context of contemporary concerns about the quality of the population in army recruitment and school selection, but also about degeneracy, segregation and sterilisation. These historical accounts portray psychology in a critical light as making social regulation and surveillance possible (Rose, 1985). The techniques of testing required and relied on the social institutions where they were used: the clinic and the school. Psychology historically underpinned the social system with its construction of developmental norms for children, becoming the judge of normality of children. Abnormality and normality became linked in the sense that what makes child development normal came to be defined in terms of what is not abnormal.

This reading of the historical relationship between scientific psychology and social policy and practices is associated with a wider critique of the role of science as a tool of reason which was supported by the state. It is part of a critique of technical rationality which points to the historic failure of scientific psychology to theorise about the context of development and challenge an oppressive and discriminatory status quo. Readings of the more recent history of psychology from this socially critical perspective also emphasise contemporary social and political factors. Ingleby (1986), for instance, identifies the US drive to optimise intellectual development through compensatory programmes as probably the immediate factor prompting the 'cognitive revolution'. This drive could be linked to two political factors: anxieties about the prospects of US technology in the 1950s and 1960s as part of the Cold War and the objective of reducing race and class tensions by increasing educational opportunities. Ingleby argues that this is the context of an increasing loss of confidence in the behaviourist model. But he also points to intellectual influences as relevant too, in particular the changes in the philosophy of science that undermined confidence in empiricist theories of knowledge associated with behaviourist models.

Ingleby's historical account leads to the grounds for the development of a social-constructionist approach to developmental psychology. The classic critique of Skinnerian behaviourism by Noam Chomsky in the field of language learning is presented as restoring mind to psychology (Chomsky, 1959). But the alternatives are seen as posing no challenge to the individualism of psychology. Chomsky's concept of language involved an inbuilt language acquisition mechanism, while Piaget's concept of development involved the individual in constructing structures in a uniform way, a form of individual constructivism. Proponents of information processing and artificial intelligence were similarly unconcerned with the 'constitutive role' of the social context in the development of cognitive processes. The historical account then points out the growing social gaps in what was then the newly emergent cognitive approach. Research on Piagetian theories began to show that social variations in the presentation of experimental tasks could lower the age when key abilities could be demonstrated (Donaldson, 1978). The significance of the social context was also reinforced by the growing emphasis on ecological validity and the move to study people in context. A challenge to structuralist models of language acquisition, whether Chomsky's innate one or Piaget's individual constructivist one, is presented by Ingleby, as coming from studies showing a growing recognition of the social relations at the foundation of language (Bruner, 1976).

Different readings of the same research and theoretical history depend on more basic commitments about the nature and breadth of psychology as a field of study and a science. Ingleby's version is to locate the trends within what was a growing challenge to the idea of psychology as a natural mechanistic science and the call from some circles for a more interpretive and social approach. A related but distinct historical reading is that the predominance since the 1960s of the cognitive perspective in psychology arises from the failure of the previously dominant conception of behaviourism to account for higher cognitive processes. This is Farr's historical reading (Farr, 1987), one which shows that our understanding of behaviourism is limited to the Watson tradition with its original methodological commitment to strict observational data. Watson's theoretical project to construct a behavioural science aimed to rescue psychology from the barrenness of introspectionism as a method of constructing a science of the mind. Farr's point is that in doing so Watson's behaviourism ignored the mind rather than attempting to explain it, as George Herbert Mead had attempted through his social behaviourism. Mead saw the mind as arising from social behaviour, in particular out of a conversation of gestures as a social process, something which occurred over evolution phylogenetically and again for individuals ontogenetically.

Farr's historical account has significance for the modern study of psychology. It shows how the dominant version of behaviourism, including Skinner's account of verbal behaviour, ignored a broader social version of behaviourism which could have included the mind in psychology. Farr's account is also interesting because it shows how Mead's theories came to be incorporated into the symbolic interactionist tradition of social psychology, which has been associated with interpretivist and social conceptions of psychology. Farr attributes this reading of Mead to the sociologist Blumer, who coined the term 'symbolic interactionism'. Farr's historical perspective is one which serves to show how a non-socially oriented science of behaviour led to a cognitive science detached from the social and behavioural aspects of psychology. It highlights the uncertain place of social processes in developmental accounts of the mind. In promoting Mead's social behaviourism, Farr is in the contemporary stream of psychological thinking which adopts a cultural or social approach. But it is important to distinguish here between the role of social processes in psychological accounts of mind and its development, and critiques of psychological theories from a socially based epistemology. This is the distinction between the content of specific theories and assumptions about the nature of such theories, their epistemological basis. It is this basis which is so formative of what counts as psychology and of the content of psychological theories. This is evident in Mead's social behaviourism, which is linked to his pragmatic critique of individualistic and representational assumptions about knowledge.

Mead, along with the US pragmatist philosopher Peirce, treated knowledge as social in origin by contrast to the Cartesian tradition which saw it arising from the individual knowing subject. Knowledge of oneself is not different from knowledge of others, and therefore the Cartesian split between self-knowledge and knowledge of others is rejected. Thoughts and beliefs in their pragmatic interpretation are seen to arise in a context of communication and dialogue, and therefore even our private thoughts and beliefs are construed as covert communication with ourselves. Knowledge in this interpretation is not belief which represents reality, but belief which guides interactions with reality and is judged in terms of their practical consequences. In explaining Mead's epistemological position, Farr illustrates how the historical course of psychology was influenced by the pervasive

Cartesian approach. He contends that the Cartesian method of radical doubt about knowledge had the effect of casting doubt on everything except the thinking subject. This meant that knowledge of others' minds was to be doubted and that mind became separated from behaviour. This led to a psychology of others which was behavioural and a psychology of the self which was mental.

This brief historical perspective shows the connections between psychological theory and explanations and philosophical assumptions about the nature of knowledge and science. This is another illustration of one of the key themes of this book, the interdependence of psychology and allied disciplines. The ramifications of different philosophical positions for psychology will be discussed later in this chapter.

Concepts of science applicable to psychology

The challenge for psychology continues to be how we can be true to our notions of our humanity and to a coherent concept of science. Our image of ourselves, our folk beliefs or folk psychology, is of agents who make sense of their lives and generate intentions. These folk beliefs are institutionalised into our legal and political systems with notions like responsibility and voluntary action. To those who deny these crucial common-sense notions there is no ultimate proof: we simply say, with Bruner, 'But, that's how it is, can't you see?' (Bruner, 1996: p. 16). Yet our dominant concepts of science are of causal determinism which, when applied to human actions, is incompatible with folk beliefs about agency. The classic historic attempt by Descartes to retain scientific mechanism and human agency was to separate physical from mental things and presume they operated by different principles. But even in his own time the weaknesses of this dualism were recognised by other philosophers, and the mind came to be cast as part of the causal, mechanistic physical realm.

Aversion to mechanistic scientific forms of psychology stems from this deep attachment to beliefs about human nature as purposive and behaviour as based in beliefs and intentions. A human science of the mechanistic kind offends these cherished beliefs. To explore what is at issue here, it is useful to consider the place of the principle of determinism in human behaviour. There are different versions of this principle that apply to psychology – as Eysenck (1972) has pointed out – which have significance for the relationship between causal mechanisms and human agency. The 'strong' version holds that all human behaviour is determined by psychological laws or mechanisms. These laws operate on people through heredity and the environment. However, this assumption can be seen as metaphysical in the sense that there is no empirical evidence for it. And, as many commentators have pointed out, the strong form of determinism has been questioned even in physics since the development of quantum mechanics, as expressed in Heisenberg's uncertainty principle. Eysenck and other empirical psychologists have therefore tended to opt for a weaker version of determinism which assumes that actions are determined in part. Thus it becomes an empirical question how far deterministic explanations can be extended. The weaker version of determinism assumes that there are causal factors which affect behaviour, but leaves open the extent to which behaviour is determined by prior causes. The weak version is then open to different stances which have significance for the nature of psychology. For some there is the expectation that further and powerful causal explanations will be found; for others, that many actions have reasons, and that causal factors are necessary but not sufficient for explanation.

Assuming some limit to the role of causal mechanisms in human behaviour does not mean that the alternative to determinism is that behaviour is a matter of chance. It is to presume that people are agents of their own behaviour, in the sense of selecting their own goals and determining their own behaviour. This is the issue of the human versus external determination of behaviour. In considering the self-determination of behaviour the question arises how much freedom there is to select goals and actions. Is the selection of goals and actions itself determined by some causal mechanism or is there some uncaused agent which selects? The idea of an uncaused agent, which has been called a 'ghost in the machine' or an homunculus, has its historical origins in religious and metaphysical thinking. However, it gives rise to long-standing problems about the connection between the mental and physical, the mind–brain problem, and the nature and origins of human agency.

One of the interesting implications of the 'cognitive revolution' in psychology has been that a particular mechanistic version of the mind and what is mental has been reintroduced into psychology. This has softened the tension between external determinism and human agency. The cognitive information-processing framework presumes a form of computational determinism in which specific rules govern processing. This is an internal determinism and can be linked to ideas of human agency, even though a caused agency, which is part of a larger system of rule-governed processes. A computational model provides a deterministic framework which can incorporate a particular version of agency and autonomy, even if it is still incompatible with ideas of uncaused agency or original agency (Dennett, 1995).

But, as discussed before, there are still fundamental differences between a deterministic computational and an interpretivist model. Central to this difference are their respective knowledge aims, which have moral implications. A deterministic model seeks to identify and understand causal mechanisms, as this provides the means to predict future events and behaviour and therefore to intervene to control outcomes. An interpretivist model seeks to understand the meaning of behaviour from different perspectives. Agency and the construction of meaning are the presumed ways of proceeding. This difference can be seen to reflect an active versus a more passive stance to humanity: the deterministic scientific stance is active in its aims of intervening to control, an activity which depends on mechanism. The interpretivist stance is more passive in its aim of understanding, which follows from its recognition of and respect for agency and self-determination.

It is this acknowledgement of others' agency that has been at the root of the criticisms of scientific psychology. Harre et al., for example, argue that what is offered as scientific psychology is not only less useful than it could be, but can be harmful and morally obnoxious (Harre et al., 1985, p. 17). One of the main points is that such psychology transfers what has traditionally been within the moral sphere into the causal-technical sphere. This can be seen to relieve people of responsibility for their actions by casting them in passive roles subject to external mechanistic processes. A strong form of determinism leaves no room for options and alternative actions and therefore no self-determination. It is this fear of diminished human agency which is one of the main reasons for criticisms of mechanistic psychology. The abhorrence for strong versions of behaviourist psychology, such as those promoted by Skinner (1971), derive from this threat to traditional ideas about freedom and dignity.

But this attack on a deterministic human science as undermining human responsibility has a historical background in Christian theological ideas about the relationship between God and humanity. Christianity has assumed that people have responsibility for their actions and that this depends on their having some self-determination. Moral responsibility has depended on some acceptance of human agency, that 'ought implies can'. However, acceptance of an omniscient and omnipotent deity also implies that God knows, understands and controls what humans do. This has posed a continuing paradox and a wish to resolve the tension between external determinism and human agency. There are parallels and continuities between this theological issue and the tensions between different kinds of psychologies. The development of science can be seen as an attempt to generate the kind of knowledge associated with a god-like stance and perspective. Scientific psychology can be seen therefore as a secular embodiment of this attitude towards human experience and actions. This analysis suggests that there is a long history of regarding others' presumed knowledge about humans as a threat to ideas of human agency.

This parallel has further relevance to debates within contemporary psychology about the relationship between causal mechanisms and human agency. Theological ideas attribute human agency and responsibility to God's agency. So derived, human agency is made possible by God's agency. It is possible that the relationship between causal mechanisms and agency in psychology can be construed in a similar mode. Causal mechanisms, rather than being seen as opposed to human agency, can be taken as giving rise to human agency. But this would be a caused agency, with self-determination operating within certain constraints. The effect on our ideas about humanity would be to revise our concepts of autonomy and responsibility as interlinked with causal mechanisms, not as opposed to mechanisms. It would imply that we would have flexible ideas about which behaviour was regarded within the moral and which within the causal-technical sphere. Treating a person's behaviour as the outcome of a causal mechanism – that is, as not under direct control – does not necessarily relieve him or her of responsibility for the outcome. It could mean that their responsibility shifts from direct control of the outcome to adopting some techniques for achieving the outcome. The thrust of this position is to accept the criticisms of psychologists like Harre that psychology cannot operate outside an understanding of its social, historical and moral context. But a causal mechanistic psychology need not be incompatible with ideas of agency and autonomy. Quite the reverse: the deterministic presumption could not be used to intervene and control if we did not assume that there was a human agency which actively sought knowledge of causal mechanisms and used this to identify techniques for intervening.

Critiques of scientific psychology

Harre et al. have mounted a critique of contemporary psychology over the last two decades in an attempt to develop a 'new' psychology (Harre et al., 1985). This critique identifies four main weaknesses in mainstream psychology: scientism, individualism, universalism and causalism. The question of causalism has just been discussed. Scientism is the accusation that in its dominant mode psychology deliberately draws on the methods and vocabulary of the physical and biological sciences, when they may not be appropriate. Scientific terms can come to replace everyday terms for our working psychological judgements, and in the process come to lose the subtle nuances of meaning. Scienticism is also about the use of experimental methods as the sole method of empirical inquiry. This is related to a facile universalism which assumes that because experimental methods are used the results represent universal features of functioning. Harre and many others argue from a substantial base drawing on anthropology and cultural psychology that cultural differences are significant, being evident in the role and influence of different languages on psychological development. However, while Harre's position does not deny that there are some general conditions of human life set by biological and environmental factors, it is counter to a facile universalism. It reminds us that some apparently obvious universals can turn out to be local in origin.

Individualism is shown in much contemporary psychology in the assumption that each person is a unit with certain characteristics, in which processes take place separated from social contexts. Handy (1987) has summarised this critique of individualism in psychology in terms of the indivisible link between the person and social context. It assumes that human subjectivity and action are 'constituted within and through social structures' (Handy, 1987, p. 164) while being producers of these structures. This is a critique of the person as a distinct psychological entity in favour of an interactionism which replaces the person as a unit by the person and social context as a unit. Handy argues that it is still possible from this perspective to identify individual differences, provided it is accepted that 'individuality is acquired within a social context and still reflects the indivisibility of the person and their socio-historical context' (p. 164).

Critiques of individualism in psychology are of considerable significance, because they directly address the field as a distinct discipline and its relationship with other social sciences, especially sociology. These critiques embody holistic thinking in emphasising the connections between entities rather than the entities themselves. But it is not often made clear what is entailed by the indivisibility of the person from the context. Does it mean that there is no continuity and integrity of personal processes across different contexts? It is unlikely that critics like Handy mean this because the person would then reflect the immediate context, leaving no place for personal agency and continuing identity. And this would present them with an unacceptable consequence of their critique of individualism. So the rejection of the concept of a person as thoroughly passive has considerable theoretical significance. It implies that a coherent concept of the person will include personal characteristics and processes which can in principle be continuous across contexts and over time. But this is not to adopt a concept of the person which stands outside social context, as a thoroughly independent and active agent untouched by social context. Construed in these terms the link between person and social context is more one of interconnection and mutual interaction than of indivisibility.

The concept of a person as part of an indivisible person–social context unit is also untenable, as it keeps out more than merely over-individualistic notions of the person. It treats the social context as homogenous. In doing so it does not distinguish between micro-social, interpersonal and small-group phenomena, such as families and dyadic relationships, and the macro-social, large-scale institutional phenomena, such as civic organisations and governmental agencies. It can also slip into treating the person as a speaking, thinking and reasoning being and ignore the bodily biological aspects of personal being. It is more useful to consider the person as connected with the micro-social context as one unit amongst other units of analysis. What is agent and what is context varies depending on the level of analysis. From one perspective the family can be the context to the child as a person, but from another level of analysis, social policy legislation and social service agencies can be the context of the family as a social group.

Critiques of individualism in psychology arise from wider criticisms of individualistic values with their origins in socially oriented political philosophies. In this critique individualistic values are associated mainly with the pursuit of self-interest as brutish competitiveness, selfish egoism and alienation from society. Any psychology which focuses on the socially separate individual is then implicated in the creation and perpetuation of these values. This is attributed to the theoretical focus on psychological characteristics and processes – for example, characteristics like self-esteem and processes such as cognitive appraisal and coping. The psychological focus is taken to imply that well-being requires individual change with the stress on self-direction. Change becomes the responsibility of the individual rather than any collective or social agency. Individuals are seen to pursue self-interest rather than wider social interest, which is taken to imply that psychology is based on individualistic values.

This reading of the policy and practical implications of psychology stems from a serious confounding of different versions of individualistic values: those found commonly in our society, a narrow and egoistic self-interest, and those expressed in an ethical and humanistic individualism (Waterman, 1981). It also misrepresents the empirical content of much psychology which actually shows links between self-enhancement and enhancement of relations with others. Critics of individualism in psychology tend to ignore the distinction between competitive, self-contained and alienated individualism, on the one hand, and the ethical individualist values associated with many psychological theories and theorists, particularly of humanistic persuasion, on the other. These are the values of self-knowledge (know thyself and become what thou art), freedom of choice, personal responsibility and respect for others. It should be clear that such individualist values go beyond narrow self-interest and conceptually imply the promotion of interdependence.

A cursory analysis of the actual empirical basis of much psychological theory of individual development also shows that enhancement of personal characteristics is often associated with improved interpersonal relationships (Waterman, 1981). The example of self-esteem can illustrate the point. Though there has been much concern about the theoretical and empirical basis of this concept in psychology circles (Wylie, 1979; Burns, 1982), it is a concept with a humanistic philosophical background. It is also one which has increasingly been adopted within everyday psychological language and analysis by lay people and professionals in human services. Over 50 years ago, Fromm (1939), from a humanistic psychoanalytic perspective, linked self-esteem, as a characteristic of self-regard and self-acceptance, to acceptance of and regard for others. Of course, self-esteem was not construed as arrogant self-importance and vain pride, but as a self-acceptance which included knowing one's own strengths and weaknesses and approaching them in a positive way. It is interesting that empirical attempts using quantitative methods to assess self-esteem through inventories have also shown the links between self-esteem and positive relations with others (Burns, 1982).

However, critiques of mainstream scientific psychology over the last decade have been extended to a more fundamental questioning of the nature of psychological inquiry as part of a wider social-constructionist philosophical position (Gergen, 1985). As outlined by Gergen, social constructionism is about 'explicating the processes by which people come to describe, explain, or otherwise account for the world in which they live' (Gergen, 1985, p. 266). This has the far-reaching implication that what have been taken as psychological mechanisms and processes are removed from within the head and placed in the sphere of social interaction and discourse: 'each concept (emotion, motive, etc.) is cut away from an ontological base within the head and is made a constituent of social process' (p. 271). This presents a clear challenge to traditional psychology claims about cognition, motivation, perception and so on. What had been taken to be psychological processes become derivatives of social interchange.

Gergen has identified several broad assumptions in work informed by the social constructionist orientation. The first denies the basis of knowledge in empirical experience and induction. This expresses the more recent views of philosophers like Quine (1960), Kuhn (1970) and Feyerabend (1975), that scientific theories do not represent or map reality. These authors question whether words can represent things and whether meaning derives from real-world referents. They focus instead on language use and conventions as primary sources of meaning. They refocus attention on the primacy of language and text in our conceptions about knowledge and understanding and locate these within a cultural and historical context. This forms the second assumption of the social-constructionist orientation: that what counts as knowledge and understanding is a social product or construction of interchanges between people within particular cultural and historical contexts. Applied to assumptions about psychology and the mind, this invites us to consider the social origins of what we take for granted about our psychological functioning. This cultural-relativist view also calls into question whether psychologists can step outside the understandings of their cultural setting. The implication is that this could set limits to what psychologists can say.

This leads to the third social constructionist assumption that the prevailing forms of understanding derive from the social processes of communication, rhetoric, negotiation and conflict. Observations become a less significant guide to descriptions, explanations and attributions as the working rules of inference become ambiguous and are subject to their users' interests. What Gergen has set out is what has come to be called a *post-modern* position, in which concepts like truth come to be seen as ways of warranting one position and discrediting another. Like other areas of knowledge, and especially alongside other social sciences, psychology then comes to be cast as a field of knowledge and understanding with social control functions. These are ideas which have been expressed by British psychologists who adopt a critical perspective, such as Walkerdine (1984, 1988). She draws on the European ideas allied to the social-constructionist orientation and philosophical positions which have switched from an experience-based to a socially and linguistically based epistemology. In particular she draws on the work of Foucault, who was interested in the production of discourses, such as psychology, as historically generated bodies of knowledge (Foucault, 1980). Walkerdine's argument is that psychologists like Piaget, with their scientific accounts, are implicated in the construction of modern social practices through their claims to be telling the 'truth' about children. In Piaget's case the focus on the development of reason represents an interest in promoting reason as a form of regulating children and their development. This is part of a wider agenda concerned with promoting reason and self-regulation in managing social and political affairs. What is asserted as natural comes to be revealed as produced for ideological and value purposes.

Walkerdine uses Foucault's idea of veridicality to refer to the creation of truth in scientific psychological discourse as a way of questioning the dominance of reason in human affairs and our relationship to nature. In her feminist view, social and unconscious emotional aspects are left out of this kind of discourse. It questions the privileging of objectivity and control over the ambiguities and ambivalence found in education and wider social matters. It is in this context that she uses Foucault's idea that scientific discourse creates objects which are claimed to be real but which never existed in the first place. As Walkerdine (1988, p. 202) asserts: 'Veridicality marks the idea that what is claimed as real is the biggest fiction of all.'

She uses Foucault's idea that theory creates its own truth as a critique of child-centred pedagogy which has to be seen within a wider context of post-structuralist thinking. Ideology is not seen in this framework as a distortion of reality; ideology is seen rather as a form of discourse which creates or produces reality. This is what lies behind Foucault's linkage of power and knowledge, which assumes regimes of truth which regulate society by producing the terms in which the validity of discourses is assessed. A most important part of the post-structuralist position was its critique of what were then current Marxist critiques of power as coercive and repressive. In the critique of power as repressive, emancipation involved becoming liberated from coercion. Those who repressed and those seeking liberation from repression were treated as agents. These assumptions have been questioned in the post-structuralist critique, which recognises that overt conflict does not necessarily characterise the operation of power. Power is seen as productive in the sense that it involves the production of agents by constructing their mentality, feelings and aspirations.

The post-structuralists, as Ingleby (1986) has pointed out, have been interested in the concrete social effects of discourse. Psychologists are involved in more than the development of knowledge, they are involved in the very running of society itself. Practices such as IQ testing and child-centred pedagogy are seen to create a population disciplined in certain ways. Psychologists as professionals come to be seen therefore as socialisers and assume functions in relation to families and schools. Their function is not to take over, but to study, theorise and advise parents and teachers. Parenthood becomes a skill which is regulated through scientific accounts of how children develop and what is best for them (Burman, 1994). As Ingleby (1986) points out, earlier psychology was concerned with identifying and excluding the inadequate and defective. This has become replaced by 'normalising' practices focused on the promotion of healthy development. In this light developmental psychology can be seen to illustrate Foucault's point about the move from repressive to productive power.

Part of the post-structuralist critique of humanistic and rationalist approaches is directed at the privileged positions given by these Enlightenment philosophies to the unitary self and human agency. The Cartesian divide between agents and their behaviour is rejected from a position which denies that there are human characteristics outside or prior to the social context. But this stance has its own problems, as there is an inconsistency between denying a conception of human nature and rejecting contemporary assumptions about autonomy and unitary agents. The problem is that individual powers are inscribed in many parts of contemporary social life, for example, in the law and in person-centred teaching and therapeutic practices. It is not open to the post-structuralist to deny this by referring to what people are basically like, their human nature. According to the post-structuralist position, these person-centred practices create the autonomous individual, so individuality cannot be construed as less than real, because reality is what is produced through the operation of these kinds of discourses. Subjectivity cannot therefore be denied a reality, even if it is seen to originate from without and not from within. This is an inevitable implication and problem for a position which disconnects language and discourse from a reality which is denied any discourse-independent status.

The post-structuralist critical perspective is relevant to more current social conditions in Western societies in which overt repressive power is less evident. But its concept of ideology as productive of social reality leaves it without the critical leverage of longer-standing critical perspectives which draw on Marxist and materialist philosophies. Ideology in the materialist tradition is partly about false consciousness and distorted views of reality which serve some dominant social interest. Sampson (1981) has long argued from this perspective that much of current psychology in the cognitive psychology tradition operates as an ideology in the reality-distorting sense. There are two elements to cognitive psychology which represent the values and interests of the social order, what Sampson calls the subjective and individualist reductions. The subjective reduction gives primacy to the structures and processes of the knowing subject rather than the objective and material conditions; the individualist reduction gives primacy to the thinking and reasoning of individuals over social and historical processes. These elements have their origins in the Cartesian philosophical tradition, which based knowledge on the individual knowing subject. Sampson's position is that the individualist and subjectivist reductions act to conceal the social and material origins of human behaviour. This critique of cognitivism questions the origins of mental powers within the individual and gives priority to the 'we think' over the 'I think': a tradition allied, as noted before, with the work of Vygotsky, Mead and others.

Sampson's points can be illustrated in his critiques of what has passed as interactionist theory and the tendency to reify psychological constructs. Interactionism, for example in Piaget's developmental account, is presented as the interplay of subject and reality in the developmental process; but Sampson argues that it is still the subject which is given primacy, with reality being represented as having a passive part in the process. The reality or object in the interaction continues to be seen from the perspective of the individual subject, and not in terms of how it actively contributes to the developmental process. Social reality is not treated as having an independent dynamic of its own. A second example given by Sampson is the process of reifying psychological constructs and processes, such as those involved in delaying gratification through hot-and-cool ideation in children (Mischel, 1979). 'Cool' ideation, which focuses on abstract thinking as a substitute for the unavailable concrete reality, has been shown by Mischel to facilitate delay of gratification in children. Sampson's point is that this representation of self-control in children involves a denial of reality which is presented as a fundamental aspect of human nature. Such processes of cognitively mediated self-control are more accurately seen, he contends, as a reflection of a particular social and historical context where delay of gratification is central to the efficient functioning of the economy. Sampson is making the point that there is a risk of portraying psychological processes which operate within particular socio-historical contexts as universal cross-cultural features of human nature.

Another allied source of critique of scientific psychology is feminism. Feminist scholars have criticised positivist scientific methods for a bias towards pathologising women and affirming their deficiencies and subordinate role to men. The ignoring of social context in methodology has been criticised, as has the failure to consider the construction of knowledge about women. Psychology has been portrayed as particularly resistant to the influence of critical and post-modernist theory (Riger, 1992). From a feminist perspective, there have been critiques of the contribution of experimental studies to psychological knowledge along the same lines as those mounted from the relativist position discussed above. Feminist psychology comes therefore to represent its own role as challenging the realist position of patriarchal science (Nicolson, 1995). It is clear that the feminist perspective is relevant to the study of psychology generally and constitutes an important perspective on what is conceptualised as research and knowledge, on the one hand, and on what are important substantive areas for study, on the other. The development of a feminist perspective in and on psychology is also important for our understanding of the nature of psychology as a field of study and an academic and service profession. Some feminists trained as psychologists reject what passes as psychological knowledge and methods because they are seen to obstruct them in their projects. Other feminists have founded sections within national psychological associations, though not without resistance. Of course, there are also different versions of feminism which change over time in response to social and political developments. But what the feminist perspective has contributed to psychology has been not only the introduction of a more social and critical stance, but also connections to other allied disciplines such as philosophy and sociology. Feminist psychology therefore illustrates how psychology overall has come to diversify and include strands which are mutually critical of each other.

Much of the critique discussed in this section questions the universalising aspirations of psychology by locating theoretical portrayals in psychology within a particular social and economic context. This asserts the primacy of the social over the individual and questions the focus on independent subjectivity in psychology by invoking either the dominance of material and social interests or the pervasiveness of language and discourse in creating the subject. But, as argued above, there are serious problems with the other extreme of relativising psychology. To treat the individual person as a wholly social creation is to ignore the biological basis and origins of humanity. Psychological processes can be seen to originate socially from internalising interpersonal joint interactions, but the process of internalising is undertaken by an individual with a neural system located within her or his brain. However much mind might be construed as social in nature and origins, there is no easy way of ignoring its physical embodiment within a physical frame. These points will be elaborated in a section to come.

Psychology as common sense

A common response from non-psychologists to psychology is that it is like common sense, or even nothing but common sense. This dismissive response might be related to the fact that the subject matter of psychology is something which is familiar to everyone. Psychological concepts and assumptions are common in everyday life and activities, to such an extent that it has been argued that everyone is a lay psychologist. But to see it this way is to give priority to psychology as a formal discipline, one which has tried to go well beyond common-sense understandings. The scientific psychology which has been built up over the last century has made a point of abandoning everyday common-sense psychological categories and understandings. In trying to understand the common sense–psychology relationship, Harre et al. (1985) have identified four possible forms. One is that there is no connection between scientific psychology and common sense. This position implies that scientific psychology uses a language and adopts a set of assumptions which cannot be translated into common-sense knowledge and is therefore largely unusable. A second kind of relationship is that scientific psychology can be translated into common-sense knowledge, but the implications are found to be morally obnoxious and are therefore rejected. The usual example referred to here is Skinner's operant psychology, which is read as reducing human behaviour to that of automata and from a humanistic viewpoint rejected as demeaning. Skinner's psychology has come, as mentioned before, to represent a psychology which assumes an overt form of causal determinism. This is partly because it focuses on the relationships between the environment and behaviour while rejecting internal mental processes and states as causal. But it is not in principle different from other cognitive theories of a causal-deterministic nature. From the everyday perspective that humans have some control over their thoughts and actions, it may seem that cognitive theories are consistent with this kind of human agency. But, as explained in the introduction to this chapter, this does not follow. Computational models in psychology associated with cognitive theories and cognitive science are no less deterministic than radical behaviourism. The difference is between more and less complex models and between more overt and more covert kinds of determinism. It may be that the more complex and covert models evoke less fear of portraying human beings as automata. But this may be a superficial perspective which hides the real nature of a deterministic model. This analysis can be linked up with ideas associated with the post-structuralism of Foucault, discussed above. He identified a trend for the human sciences to be used for social control less overtly and coercively, and more covertly, by producing working assumptions about what counts as authoritative knowledge about human nature and what is normal. Thus the rejection of scientific psychology from a moral viewpoint is central to the fundamental question of the nature of psychology and our views about ourselves. It is a question of how much we hold on to beliefs which express human aspirations for agency and control and how much we moderate these by taking account of what we can acknowledge dispassionately about causal processes determining how we think, feel and behave.

A third kind of relationship between common sense and psychology is to see scientific psychology as falling within the bounds of common-sense knowledge. From this perspective, psychology is a re-description of common sense concepts and principles set out in invented terms which sound significant and insightful. This is the view that psychology is largely what we already know – truisms dressed up in jargon. However, it is a position which can be used constructively to illustrate that much psychology can be represented as the systematic exploration of semantic rules. This is where the philosophical distinction between analytic and synthetic statements is relevant. Analytic statements are true by the definition of the terms. So, to use the usual example, in the statement 'bachelors are unmarried men': we do not need to do an empirical survey to find out about this relationship. By contrast, a synthetic statement is true because empirical evidence supports the relationship. For instance, an empirical survey would be relevant to testing the statement that 'most bachelors are in the below-40 age group'. Smedslund (1995) has developed a view which questions whether psychology can be represented as the accumulation of empirical generalisations that are mainly synthetic statements. His view is that 'what is good in psychology is not new', and that our natural language has psychological common sense built into it. By psychological common sense he means those psychological statements which are true because of the meaning of their words. Such common sense is not open to refutation because it consists of analytic statements, which are true by definition. Smedslund uses a statement containing psychological common sense, such as 'a person is surprised if and only if and to the extent that she or he has just experienced something unexpected' to illustrate the point. His position is that it is true by the definition of what surprise is and therefore is not open to empirical investigation. From this he comes to characterise the empirical study of such relationships like this as pseudo-empirical and to make two strong assertions about psychology. Firstly, that 'plausible hypotheses in psychology are always based on meaning relations between constituent variables and hence are not empirical', and secondly, that 'psychologists always believe that their hypotheses are empirical' (p. 202). Smedslund has over the years tried to show that well-known theories in psychology, such as those dealing with self-efficacy, learned helplessness, attitudes and behaviour, cognitive development and so on, can be shown to support his position.

The implications of his position are significant for the future of psychology because they mean that psychology becomes a formal non-empirical discipline which elaborates the meaning of psychological terms, and which he has called 'psychologic'. This 'psychologic' attempts to systematise the conceptual framework embedded in ordinary language. It contains axioms, definitions and derived propositions. From these it is possible to work out the outcomes of psychological interventions. Empirical study is therefore relevant to investigating the particulars of a person in a given situation, to work out the implications from psychologic propositions. Difficulty in prediction is then seen not as ignorance of empirical psychological generalisations but as a lack of particular concrete knowledge. In this conception of psychology, empirical work is also useful in evaluating the usefulness of methods and procedures. But experimental methods lose their traditional function of discovering invariant empirical generalisations, for it is argued that meaningful relationships involve variables which are already conceptually related.

Smedslund's approach of seeking the analytic propositions expressed in the semantics of everyday language is a reminder of how much of contemporary psychology is imbued with the empirical tradition. However, there are questions about the relevance of his approach to modelling psychologic on the logic and proofs used in Euclidean geometry and doubts about whether semantic relationships are clear-cut. As Harre et al. (1995) have pointed out, semantic relations are more like a web of loose relationships. This implies that the analytic relationships which form the basis of a psychologic are not so easily identified and may need to be supplemented by conceptual work to clarify the nature of these relationships. Smedslund does not rule out the possibility of finding empirical relationships not already contained in the definitions and axioms implicit in ordinary language. Rather, he challenges us to find empirical generalisations which are general, empirical and valid. If there are such generalisations, he suggests that they will have to be resistant to falsification by learning and are more likely to be fixed biological principles or boundary conditions which are outside the domain of psychology.

Gage (1991, 1996), whose position was outlined in the previous chapter, has also confronted this question of the empirical contribution to generalisations in the social and psychological sciences. He makes a distinction between the obviousness of generalisations and their trivial nature. He has also shown that what appears obvious and plausible can be contradicted by empirical evidence and that even quite contrary generalisations can appear similarly plausible. But it is not this aspect of psychology which is relevant to Smedslund's view that empirical study can add little of significance to relationships which are true conceptually. Gage takes the view that even if some generalisations are conceptually true, empirical study can enhance them with specifics about the extent of the relationship under different conditions.

Gage defends the contribution of empirical work from a technical perspective which aims to find out what interventions can improve learning outcomes under what conditions. This is in a different tradition to Harre et al.'s programme, which assumes that 'systematic, careful, sceptical and rigorous scientific research could be used to extend and correct the domain of common sense psychology' (Harre et al., 1985, p. 15). This is the fourth possible relationship between common sense and psychology. In this version the task of systematic study is to make explicit the psychologies of every day and then undertake empirical study in the light of this understanding to develop and extend this body of knowledge. Harre et al. summarise this position neatly by referring to common sense as the literature, as that part of the body of knowledge available to the systematic study of psychology. This conception of psychology as a systematic field of study has much to commend it because it retains a critical distance for psychology from everyday notions and assumptions while recognising their interdependence and interaction. However, it does not address issues concerned with what is implied and required by calling a systematic study 'scientific'. Nor does it provide a perspective on how everyday or folk psychology interacts with the systematic study. These issues arise because everyday psychology is a complex mixture of notions and assumptions which have been developed over the years in response to how people lead their lives on a day-to-day level, but also in response to wider issues about our origins and place in the universe. This inevitably leads to philosophical questions which will be dealt with briefly in the next section.

Philosophical ideas of psychology as science

Much has already been said about the lack of theoretical unity in psychology and the aspirations for a scientific treatment of the field. Science has assumed considerable importance in Western societies and is considered to be one of the great human achievements of the last two centuries. There is no doubt about its impact on our understanding of the natural world and therefore our place in it. It has also influenced our technologies and had an immense impact on all areas of our lives. It is hardly surprising that the study of social and psychological affairs should adopt some, if not all, of the hall-marks of this successful endeavour called science. The problems arise because there are uncertainties about whether the characteristics associated with the more successful empirical sciences, such as physics or biology, are applicable to the study of human experience and actions. Central to these sciences are assumptions and methods which are considered to hold the key to explanatory success. One assumption is the autonomy and authority of facts. Facts relate to what is the case and form the basis for deriving and testing explanations of phenomena and predictions of the future. Scientific methods, which are designed to be well defined, systematic, objective and clear, are central to this process of comparing ideas and explanations with evidence. The knowledge derived from these systematic empirical methods is open to revision, and therefore the scientific method is considered to have the power to self-correct and adapt to new circumstances and fields. Though the idea of science is associated with these methods, they have to be judged in terms of their adequacy for the aims of science. These are theoretical aims: to enhance understanding and explanation.

Much has been said over the last half century of the idealised nature of the scientific method. Scientists in various fields have been shown to depart from the procedures in the classical view. That scientists do not always abandon their theories in the face of contrary facts and evidence has become more widely known. Scepticism about the autonomy of facts and their role as the ultimate arbiters of theory has also become more accepted. Much of this has been in reaction to the development of *logical positivism* in the early part of the twentieth century. Positivism has its origins in empiricist epistemologies which base knowledge on sense data. In the logical formulation of positivism, the meaning of any statement is founded on its empirical verification. This means that theoretical terms without direct empirical content have to be linked through a deductive network to empirical observations. Another feature of positivism is its belief in the unity of different sciences through the use of the same methods.

Critiques of positivism have been directed at assumptions about the nature of our mental states and their position at the foundation of knowledge. This has been called the *myth of the given* (Sellars, 1963): the central but false idea in Western epistemology that we have direct awareness of our mental states. It is the myth that we have privileged access to these mental states in an infallible and incorrigible way. The myth of the given is related to the critique of the mind as an internal theatre. This is the Cartesian model of the mind, associated with mind–body dualism in which there is internal observation of mental objects, through a process of introspection. This is an important point, for the early history of modern psychology was marked by the failure of the introspectionist project. This called into question the assumption that one can simply read off one's own mental states. But the myth of the given is also connected to empirical positivist epistemology, which takes true knowledge to be based on what is presented to our senses, what is given to our inner eye. The implication is that critiques of the idea that our mental states are infallible undermine confidence in empirical positivist assumptions.

The general thrust of this critique of empiricism and positivism was that what was taken as incorrigibly given was really theory laden and therefore fallible. Thus 'knowing' came to be seen as making true statements and predicting what would happen, rather than having evidence based on sense data. This thrust was in line with positions developed by philosophers like Quine (1960) and Wittgenstein (1953). Quine argued that empirical statements (synthetic) could not be distinguished basically from conceptually true ones (analytic), as meaning is grounded in usage, and therefore that no knowledge can be completely independent of theory. Quine also argued that when there was a conflict between theory and observations, single statements about the external world could not be isolated and tested. Experience confronted knowledge as a system of statements that could be accommodated by adjustments to the system. The implication was that though empirical data were relevant to testing systems of knowledge, they could not provide the infallible foundation sought by empiricist and positivist traditions. Wittgenstein's work is relevant here because his early position was along logical positivist lines: language pictured the world. However, in his later work he criticised his own earlier views that propositions could be considered in isolation and that there was a context-free link between proposition and fact, or language and reality. Language came to be seen instead as getting its meaning from the context of its use in what he called language games. Language was itself a form of activity, it was a form of life. Meanings were rooted in public language, which provided the terms with which one made personal sense of one's experience and the world. The implications of this language-focused position are significant for conceptions of knowledge and science. Rather than seeking timeless foundations, the social origins of knowledge were identified and science came to be seen as a social institution, where practices change depending on context.

This turn away from sense data as the foundation of knowledge to language as a social institution undermined the role of observation as the arbiter in science. Observation came to be seen as theory laden; what was observed depended on having relevant concepts and background assumptions. But there was still the question whether observations reflected the facts; whether there were facts independent of theory, one of the core tenets of positivist philosophy. The motive for this distinction was to seek a way of separating science as true knowledge from pseudo-science. This was an important distinction, as it was the basis for the continuing effort of empirically minded philosophers to develop an epistemology which could justify the legitimacy of scientific knowledge. It has particular relevance in this chapter to different conceptions about the nature of psychology; whether psychology can be given an empirical scientific treatment or whether it is better conceived in social constructionist terms as a social institution with particular social and technical functions. Critiques of positivism in psychology sometimes ignore the fact that there were subsequent attempts to salvage the empirical tradition and the ideal of demarcating science from pseudo-science. This was the significance of Popper's falsification notion (Popper, 1979), which justified knowledge on the grounds that it could survive repeated attempts at empirical falsification. Popper's response was to give up the search for a secure foundation for knowledge in empirical facts by rejecting induction and verification and so abandoning the quest for certainty. Nevertheless, Popper held on to the idea that falsifiability was the hall-mark of rationality in that it subjected ideas and statements to critical and public tests. The knowledge claims of competing theories could therefore still be tested, which was one of the personal interests of Popper, especially in relation to the scientific nature of Freud's psychodynamic psychology. This philosophical position, about scientific knowledge as conjectures which withstand refutations, came to be presented as an evolutionary conception of knowledge in which the fittest hypotheses and theories were those which survived empirical falsification.

The Popperian focus on critical rationality based on empirical falsification can be seen more as a prescription for knowledge production than an accurate description of how scientists have proceeded in practice. The focus amongst other philosophers of science was less on justification for knowledge than on how theories were generated and tested. This is where the work of Kuhn has been so influential on our ideas about science in general and about the status of psychology, in particular his use of the notion of paradigms to refer to the self-perpetuating and collectivist aspects of science as a social and historical practice (Kuhn, 1970). Though there have been doubts about what was involved in a paradigm, Kuhn's intention was to show that paradigms were incommensurable. This term refers to the impossibility of making a rational comparison between competing paradigms. It implies that there is no definitive and rational way of deciding between different paradigms, so calling into question a demarcation between authentic science and non-science. It is a position which opens up a relativism as facts themselves are considered to be part of paradigms and therefore cannot be invoked to decide between competing paradigms. Kuhn's work has been interpreted as showing the significance of cultural and historical processes in scientific change. Paradigms are able to accommodate results which are hard to explain, by either invoking supplementary assumptions, denying the validity of the results or putting aside the results for later consideration. Paradigm changes are therefore seen to come about for social and non-rational reasons.

Kuhn's work was open to two contrary responses. One, associated with Lakatos (1970), took on board Kuhn's historical perspective about the collective and dogmatic aspects of science, but attempted to retain the criteria of scientific rationality by applying this not to specific theories, but to research programmes. Research programmes were taken to involve hard-core assumptions which were not open to criticism, but also contained auxiliary hypotheses which were open to refutation. Programmes which could anticipate events and novel facts were progressive, while those which had to invent hypotheses to counter negative results were degenerative. A decision between programmes or paradigms might have to wait till rival programmes had been developed and tested. But this response to Kuhn was positive about the prospects of a rational basis for scientific demarcation and development. The other response was to build on the relativism in Kuhn's socio-historical views about science, and is best known through the views of Feyerabend (1975). A clear demarcation between rational science and non-science was rejected by Feyerabend as paternalistic and arrogant. Observations were considered to be theory laden and theories were seen as productive of their own supporting evidence, based on the resources and power of scientists in dominant research positions. A methodological position of 'anything goes' was advocated as a way of undermining philosophical attempts to police for society what counted as authoritative science.

These differing philosophical positions about the nature of science were developed partly in response to major changes in physics and the natural sciences during the twentieth century. But, as mentioned before, they were also relevant to issues within the social and human sciences where claims were made for the authority of certain fields of study, such as Marxism and psychoanalysis, in the name of science. These moves within the philosophy of science are relevant to the discussion of psychology in this chapter, as they highlight several important points about the theoretical diversity of the field of study called psychology. The idea of a paradigm, loose as it is, does call attention to the social, professional and institutional aspects of scientific fields of study. Paradigms involve not just theoretical assumptions but also commitments to methods, procedures, professional practices and ways of approaching the field. Paradigms are like world-views, into which scientists become initiated through their education and professional training. These trends in understanding science can be seen therefore as introducing the human and historical contexts into the institutions of science, including those of psychology. This is a welcome counter to the almost religious authority and infallibility attributed sometimes to science in a secular age. But that is where different positions emerge, between those who acknowledge these social aspects in order to protect a sustainable commitment to empirical rationality and those who see this leading to all-out interpretivism or constructionism.

Constructionist, realist and pragmatist views of psychology as a science

As discussed before, social constructionism represents a philosophical approach to science in general and to psychology in particular. It is opposed to realism in the sense that it denies that psychological knowledge represents or corresponds to psychological states or processes in the world. It assumes that we cannot map or mirror human realities in a definitive way. What positivist psychologists have called scientific knowledge comes therefore to be seen only as the product of social construction. As Gergen (1985, p. 266) has asserted, 'Social constructionism views discourse about the world not as a reflection or map of the world but as an artifact of communal exchange.' Language and discourse function, in this view, to create and change social relations, and if they represent, this is only within a form of social life. As discussed before, this position supports a critical psychology that questions the mainstream topics and concepts of empiricist psychology. Psychological understanding, therefore, is not dependent on the nature of psychological states and processes, but on the social processes of communication, conflict and negotiation. There is no objective understanding in psychology, because reality is itself negotiable and there are different perspectives and meanings which can be attributed to experience and actions. This means that in this view interpretation is a key to psychological understanding.

In its exposition by theorists like Gergen, social constructionism poses a basic threat to the security of a scientific basis for psychology. It questions whether psychology is about establishing objective knowledge about psychological phenomena, by questioning the processes of warranting theoretical explanations. As Gergen explains:

> constructionism offers no alternative truth criteria. Accounts of social constructionism cannot themselves be warranted empirically. If properly executed, such accounts can enable one to escape the confines of the taken for granted. They may emancipate one from the demands of convention. However, the success of such accounts depends primarily on the analyst's capacity to invite, compel, stimulate or delight the audience, and not on criteria of veracity.
>
> (p. 272)

Gergen recognises that some psychologists want to avoid this form of social constructionism because it is relativistic and opens up an 'anything goes' approach to the field. However, he denies that the relativism of social constructionism implies an anything-goes approach to evaluating knowledge in psychology. He asserts that any knowledge claims have to be intelligible to others in a community and that therefore what is taken to be scientific activity will be governed by normative rules.

Social constructionism can be seen to make an important contribution to our understanding of the nature of psychology; but when it is presented as denying the prospect of objectivity as an epistemological aspiration, it runs into a self-defeating and nihilist position. It is possible to recognise the importance of the social construction of reality without denying that there is some external reality, along the lines suggested by Searle (1995). He distinguishes between the nature of judgements or statements in the domain of language or discourse, epistemology, and what exists, ontology.

Figure 2 illustrates these epistemological and ontological dimensions. It shows that some statements can be considered as objectively true insofar as they are consistent with the facts, while other statements may be subjective

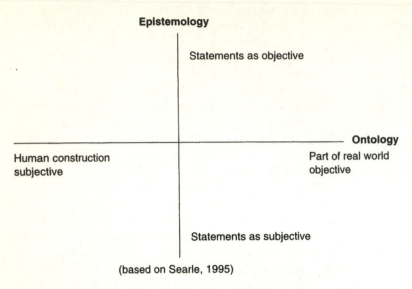

(based on Searle, 1995)

Figure 2 Two independent features of our relation to the world

because they express personal perspectives. Independently of this distinction, some things can be considered to exist objectively, in the sense that they exist independently of any human attitude or knowledge of them, while other things are subjective or related to some human use. Some features of the world, such as the existence of a mountain, can therefore be regarded as intrinsic and do not depend on any human construction for their real existence. Other features of the world, by contrast, may depend on human construction or use, being ontologically subjective, but can be described in epistemologically objective terms. For example, that someone is a teacher is a social construction in the sense that this attribution derives from human aims and institutions, but this subjective ontological feature can be represented by objective statements. Searle's point is that the social construction of reality depends on there being a reality. Psychology, like other fields of study, does not therefore have to choose between recognising the human or social dependence of certain features of the world and making objective statements about these features.

The problems with realism and objectivism, which I have discussed above, have highlighted the limits of positivism as a philosophy of psychology. They have also illustrated that there are no absolute foundations for psychological knowledge, and have shown that claims for objectivity involve wider value issues which are related to the social functions of the discipline. But these problems do not mean that we have to accept that psychology cannot aspire in principle to some degree of objectivity. They do not imply that showing the social aspects of personal experience and action means that there are indefinite versions of the truth and no prospect of a rational basis for rejecting some versions and perspectives. This is not to say that truths in the field of psychology are easily decided, or that psychologists have some privileged and exclusive access to such truths compared to other commentators on the human scene. It is to say, following the commonly heard argument, that a purist relativism is self-defeating for the following reason: to assert the truth of a statement which declares that no statement can be true undermines the statement of the relativist position itself.

This form of relativism, which has been called judgemental relativism (Bem and de Jong, 1997), assumes that all claims to knowledge have equal validity. As Gergen mentioned above, relativists often claim that their form of relativism does not mean that 'anything goes'. For them relativism means opposing absolutism in knowledge and seeing knowledge as rooted in a particular time and culture: this is what has been called methodological relativism, thus social constructionism. But even this claim – that what is true for one culture or period of history cannot be true for another culture – is incoherent. The reason relates back to the question of incommensurability raised in the section above about scientific paradigms. The problem for this position is that any comparison of different theories or knowledge claims requires some way of translating one claim into terms which are comparable with the other claims. This implies that some neutral standpoint is assumed in which an independent position can be taken. And of course this is not allowed in a relativist position which cannot distinguish between different truth claims.

The retreat from assumptions about reality to the dominance of language and discourse, in some contemporary approaches to the social and human sciences, leaves a field like psychology in a state of flux and radical uncertainty. Language becomes our major access to the world, based on the assumption that there is nothing outside the text and that statements can only refer to each other and cannot be about the world. The problem with this contemporary position is that it confuses knowledge with language; knowledge is usually expressed in language, but it is not the same as language. Knowledge can be considered more fruitfully as a human relationship to the world. Knowledge may be in error and is therefore not certain, but nevertheless it is about relating to the world. As Bem and de Jong (1997) point out, relativists tend to ignore subject–object relatedness and to replace it by subject–subject relatedness, that is, by social conventions and practices. Thus knowledge claims in a field like psychology come to be treated as nothing but social constructs subject to power and ideological interests. This is an unjustified conclusion, for it turns everything into a social practice and ignores that practices themselves are also object-related.

Underlying this denial of subject–object relatedness is the relativist criticism of the correspondence theory of truth, which asserts that true knowledge is the correspondence between statements and states of affairs in the world. Relativists claim that there is no independent way of comparing statements with the world, because the only access to the world is through statements themselves. Though this critique is widely shared, it is possible to assume some form of realism without subscribing to the correspondence approach to truth. Another problem with the correspondence approach is that it is too focused on language: the world is mirrored in our thoughts and statements. But it is interesting, as Bem and de Jong (1997) point out, that both relativists and correspondence theory realists share the assumption that our relationship to the world is through language and theories. Both views ignore the fact that there is another perspective on knowing, which is not exclusively theoretical or intellectual. This is to regard knowing as an active relationship to objects or entities in the world: what has been called a pragmatic position, which cuts through the locked opposition of realism and relativism, of objectivism and subjectivism.

There are different versions of the pragmatic position, a philosophical position associated with John Dewey. It focuses on knowledge as guiding actions in our coping with the world, rather than as copying the world or as arbitrary social constructions. For example, the contemporary US philosopher Putnam (1990), who accepts that it is not possible to describe the world in an absolute way independent of a human perspective, does not see this as leading to relativism. His internal or pragmatic realist position assumes that our changing knowledge can only be justified by its success in relation to our values and interests. But the world is neither the product of human will nor of tendencies to discourse in certain ways. Rorty (1979), another US philosopher in the pragmatic tradition, sees knowledge as a tool for dealing with reality. Pragmatism, according to Rorty, is anti-representational in the sense that language cannot be compared with reality. But knowledge, although arising within language and discourse, is in relation to the world. What the renewed interest in pragmatic views has to offer, therefore, is a turning away from absolute foundations for rationally based knowledge without letting go of a relatedness to reality. Knowledge is about skills and practices, with the sciences as a systematic and exploratory way of coping with the world. What is real is not what is represented in language, but what emerges in our interactions and manipulations of the world. This means that *knowing how* – our skills and practices – precedes *knowing that*, our theoretical knowledge. It is an approach which assumes that, although there is no uninterpreted reality, reality comes to be grasped through practical interactions: 'the world is what shows up in our practices' (Bem and de Jong, 1997, p. 79). As these authors explain, the absence of absolute criteria and foundations for rationality does not imply an absence of rational discourse.

Biological and evolutionary perspectives on psychology

In acknowledging how a pragmatic philosophical position breaks through the dichotomy between social constructionism and scientific realism, it is possible to see how knowledge comes to be linked to pre-linguistic interactions between humans and the world. Knowledge is about how humans interact with the world in their actions, not just in intellectual terms. So if knowledge is seen to grow out of personal and social interactions with the world, then thinking and knowing are related to doing and coping. Mind is connected to actions, development over the individual life-span and with biological evolutionary origins. A pragmatic philosophical approach to psychology therefore links psychological states and processes to developmental and evolutionary origins. Historically, there are several theoretical traditions within psychology, such as the Piagetian and Freudian developmental psychologies, which have tried to base psychological processes, whether of an intellectual or emotional nature, on biology. These traditions have a particular significance within psychology because they link the functioning of the mind with the body, a topic which has been at the centre of attempts to apply scientific methods to human experience and actions.

Freud's psychodynamic theories of psycho-sexual development are of particular interest, as they were presented as attempting to place human development in the tradition of Darwinian evolutionary theory (Sulloway, 1992). The biologically based instincts of sexual reproduction and survival were seen to underlie the stages of individual development. The instinctual elements within personal functioning came to be represented by the id, operating on the pleasure principle of seeking instant gratification. The socially responsive elements were represented by the ego, operating on the reality principle of rational deliberation, and the superego, as an internalised overseer. The conflicts between the ego and id were seen to be the source of repressive moves to ward off negative feelings and their associated cognitive representations. In this way mental functioning was seen as influenced by defensive processes, putting individuals in a position where they were not fully aware of the factors affecting their experience and behaviour.

That important psychological processes were outside and inaccessible to conscious awareness has been seen as one of the most significant knowledge claims made in the field of psychology over the last century. Freud himself represented it as the equivalent of the Copernican revolution for the human sciences. The status of Freudian psychodynamic theories about unconscious processes is important for the discussion in this chapter about the nature of psychology as a science. Freud's background was in medicine and as a medical research scientist; his psychological theories were based on case studies arising from clinical practice. His model of conscious, pre-conscious and unconscious processing was not based on systematic empirical investigations, and he was reluctant to consider independent attempts to investigate his conclusions by empirical research methods. The outcome has been that Freudian ideas have been subjected over a long period to criticism for their lack of empirical grounding, by psychologists of a more behaviourist orientation (Eysenck, 1985). The concept of an unconscious has also been criticised from a philosophical position for being unfalsifiable. This criticism relates to what counts as independent evidence for or against identifying a psychological process as unconscious. Freudian theories have also been seen to perpetuate a Cartesian model of the mind in which there is some inner person or homunculus which controls conscious processes and interacts with unconscious ones.

More recently, there have been some serious and sustained allegations about the professional ethics of Freud's psychoanalytic practices and distortions of his theoretical formulations in relation to the abuse of his young adult patients when in childhood (Masson, 1984; Webster, 1995; Crews, 1997). Though these contemporary debates are important and interesting, they are not directly relevant to the present discussion about the place of conscious awareness in psychological processes and the relationship between mental and bodily processes. More relevant to this discussion is the growth of experimental research about cognitive processes which has shown that people have restricted access to their internal mental states (Brewin, 1993). For example, behaviour can be influenced in ways that individuals cannot report, by external events and by internal rule systems. So, as Brewin points out, it is no longer contentious that there are important psychological processes of which individuals might be unaware. But this is not the same unconscious as Freud was dealing with. In his formulations, the unconscious was not just about thoughts and feelings which were outside conscious awareness but could be retrieved or accessed. His unconscious contained memories associated with childhood experiences that were often associated with powerful emotions, and were not admissible to conscious awareness. This has been called the dynamic unconscious and is associated with the repression of ideas and affects from conscious awareness.

There is continuing controversy about whether experimental evidence can be produced to show the presence of a dynamic unconscious, as the reviews by Dixon (1981) and Brewin (1993) illustrate. It has been argued that emotional arousal accompanying traumatic experiences may affect the registration and storage of events, rather than traumatic memories being excluded or repressed from conscious memory. Nevertheless, there is experimental evidence showing the operation of an analogous process to repression, what is called perceptual defence in response to emotionally disturbing words. Dixon (1981) has also produced a model of defence processes and linked these to neural pathways in the brain which could mediate them. Whether direct experimental evidence will be found to support the presence of a dynamic unconscious is still an open question. It is an important one, especially with the emergence of allegations that psychotherapists have placed false memories in their vulnerable clients (Crews, 1997). However, there is less controversy about the presence of non-conscious processes influencing thinking and behaviour. It has led to the proposition that there are two parallel psychological systems which process information: *automatic* processes, which operate outside awareness, and *conscious or control processes*, which are deliberately set into motion by individuals. Brewin links these two systems to distinct theories in psychology, the behaviourist theories of Pavlov and Skinner and the social learning theories of Bandura and Mischel.

The behaviourist tradition has regarded conscious beliefs and feelings as by-products which have no causal influence in their own right, what have been called epiphenomena. The social learning tradition, which has been more in line with common-sense ideas about actions, has seen conscious goals and plans as important influences on the self-regulation of behaviour. So here we have two kinds of theoretical traditions cast as providing accounts of quali-tatively different but interacting kinds of behaviour, what Brewin calls regu-lated and unregulated behaviour. Unregulated behaviour is more stereotyped and is in response to identifiable environmental stimuli; individuals may be unaware of these actions and unlikely to provide an accurate account of what they are doing. Regulated behaviour is by contrast more flexible and adapts to changing circumstances; individuals can usually give an account of their action by invoking some goal or intention. In practice, actions are controlled by the two systems, sometimes in a complementary way, at others in con-flicting ways.

This kind of dual processing theory is important because it attempts to link ideas about human agency and intentions in human action with what we know about the determinism of some human actions. But it does not directly address more fundamental questions about how mind and human agency arose out of biological evolution. This brings us back to issues raised earlier in the chapter about the relationship between physical systems gov-erned by mechanistic determinism and by human agency and consciousness. It is here that developments in evolutionary biology, building on Darwinian ideas, have introduced some challenging and exciting ideas about the nature of minds and consciousness and their biological origins (Dawkins, 1989; Dennett, 1995; Pinker, 1997). As a philosopher who has taken up Darwin's ideas about the natural origins of life, Dennett has tried to explain how the evolutionary ideas of natural selection can be applied to understanding the origins of human agency and consciousness. He presents these ideas as dan-gerous even a century after the battle between Christianity and Darwinian evolutionary biologists, because they threaten continuing beliefs about the mind as something which cannot be connected to the mindless mechanical processes of natural selection. Dennett claims that there is still some con-temporary belief in Cartesian dualism, in assumptions of a homunculus as an inner agent directing actions and of human intentionality as arising inde-pendently of natural processes. He contends that these strands derive from the continuing residue of metaphysical religious ideas which attribute the origins of life to an external designer having an original intention.

Dennett's approach to the natural origins of human agency is to identify the birth of elementary forms of agency in the behaviour of the first self-replicating macro-molecules. These basic building blocks of organisms are in the strict sense mindless, being unaware of what they are doing. But these molecules are systematic and operate control systems, being sensitive to variation and opportunities. Dennett's point is that since humans are the descendants of these self-replicating robots, these molecules show an early form of agency. Dennett calls all these systems, whether artifacts, animals or persons, intentional systems. (By this he does not mean to treat them as if they had conscious thoughts and feelings.) This way of regarding physical and biological systems allows the adoption of what he calls the intentional stance, a strategy of interpreting the behaviour of a system *as if* it were a rational agent who governed decisions in terms of beliefs and desires. The reason for anthropomorphising is to predict the actions of the system. The significance of the intentional stance can be understood in the context of two other stances of prediction, what he calls the physical and the design stance.

The physical stance is the standard approach of the physical sciences, in which we use the laws of physics and the constitution of things in order to predict. Dennett sees the physical sciences as applying to all matter, whether organic or inorganic. However, some physical objects which are designed to perform certain functions are subject to more sophisticated types of prediction than others which are not so designed. The design stance becomes useful if it is assumed that the object performs its designed function properly. This stance therefore provides a short cut to prediction without having to adopt the more laborious physical stance. It is a stance which applies not only to physical artifacts, but also to living things and their parts. The intentional stance can be seen as a version of the design stance. Its adoption is more useful when the artifacts are even more complicated, such as chess-playing computers. Adopting this stance does not mean that the physical or design stances are not applicable to predicting the behaviour of these artifacts, just that the intentional stance is a short cut to predicting the moves of the chess-playing computer. Nor does it mean that by adopting it we regard such artifacts as if they are really like us.

Dennett wishes to show that through evolution the brain, although it is an automaton, reaches a level of complexity and sophistication such that it operates as a fully fledged intentional system and can be regarded from the intentional stance. This is a view which is criticised by philosophers such as Searle (1992), who deny that automata have real intentionality. They are only willing to accept that at best automata have an 'as if' kind of intentionality. The problem for Searle's view is that if humans are descended from automata, then it is hard to deny that humans are also composed of automata. His denial springs from his assertion that humans have real intentionality, a property which cannot be attained through the process of building better algorithms. Dennett attributes the hostility to artificial intelligence to the metaphysical belief that minds have original intentionality and are not the outcome of a natural evolutionary process.

Dennett also suggests how brains might have evolved to operate a sophisticated kind of intentionality. He presents an idealisation of this possible process in terms of the design of a tower floor by floor, calling it the *tower of generate-and-test*, a Darwinian change process. Each floor represents an advance in cognitive power, starting with Darwinian creatures in which blind mutation and natural selection generated novel and adaptive designs. Amongst these were creatures which had greater phenotypic plasticity, meaning that the organisms were not fully designed at birth. Aspects of design could be adjusted from experience of events which occurred. He calls this subset of Darwinian creatures 'Skinnerian creatures', as they operate by the principles of operant conditioning or learning. Dennett reminds us that there has been a tendency to underestimate the power of such learning, and that the current interest in connectionist networks testifies to the flexibility of simple networks adjusted by experience. However, there are some cognitive tasks, beyond recognition, discrimination and generalisation, which do not require trial and error. The next floor in Dennett's tower belongs to the Popperian creatures which survived because they could make better than chance first moves. This involved a pre-selection process in which an inner environment, which had information about the external environment, previewed and selected possible actions or hypotheses. As discussed above, Popper saw his position about scientific knowledge as part of a wider evolutionary theory of cognition. Popperian creatures had this ability to install information about the external environment so that it could be used to pre-select from various possible moves. This relates to what has been called latent learning, a kind of learning about the environment which was not rewarded by detectable reinforcement. It was an area of learning which was not readily accommodated by operant learning models. The next floor of the tower is inhabited by creatures which had inner environments that were informed by the designed portions of the outer environment. This sub-set of Popperian creatures are called Gregorian creatures (named after the psychologist Richard Gregory): they use designed artifacts or tools to enhance their powers. Dennett recognises Gregory as the psychologist who observed how tools 'enhance potential to arrive safely and swiftly at smart moves' (Dennett, 1996, p. 99). Words and other mind tools gave the Gregorian creatures an inner environment that made it possible to develop more subtle generators and testers. By importing mind tools from the cultural environment, the Gregorian creature acquired foresight and could operate beyond the immediate options. It could draw on the accumulated knowledge of others and did not have to design afresh, with all the associated risks. This is where language comes to have such an important role in human functioning, leading to what Dennett considers to be the final step up the tower. This is the floor where the kit of mind tools enables the deliberate generation and testing we call science.

Dennett's ideas are important for the discussion in this chapter, as they show that psychology can be linked in most fruitful ways to current ideas in Darwinian thinking about evolution. His ideas naturalise our ideas about the mind and psychological processes and help us consider the relationship between mind and matter as less problematic than when cast in dualist Cartesian terms. These ideas are also important because they illustrate how biological systems like the brain can evolve to operate with language and the accumulated wisdom of culture. They are relevant to the present discussion of psychology as a field which stands between the biological and the social sciences. The biological sciences have become identified with the natural sciences, which have been presented, as discussed above, as different from the social and human sciences. Dennett identifies this basic difference in terms of the physical and intentional stances. He represents the intentional stance as a form of the design stance, and then shows that they are compatible but have different uses. In this way he proposes an integrated framework for understanding the place of mind in nature.

Dennett's account is informed by his philosophical background, but also by his knowledge of the biological and social sciences including psychology. It is interesting that some similar views have been presented by Edelman (1992), a neuro-biologist also conversant with philosophy, cognitive sciences and psychology. Edelman's interest is in undermining the idea that the mind can be understood outside a biological framework. He directs his argument against what he and others have called cognitivism, the approach to psychology which assumes that psychological functioning operates according to algorithmic computational principles. In this model, the brain is the hardware and the mind is the software which runs the computational system. This model has also been known as functionalism, the view that psychology can be described in terms of the functional organisation of the brain. The focus of functional theories, or what are more commonly called information processing theories, is on the algorithms which determine processing and not the physical system in which processing takes place. It is interesting that these criticisms of cognitivism come from a biological and evolutionary perspective. They contrast with other criticisms of cognitivism which focus on the individualism of information processing and its detachment from the social context of cognition, which were discussed above. But Edelman's critique of cognitivism draws on philosophical ideas which were also influential in the social critique. He identifies the central idea of cognitive psychology as mental representations, those abstract symbols which are processed and are assumed to be related in determinate ways to objects in the world. These symbols derive their meaning by being mapped onto defined and fixed objects. His point is that this conception of mental representations assumes that there is some independently identifiable objective reality to which they can correspond. This argument relates back to the previous discussion of the weaknesses of a correspondence theory of knowledge. If there are difficulties in identifying such clear mappings between representations and objects, then the central cognitivist idea is in trouble. Meaning has to be found in some other way. Edelman's way is to consider how the mind reveals itself in humans who have bodies which have evolved through natural selection. The links with Dennett's ideas are clear.

The core of Edelman's critique is that the structure, function and diversity of the nervous system are incompatible with cognitivism. The way forward he advocated is to adopt a Darwinian framework which considers the brain's functioning in the conceptual terms of populations, their variations and selection processes. This is contrasted with typological thinking in physics, in which variation is considered as error and not the source of novelty and change. In this 'neural Darwinism', the brain is regarded as operating as a selective recognition system using the same selection principles which apply in immunology. This means that psychological functioning does not have to rely on some inner man or homunculus to read or recognise information. Assuming that there is initially some diversity of neurone groups in the brain, then the most adaptive group will be selected. On this basis, he proposes an account of psychological functioning which includes perception, memory and higher-order consciousness linked to language arising out of socially constructed processes. Edelman also contends that the Freudian notions of repression and unconscious memories can be given an interpretation consistent with his model of consciousness as biologically based.

In this brief discussion of some biological and evolutionary ideas and their relevance to the field of psychology, I have tried to illustrate some of the significant current connections between ideas in psychology and philosophy on one hand, and biology on the other. When these illustrations are placed alongside the discussions in previous sections, it becomes evident that psychology is one amongst several interlinking fields and that its theoretical principles are strongly influenced by dominant frameworks in these fields. And, as I mentioned in the introductory section to this chapter, this makes psychology a field where there are different and often incompatible theoretical concepts and principles. In the final section of this chapter I will discuss some approaches to making sense and perhaps even integrating this diversity.

Ways forward

As explained in a previous section, some psychologists have taken the philosophical critiques of positivism and empiricism as grounds for retreating to a social constructionism which is critical of the very project of finding causal explanations of psychological phenomena. But this has not been the only response to the weakening of logical positivism. For instance, Manicas and Secord (1983), in acknowledging that there was no pre-interpreted given in empirical data and that a correspondence theory of knowledge had to be rejected, saw this as no reason to give up the basic scientific aim of trying to construct causal explanations of phenomena. They adopted a position of fallibilist realism (drawing on the work of Harre, 1972 and Bhaskar, 1979), which assumes that there is an external reality, but one that we might be wrong about. Things in the world are complex composites, by which they mean that the world is stratified into levels and that things at each level have their own causal properties, which are different from the causal properties of their constituents. In this realist position, scientific explanations relate not to events and generalisations about them, but to causal properties of structures or mechanisms. This means that science tells us about how these mechanisms operate under given conditions and that explanation is not the same as prediction. Prediction may not be possible, as the particular conditions may not be known in advance in the open world outside experiments. How-ever, explanation may be possible after the event by invoking alternative causal mechanisms and the particular conditions of the event.

When Manicas and Secord apply this position to psychology, they draw several significant conclusions. First, individuals are complex and particular and therefore their behaviour results from different mechanisms at different levels. This puts an end to the hope that behaviour can be simply explained by reference to simple psychological laws which relate antecedents to consequents. Explanations of behaviour are therefore a multi-disciplinary effort. From this perspective, they propose that the realistic approach to psychology means that it is 'a family of related sciences with different tasks and methodologies' (p. 405). They also argue that controversies about the role of consciousness in human behaviour have mistakenly seen the aim of psychology as seeking explanation through principles or laws of behaviour discovered experimentally. From their perspective, humanistic psychology is correct in requiring that human agency and consciousness be part of expla-nation, but they see this as compatible with the operation of psychological principles, construed in realist terms as statements of the causal properties of psychological mechanisms. These authors remind the behaviourists, who see consciousness and agency as epiphenomena, that psychological principles relate to the causal properties of mechanisms and not to specific behaviours. Psychology is about causal powers, but their actualisation depends on knowl-edge about individuals and their circumstances. From this they draw the key conclusion relevant to this chapter: that in order to explain actions in real-life circumstances, other frameworks of accounting are necessary. One speci-ality is concerned with understanding people in terms of their individuality and history, a hermeneutic or interpretivist psychology. Another speciality, social psychology, focuses on the actions of individuals in social contexts. This takes one into the allied field of sociology, where the focus is on aggregates of people and social institutions and processes.

Manicas and Secord, along with Harre, see social psychology as a mediat-ing discipline which focuses on the interaction of the individual with others in the context of social institutions. But they consider the dominant themes to focus inward, on cognitive processes (attitudes, attributions etc.) rather than outward, on social situations and structures. They also question whether social psychology as a mediating discipline is best served by experimental methods. Even if social variables can be included successfully in experimen-tal designs, they point out that experimental psychology can only partially explain everyday behaviour. Phenomena in open systems require knowledge of contexts and biographical and historical details. They propose instead that social psychology acts as a mediating discipline by considering the indi-vidual as a person who is an agent with plans, purposes and motivations, and that behaviour should be considered from this hermeneutic position. Theirs is a very interesting conceptual move. It distinguishes a psychology which seeks causal mechanisms through experimental methods in closed systems from a psychology which builds on the hermeneutics underlying everyday assumptions about ourselves, and then argues that neither approach is sufficient for a comprehensive psychology.

These theorists also link these two kinds of psychology to different professional roles in psychology. Experimental psychologists, with their theoretical interest in underlying causal mechanisms, create closed experimental systems for explanatory purposes. Applied psychologists, with their professional service interests in bringing about and facilitating change in the everyday world, use knowledge of such causal mechanisms, but also much beyond, relating to the individual in his or her everyday context. Knowledge of causal mechanisms is not sufficient for them to dispense with ordinary language and the hermeneutic perspective, because in open systems they need to know about the particular circumstances, both biographical and historical, under which such mechanisms might operate. It is worth recalling, as discussed above, that the humanistic and hermeneutic versions of psychology were developed by professional and applied psychologists. Putting this together with the position developed by these theorists suggests that practitioner psychologists have a dominant professional interest in hermeneutic assumptions through their involvement with the individual client or patient in everyday service. Manicas and Secord express the key point in this analysis in these terms:

> If our aim is to explain behaviour as it occurs in ordinary life there is no escaping the ordinary description of behaviour and experience. Certainly causal mechanisms and structures discovered by experimental psychology or other sciences apply to such behaviour, but by themselves they do not provide sufficient explanation, and they certainly do not dispense with ordinary language to substitute a pure scientific language of behaviour.
>
> (Manicas and Secord, 1983, p. 410)

A distinction is made between everyday hermeneutic understandings of experience and behaviour and a more systematic or scientific version. The scientific version of hermeneutic psychology has to provide systematically derived evidence for its accounts, and evidence for the use of known psychological mechanisms relevant to the individual person and of social structures that bear on his or her experience and behaviour. Manicas and Secord therefore see psychology operating under two co-existing and complementary scientific versions, experimental and hermeneutic psychologies. A co-existence position is also broadly supported by Charles Taylor, a philosopher who has criticised behaviourist accounts of psychology and argued for a hermeneutic approach (Taylor, 1964). Taylor's position is that for psychology to be a causal science it has to use data which is 'brute', meaning that it does not depend on the interpretation of the subject or observer (Taylor, 1985). He argues that most of the subject matter of psychology is concerned with

actions, motives and emotions which cannot be identified without knowing
what the person has in mind. This requires a different kind of psychology
which explores and identifies the interpretations of agents. However, he does
accept that in studies of the relationship between psychological and physical
states, independent states can be identified and related in generalisations.
Causal scientific generalisations can be tested, according to him, in the
domain which sets the boundary relations between the physical and the
psychological. But in the area of performance, which covers much of the
subject matter of psychology, the states which are related in generalisations
cannot be identified independently of the subject's interpretations. It is in
these performance or action areas that a hermeneutic science is called for.

White (1988), in his evaluation of Taylor's position, has argued that the
call for co-existence is along the right lines, but that there are problems with
Taylor's acceptance that there are intermediate areas of inquiry concerned
with 'competences' which involve the mechanistic and hermeneutic models.
Taylor considers that theories like Piaget's, insofar as they involve formalisation, belong with the causal model, but in their application are concerned
with performance and therefore require interpretation. White argues instead
for a co-existence based on a clearer distinction between two kinds of psychological phenomena, drawing on the work of the philosopher Davidson
(1980). One type involves objects, what philosophers call intentional objects, like thoughts, desires, beliefs and emotions; the other type involves no
objects, just experiences such as sensations. White argues that intentional
psychological phenomena cannot be identified independently from each other.
They have a holistic character whereby beliefs, memories, emotions and
actions (for example) are conceptually related to each other and to values
which connect the person to the wider culture. Such phenomena require
interpretative exploration and cannot be fitted into scientific law like statements. By contrast, non-intentional phenomena like sensations can be identified as discrete and occur alongside intentional phenomena, like thoughts,
and so they can be related in causal generalisations. This is a slightly different way of arguing for a co-existence, but one with no place for intermediate
inquiry using causal mechanistic and hermeneutic approaches.

Harre, another philosopher with a particular interest in psychology as a
science, has been particularly influential in promoting the development of a
psychology which is based on common-sense hermeneutic assumptions. He
presents this as marking a second cognitive revolution, to follow the first
cognitive revolution which displaced behaviourist assumptions as dominant
in psychology (Harre, 1995). He calls the new psychology, *discursive psychology* because it relates to language and symbolic interactions between individuals. However, he uses the term 'discursive' broadly to refer to all sorts of
cognitive activities which involve intentionality and are constrained by norms
governing what is correct or incorrect. He has presented one of the most
well-argued and interesting accounts of the nature of psychology as both a
scientific endeavour and as a field of study which includes our everyday

assumptions about intentionality and human agency. Though he has drawn on the social traditions of Mead and Vygotsky, which have been associated with social constructionism, his psychology is based on realistic philosophical assumptions. He explains how the social origins and context of personal functioning provide a viable alternative to Cartesian dualism, which has been so influential in the development of psychology. By presenting the mental as something essentially private, Cartesian dualism separated the mental from scientific study, which required public observational evidence. Behaviourism, which translated the mental into observable behavioural terms, was therefore a way of bringing psychology into a scientific frame of reference. But even the cognitive revolution which introduced information processing still hung on to dualistic assumptions and the resulting explanatory problems generated by them. Cognitive representations became the focus of study, but there still remained the question of how and who registers these internal representations, the question of the inner person or homunculus.

Though not alone in making these points about the Cartesian influence, Harre has expressed them in such a way as to show that its problems and an alternative are evident. He has pointed out that Descartes and his successors treated the mental as subjective in the sense that it is essentially private and not available to others. As Farr (1987) argued in a similar vein, and as I discussed above, this Cartesian influence has not been conducive to the development of the social and human sciences. Descartes's system of radical doubt left him acknowledging his own mind and existence (*cogito ergo sum*), but doubting the existence of others' minds. This led to a psychology of others as behavioural, because others' mental states and processes were assumed to be unobservable. It also led to a psychology of the self or first person as a purely subjective field which was liable to criticism for being unscientific. Along with other philosophers of mind, Harre has questioned this identity between the mental and the subjective. His position is that much of what we call mental is as observable to others as it is known to oneself. From this he claims that more basic than the distinction between subjective–inaccessible and objective–observable is the distinction between the public display of the mental and its private reservation. This cuts through the idea that there is a basic difference in kind between the mental and the physical. From this he identifies a key dimension of psychological space as concerned with the display of psychological processes. The other dimension he identifies as the location of these processes, whether in an individual or collectively between two people or in some group. The assumption here is that psychological processes can be located as taking place in some collective of people, as when remembering or reasoning may take place in a group. With these two dimensions, Display and Location, Harre constructs a two-dimensional psychological space for making sense of psychological concepts and development (see figure 3).

The main assumption of this model is, following the ideas of Mead and Vygotsky, that development is a process of appropriation or internalisation

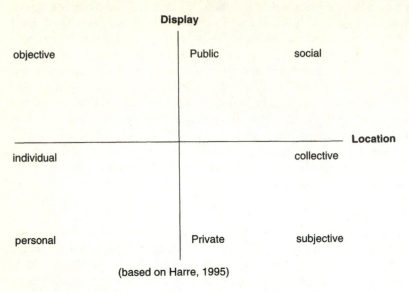

(based on Harre, 1995)

Figure 3 Two-dimensional psychological space based on display and location

of collectively located and publicly displayed processes to private display and then to individual location. This presumes two important positions: that what is taken to be the privacy and subjectivity of mental processes arises from the transferring of the interpersonal to the intrapersonal, and that social processes are previous to mental ones. As Harre has put it, minds come into existence by 'fencing off' part of public conversation as a private and individual domain. The mental has therefore the characteristic of being in the form of an internal dialogue, a position which respects the individuality and privacy of human experience, while connecting it to social and observable processes.

As I outlined in the section on historical aspects of psychology, Farr (1987) has argued that the failure of both the early introspectionist and later behaviourist projects were due to the fact that the mind and behaviour were conceived in non-social terms. Farr argues for a model of psychology which incorporates both mind and behaviour and which is social in nature, what he calls a social psychology. The current interest in cognitive psychologies and cognitive science is, for him, half way to making psychology once again a science of the mind, which would be both behavioural and social in nature. To achieve this, Farr wants to revive the interest which Mead had in the 1930s in the social and linguistic origins of the mind. For Mead, mind arose through communication by a conversation of gestures in a social process, and he saw language as an expressive form of behaviour, drawing on Darwin's idea that emotions are communicatively expressive. However, for Mead this focused only on the perspective of the observer and not of the actor. He managed to link these perspectives by showing how language as an expressive behaviour evokes a response in the mind of the speaker comparable to what is evoked in listeners. Language then becomes in evolutionary terms a more complex mechanism for communication than gestures. The key point here is that we are, as Farr (1987, p. 11) puts it: 'more self-reflexive in the auditory modality than we are in the visual modality. The divergence in perspective between actor and observer is much sharper than that between speaker and listener.'

The human sense of self, from a Meadian position, is seen to derive from this special feature of the auditory modality, so that expressive behaviour forms impressions not only in other listeners, but in the actual speaker as a listener. For Farr, psychology took a false turn by separating what psychologists observe others doing from what they can tell about the meaning of their actions. It is interesting that Farr also links Mead's and Freud's theoretical approaches insofar as they both identified the meaning of an act as the response elicited in others. He portrays Freud as a research physiologist, who initially used the visual modality and then switched to listening to his patients in his clinical practice, using the auditory modality. Psychoanalysis was the theory which Freud generated to make sense of what he heard and observed, though mainly based on what he heard and the meaning it evoked in him. In this way we can understand how Freudian and other psychodynamic theory deals with the meaning of processes and actions which may not correspond with the actor's expressed intent. What psychoanalysis and Mead's social behaviourism have in common is that they deal directly with the question of meaning in psychology.

As discussed earlier in this chapter, Bruner (1996) has argued in favour of a co-existence between what he calls the computational and the cultural approaches to the mind and psychology. Bruner recognises that hermeneutic meaning-making is incompatible with information processing, which assumes pre-fixed categories and processing rules which are specified in advance. This computational model is built on reducing messy or fuzzy categories, leaving no room for ambiguity, which is the very essence of the constructivist assumption in the cultural model. As Bruner explains, for any ambiguous word to be processed in a computational system, there would need to be some device to look up alternative meanings and their relationships in different contexts. This would require a storage system of different kinds of contexts linked to different meanings of the term. This introduces the prospect of a potentially infinite number of contexts which cannot be easily dealt with in a finite computational system. Yet, as Bruner points out, the two models have some connections. Once meanings are defined, computational systems can deal with them. This might lose some of the subtlety of meaning, but then such formalisation is what science is about; focusing on the general across contexts means losing the detail of the particular in context. But there is also a relationship in the other direction, from computationalism to culturalism. There seems to be no option but to interpret the output of computational models so as to make some sense of them.

What Bruner is picking out here is that there are two different models based on incompatible principles which are interconnected.

Bruner asks the important question about interpretive processes, which pertain especially to the function of psychology: whether interpretation as a process can be explained in causal terms. If it can, is it just another fact of nature subject to causal scientific explanation? In supporting a separation between explaining and interpreting, Bruner points to some of the features which keep them apart. Causal explanation aims to identify necessary and sufficient conditions that enable us to have certain mental states, for example. Such explanations allow prediction, whereas interpretation is after the event, from some person's perspective, context dependent and historical. But Bruner urges us to resist the temptation to split the two complementary processes and see the study of the mind as divided neatly between interpretivist humanists and neuro-scientists, with psychologists locked out. This splitting should be resisted, he argues, because causal explanations do not exhaust interpretations, nor do interpretations exhaust explanations. Such explanations merely provide a basis for interpretivists' interpretations. Similarly, interpretations offer ideas which can be cast in well-defined propositional form in the search for causes.

Bruner, like the other theorists referred to in this section, is arguing against an either–or approach to psychology, whether exclusively biological, computational or cultural-interpretive in position. Though Bruner locates himself personally on the cultural side of the difference, he is keen to promote a psychology which focuses on the interaction of biological, evolutionary and individual psychological and cultural perspectives. He sees the question of 'intersubjectivity', that is, how people come to know what others have in mind and how to adjust to this, as providing an important agenda for psychology. Though this is seen to be central to a viable cultural psychology, he recognises that this will depend on knowledge about primate evolution, neural functioning and mental processing capacities. Bruner acknowledges that psychology will in the end depend on understanding the interplay of biology and culture. In a similar mode to Dennett, he sees culture as an outcome of evolution, and sees culture as having some autonomy but nevertheless as constrained by biological limits and predispositions. To quote him directly:

> The dilemma in the study of man is to grasp not only the causal principles of his biology and evolution, but to understand these in the light of the interpretive processes involved in meaning making. To brush aside the biological constraints on human functioning is to commit hubris. To sneer at the power of culture to shape man's mind and to abandon our efforts to bring this under human control is to commit moral suicide.
>
> (Bruner, 1996, p. 184)

Though Bruner's concerns are with psychology as a discipline, his emphasis is mainly on the complementary nature of different accounts of psychological or mental processes. By contrast, Fraser Watts, when president of the British Psychological Society (BPS), was interested in the discipline and its promotion by a national institution (Watts, 1992). His concern was that psychology could be falling apart along three distinct but connected lines of fragmentation. None of these areas of concern are new but they take on different forms in different periods. The first area is the different lines of inquiry, from the social to the biological. However, as Watts points out, the recent increase in cross-disciplinary activities, such as cognitive science, neuroscience and social sciences, shows up the divisions within psychology. Already in some universities there is no identifiable psychology department, as psychologists have been distributed amongst other subject groupings. Watts considers that this is a significant loss, not just out of nostalgia for psychology as a discipline, but because there is a need for a coherent discipline that takes an integrated view which brings together social, biological, cognitive and affective aspects within a single frame of reference. Watts is clear that there has not been much coherence within psychology and that staying together has been more a matter of convenience. But his argument is that unless some coherence is built within psychology, the development of allied multi-disciplinary studies will draw psychologists away. The distinctiveness of the discipline, in his view, should be such that psychologists in different fields can communicate with each other. He suggests that two main distinctive features, a commitment to empiricism and a concern with human processing, could provide some commonality across the range of different lines of inquiry.

Watts identified the second area of fragmentation in the divergence of methodological approaches. This is related to the first area, but is worth considering in its own right. As discussed in previous sections of this chapter, different methods make claims to be 'scientific'. Watts is interested in how to retain different methods for different kinds of inquiry, while integrating these different modes. To do this, he suggests that we give up the idea that some methods are objective while others are subjective. He agrees that it is more accurate to consider that methods differ in terms of what the inquiry is looking for: an interpretative approach for meanings and reasons, an experimental approach for causes. Both are interested in achieving objectivity in their own ways. What we need is a clear distinction between 'objectivity' meaning the use of systematic methods of inquiry and 'objectivity' meaning an assumption about phenomena to be investigated. Interpretive methods are objective in adopting systematic methods, but do not assume the realism found amongst those seeking causal explanations. In adopting a methodological eclecticism, Watts recognises the differences between methods, but considers that many fields within psychology can be investigated by radically different methods. This implies that an exclusive set of methods or a methodological purity cannot be accepted, whether from classical experimentalists or those proposing alternative or critical psychologies. As Watts and others in the wider social and educational research fields have argued, there is a complementary relationship between quantitative and qualitative data and its collection and analysis. Qualitative data can be quantified at some stage of the research process, and (as some argue) might well benefit from such quantification. Similarly, quantification depends on prior qualitative analysis, and easy and premature quantification can conceal poor conceptualisation.

Watts's third area of fragmentation is between basic research and professional application. He considers that the gap between basic research and professional application, though serious in the UK, is less so than in the USA, where there are different national organisations representing academic and professional psychology. In the UK, there has been a tradition of high-quality applied research producing outcomes which have had theoretical implications and service use. Nevertheless, there are psychologists involved in basic or academically based research with little interest in applications, and many professional psychologists with scant interest in the psychological basis of their work. In line with his case for greater integration, Watts expresses doubts about basic research which is completely isolated from any practical problems. Though he recognises that findings of importance can be made in such isolation, there is the risk that these will remain unrecognised outside the discipline. This raises the question whether the value of psychology is ultimately to be judged in terms of its wider social usefulness. Watts is someone who thinks it should, but not in the narrow sense that short-term problems should determine research agendas. There is much to commend in this position, as usefulness includes practical techniques and strategies not just for resolving social and personal problems, but also for better understanding of an issue, in the pragmatic philosophical sense that there is nothing as practical as a good theory.

Practitioner psychologists also use professional skills which have little grounding in the discipline of psychology. This means that there is a need to use psychology to make sense of the problems professional psychologists have to deal with. Without this, professional psychologists find it hard to give a rationale for their service contribution as distinct from the services of other allied non-psychologist professional groups. Watts does not make this particular point, but it has special relevance to the educational psychology which will be discussed in the next two chapters. But Watts does make the important point that the gap between basic research and applied professional psychology has a strong methodological basis to it. He considers that unless there is better integration between experimental and interpretive methods, research and professional psychologists are less likely to collaborate. This means that practitioner psychologists who make use of interpretive processes should be more familiar with systematic qualitative methods, which they can learn from social psychologists. He argues that experimental work has some relevance, especially in the single-case experimental design mode. Practitioners also need to be conversant with experimental results from basic research which have applicability to their work, and could collect empirical data themselves. But basic research psychologists also need a methodological integration. This arises from the difference between the process of generating fruitful ideas, or what Popper called insightful conjectures, and the process of testing them. This is sometimes called the difference between scientific discovery and verification. The context of discovery has been linked to a more intuitive grasp of phenomena and a familiarity with them. Linking back to Bruner's account of the complementary relationship between explaining and interpreting, causal explanatory research can be considered to need more open-ended interpretive processes.

Concluding comments

I have explored in this chapter the key question within psychology of how we can be true to our notions of our humanity, to our human values and to a coherent concept of science. This raises important and difficult questions about the point of calling a field of study 'scientific'. The theoretical diversity within psychology, which was introduced in the previous chapter, has been explored further. This showed that no simple dichotomies can be discerned between broad kinds of psychological theories. Mechanistic theories are so diverse that they are not simply distinguishable from alternative theories involving constructivist and holist principles. Psychology's connections with philosophical and value questions were also discussed. The arguments about ideological issues in psychology were accepted as showing that values were at the foundation of the psychological field of study. Two broad sorts of values were suggested as helping us understand some of the differences within the field: epistemological values of participant or spectator perspectives and the well-being values of progressive or conservative tendencies. I argued that adopting exclusive positions with respect to these value differences engenders splitting and the emergence of similarly exclusive opposite positions. A purist, positivist scientific spectator approach to psychology engenders a similarly hard-line intepretivist participant approach. The case for seeing connections between participant and spectator perspectives was seen as compelling because the objects of psychology – ourselves as human beings – are also subjects who have intentionality. I also noted that a causal science model has had and continues to have a progressive form which seeks to identify alterable causal variables and promote human well-being. That well-being values influence the adoption of epistemological positions also needs to be recognised. But a causal scientific perspective, though sometimes associated with conservative values, is not necessarily so. Identifying causal mechanisms can support progressive values; they can empower and improve human conditions.

I have discussed different kinds of psychologies which arise in different institutional settings. Where professional psychologists work in service settings, such as hospitals, clinics, workplaces and schools, there are demands for psychologies which relate to the individual confronting particular types of problems. Academic psychologists based in universities have to maintain the scientific credentials of the field in relation to other scientific fields. Applied psychology was seen to relate to both the application of knowledge from basic research and the application of systematic empirical methods directly to everyday problems. But psychological theory has also been generated by practitioners, especially in the mental health area – what I called psychology-in-practice, which often involved interpretivist approaches. Historical perspectives on psychology also suggest that there are connections between broad approaches in the field and different traditions in Western thought, the ontological and pragmatic traditions. In the pragmatic tradition, psychological ideas and techniques were developed within the range of practical disciplines, including education, well before the era of scientific psychology based in universities.

In arguing for co-existence between interpretivist and causal explanatory models, it is also important to note the connections between the principles of human agency and causal determinism. Rather than setting these as simple opposites, it is possible to see how they depend on each other. From one side, causal mechanisms can give rise to human agency, though this implies that agency operates within certain constraints. From the other side, deterministic causal mechanisms cannot be used to intervene in practical settings, unless we assume some degree of human agency in actively seeking knowledge of such mechanisms. But critiques of causal scientific psychology have also centred on the individualism of mainstream psychology. The individual person is presented in the critiques as being indivisible from the social context. The problem with this way of formulating the relationship between individual and context is that it could be taken to mean that there is no place for personal continuity across different contexts, or for personal agency. The relationship is better seen as one of interconnection and mutual interaction. Indivisibility also treats the social context as of one kind, not distinguishing between micro- and macro-social levels of analysis. Other critiques have identified individualism in psychology with narrow brutish egoism. Against this I argued that there has been a confusion between anti-social egoism and the ideals of responsible individualism expressed in humanistic psychologies. What these critical psychologies, including feminist psychologies, have contributed is a greater understanding of the social uses and abuses of knowledge generated in the name of psychology. But this appreciation does not imply that the individual person should be regarded as wholly a social creation without any recognition of the biological aspects of our common humanity.

The chapter then considered different philosophical ideas about psychology as a science. The arguments of those philosophers who reject the presumed opposition of social constructionism with some form of realism were found to be persuasive. If we recognise that there are no absolute foundations for psychological knowledge while acknowledging the values at the basis of the field, this does not mean that we cannot aspire to some form of objectivity. This is where a pragmatic philosophical position was acknowledged as offering a way of giving up the quest for absolute foundations without letting go of a relatedness to reality. Reality is cast not as something to be copied by knowledge, but as something to be coped with through our discursive and non-discursive actions. Therefore an absence of absolute criteria and foundations for rationality does not imply an absence of rational discourse. In seeing continuity between language-based and non-language-based knowledge, the pragmatic philosophical tradition also connects with biological and evolutionary perspectives on the mind. I referred here to the work of Dennett and Edelman to show how it is possible to consider the brain as evolving so as to operate with language and benefit from the collective wisdom of culture. These Darwinian evolutionary ideas illustrate how mind can arise in evolution, and in so doing indicate that psychology is one amongst several interlinking fields and that its theoretical principles are influenced by those fields.

The discussion concluded with a range of different but related ideas about how to connect different kinds of explanations. What was common to all was that explanations require a multi-disciplinary effort which includes but extends beyond psychology and its sub-specialisms. As part of this position, psychology itself is best construed as a family of related but different specialisms with different tasks. One view is that experimental psychology seeks causal mechanisms in a closed system, and is therefore different from applied and practitioner psychologies which seek interpretations by building on everyday assumptions of intentionality. None of these kinds of psychology is sufficient by itself. Another theme here is the negative Cartesian dualist heritage in psychology. One useful way forward breaks the identity between what is mental or psychological with what is subjective in the sense that it is essentially private and inaccessible. This is achieved by realising that the mental or psychological can be public and observable, thus reconnecting the mind to social behaviour and reframing it as an internal dialogue – an approach which can acknowledge individuality and the privacy of experience. Another perspective on connecting different kinds of psychology has been put in terms of the co-existence and mutual interplay between computational and cultural models.

But co-existence between interpretive and causal explanations can take different forms. There is the Taylor and White position which reserves different approaches for different kinds of psychological phenomena, restricting much of the subject matter of psychology (actions, beliefs, emotions, motives) to the hermeneutic model because these intentional phenomena have a holistic character. This goes against the mainstream of scientific psychology, which formulates its accounts of these phenomena in terms of causal generalisations of discrete elements. If we accept this holistic analysis of psychological phenomena, we need to ask how they can come to be subjected to a causal mechanistic treatment. An account might take the following form. Where Taylor and White would assume conceptual connections between the elements making up intentional phenomena, mainstream psychologists treat these elements as identifiable independently of each other. For example, self-efficacy theory relates causally to self-efficacy and a person's perceived judgement of competence to persistence of striving – a behavioural construct (Bandura, 1977). Self-efficacy and persistence are assessed separately through standard and structured formats and then shown to be causally related. From an interpretive perspective, a person who has greater self-confidence will (from what we mean by self-confidence) probably show greater persistence, all other things being equal. This connection can be derived from Smedslund's psychologic, which assumes that most empirical generalisations in psychology can be mapped onto the logical relations built into the meaning of everyday psychological concepts (Smedslund, 1995). So, where interpretivists respect the holistic conceptual connections between the elements of psychological phenomena, causal mechanists treat the elements as separably identifiable and the relationships between them as contingent. The problem for the mechanists is that there are doubts about the validity of identifying these elements in the required structured formats. For example, in assessing self-efficacy, how do we know that a person's self-report to a simple question format represents his or her judgement of personal competence, unless we can test this against action implications conceptually linked to such a judgement? The answer is that we cannot know without assuming the kind of connection which self-efficacy theory aims to establish empirically. This suggests that the causal mechanistic model requires that intentional psychological phenomena be treated as discrete elements, because of an interest in or commitment to knowledge structured in a causal mechanistic mode. This mode might be worth accepting, even though the theories which derive from it are mainly translations of the relationships built into everyday psychological assumptions about performances.

This line of argument leads us to ask why such a premium is placed on the causal scientific rather than the hermeneutic knowledge mode. The obvious answer is that the dominance of the causal mechanistic model arises from the strong bias towards knowledge structured in terms of the technical interest in predicting and controlling outcomes. And, as the discussion in this and previous chapters has indicated, this is where we need to take account of the academic position of psychology in universities and the professional interest of its practitioners in acquiring and retaining expert scientific status. One conclusion to draw from this discussion is that co-existence does not mean that tensions are resolved and explanatory harmony has been achieved. Co-existence is more a matter of tolerance and a capacity to understand the rationale of different traditions. It is a call for an appreciation of the connections between different psychological traditions.

However, these are idealised reconnections between different traditions in psychology. In practice, there has been a threat to psychology by the growth of multi-disciplinary fields like cultural studies, cognitive sciences, neurosciences and social sciences, which have shown up the divisions within psychology. There have been calls for the construction of a coherent discipline of psychology, not in opposition to such multi-disciplinary collaboration, but so as to unite the cognitive, emotional, social and biological aspects of human functioning. The case for this is not based on nostalgia for a lost ideal, but on doing justice to a comprehensive and integral account of the multiple aspects of human experience and actions. The construction of such a framework, it is argued, depends partly on a methodological integration between different experimental and quantitative methods and interpretive and qualitative ones. Such a methodological integration can also be seen to be important for bridging the gap between basic research psychologists and professional applied psychologists.

It seems unlikely that research in basic psychology can thrive completely isolated from the practical problems encountered in everyday life and by professional psychologists. It has been noted that the social sciences (and this includes psychology) are essentially applied sciences in the sense, as Marx put it, that they are there to change the world, not just to interpret it (Hobsbawm, 1997). The idea that the basic researcher in psychology is a simple seeker after the pure academic truth, whether or not it interests anyone outside the field, can be attributed to the growth of the academic profession in separate institutions. It might also have something to do with a process of mystifying people outside academia. There is much influence to be gained by presenting the outcomes of research and scholarship as secure and unchallengeable knowledge that is developed by a group which stands outside policy and practice differences. The fact that psychologists, like other social scientists, have value commitments, take sides and have biases has been used to question the neutral objectivity claimed for psychological knowledge. This critical questioning is very important – personally for individuals and collectively for different traditions and models of psychology. At the extreme, however, partiality becomes a serious threat if it leads to an inability to follow the processes and outcomes of inquiry. But there are also advantages in having some degree of partiality for its potential to advance psychology by introducing debate, new topics and new questions from outside. For basic psychology this comes from applied and professional psychology within the broad field, but also most importantly from its bases within service fields like education. The answer therefore to the opening question in this chapter is that psychology depends on educational and other social and human problems for its flourishing and development.

4 A special relationship?

The whole science of human nature is but a branch of the science of education
... Nor can education assume its most perfect form, till the science of the
human mind has reached its highest point of improvement.

Mill (1818, p. 45)

Introduction

Few contemporary psychologists would regard psychology as a branch of
education, as James Mill implied in the early nineteenth century. But few
who were familiar with the history of psychology as an independent academic discipline would fail to recognise the historical and continuing links
between psychology and education. In this chapter I will consider the historical and contemporary relationship between education and psychology, by
bringing together the key points which have been raised in the previous two
chapters. In chapter 2, I examined education as a practical field which has
theoretical needs. Amongst these needs are basic assumptions about the nature
of learning, teaching and the learner, what were called meta-psychological
assumptions. I also explored the issues about a scientific basis for the art or
craft of teaching. This led into the third chapter in which I analysed basic
questions about the nature of psychology and the kind of science it can
claim to be. The diversity of the field and the incompatibility of its different
traditions were presented as threatening its coherence. Part of this tension is
between applied and so-called pure psychology. In this chapter I examine
whether there is a special relationship between psychology and education.

One question that has been asked repeatedly is how a field like psychology, which is divided within itself, can be used and applied constructively
to a practical field like education. That we are dealing with two different
fields is not in question: one is concerned with human ends and the means of
promoting them, the other with understanding and knowledge of human
experience and actions. It is acknowledged widely that psychology has influenced education in the past, though this does not mean that it has been a
good influence, as argued by Egan (1983). The question is whether it can

make a unique and worthwhile future contribution to education practice, teacher training, educational theory and research. To use the phrase which was popular two decades ago, has psychology been given away already? And has what it can offer already been taken up, on the assumption that there is not much more to contribute? I will examine in this chapter the overarching question of the continuing unique contribution and relate it to distinctions which have been made between basic-pure, applied and practitioner psychologies. Of course, this question raises further questions about the nature and relationships between these specialisations within the broad psychology field. As explained in the last chapter, the question of coherence and interconnections between these specialisations is becoming pressing, given the growth of the field and the number of psychologists involved. But the situation is more complex, because psychology is used in education, and not just by those with overt professional psychology identities. Psychology sometimes makes a contribution, which can go unacknowledged, through the work of educationalists. There are therefore also questions about how psychologists relate to educationalists and teachers who use psychology.

Educational psychology is usually referred to as a branch of psychology which emerged in the last century, and is often represented as having had a central part in the study of education (Olssen, 1993). It is represented as the original area of applied psychology, which fits with the historical development of the internal organisation of the British Psychological Society. But there are many terms that are used to refer to this branch of knowledge and understanding, which themselves reflect important professional and institutional differences. Educational psychology is sometimes given a fairly broad definition, such as that of Sutherland (1988, p. 17): 'research and the application of psychological knowledge in areas of importance to the educational system'. The implication may be that there is a body of psychological knowledge which is applied to the practical concerns of education. Others, like Ausubel, have sought to emphasise its independence by defining it as 'an independent applied discipline dealing with the nature, outcomes and evaluation of school learning, and with the various variables of cognitive structure, development, intellectual ability, practice, motivation, instructional material, society and the teachers that influence it' (Ausubel, 1978, p. v). This definition ties down the field to school learning, which for some educational psychologists overlooks the fact that the education system extends beyond the schooling phase into further and higher education. It can be concerned as much with adult as with child learning. But this kind of definition also confines the field to learning in the education system, when we know that important learning goes on at home, at work and via the media. Education goes well beyond schooling, as current ideas about life-long learning and the learning society indicate. School psychology may be a term which is relevant to practitioner psychologists who serve clients based in the school system, but practitioner psychologists working in schools in

Britain prefer a broader brief which includes work in homes and other institutional settings. They prefer to be called educational psychologists.

There are other psychologists with an interest in education who present the psychological contribution without reference to a special branch of psychology. Sutherland (1988) has commented that the early psychologists interested in education, particularly the well-known ones, called themselves just psychologists. This may be because their psychological interests went beyond education. This approach can be identified in the current application of psychology to education by authors like Fontana (1995), who draw on psychological theories and concepts from diverse fields, such as counselling and psychotherapy and personality theories. What all the above formulations of the connection between psychology and education have in common is their focus on the psychological aspect. These formulations take up the position of the psychologist, whether it is the academic psychologist, the academic educational psychologist, or the practitioner school or educational psychologist. This has often in the past been the position of those psychologists wanting to apply psychology to education. But there is the other perspective, that of the educationalist concerned with ends and means. This is the position of the teacher concerned about understanding and improving teaching or pedagogy, who wants to know how psychological ideas and techniques can enhance her or his practices directly. The term 'psycho-pedagogy' has been used (Stones, 1979) in relation to this perspective. Here, it is plain that the primary focus is on teaching, not on applying psychology: the latter, as critics have asserted, has not been strongly represented in educational psychology. That the relationship between education and psychology can and needs to be approached from these two perspectives is one of the main themes of this book. The historic relationship has been one of dominance from the psychology side, which will be explored in terms of the status of science as a discipline, the professional status of teachers compared to that of scientists and the relative roles and working conditions of teachers and psychologists.

This analysis suggests that the very terms used to refer to the field commonly called 'educational psychology' raise important questions about the relationship between different professionals, the scope of their functions, bodies of knowledge and institutional settings in education and psychology. In table 3, I have set out a broad breakdown of some of the different professional groups focusing on their educational and developmental aims, institutional setting, functions and the psychology knowledge base with which they deal.

This table is meant to be illustrative rather than comprehensive. It does not include social workers or medical doctors, but it shows the two main groups of professionals concerned with the interface between psychology and education: the academic psychologists who work in university education and psychology departments, and the practitioner psychologists who work for education authorities. What the table also shows is the areas of overlap both

Table 3 Professions related to education, psychology and development; their functions, institutional settings and psychology knowledge base

Profession	Professional setting	Functions	Psychology knowledge base
Academic psychologists	University	Teaching, research and training	Various psychologies:
	Psychology departments		Developmental and social psychology, applied psychologies, psychology in practice
	Education departments		Educational psychology, psychologies relevant to education, applied psychologies, psychology in practice
Professional psychologists			Applied psychologies, psychology in practice
Educational psychologists	LEAs	Assessment, consultation, some intervention	
Clinical psychologists	NHS	Assessment, intervention	
Mental health professionals			
Psychotherapists Counsellors Family therapists	LEAs, NHS, schools	Psychotherapy Counselling Family therapy	Humanistic, interpretive psychologies, ecological and other relevant theories
Language and communication therapists	NHS, LEAs, schools	Assessment, treatment, consultation	Psychology as contributory knowledge base
Teachers		Teaching	Diverse psychologies as contributory knowledge base
Class teachers	Schools		
SEN teachers	Special and ordinary schools		
Teacher educators and school-based mentors	University departments of education, school-based training	Initial teacher preparation	
Educational researchers	University departments of education, research centres	Educational research	Draw on relevant concepts, theories and methods

in the functions of the different professional groups and in bodies of knowledge across different settings. Psychologists in university psychology and education departments can have an interest in applied psychologies and practitioner psychology. Clinical and educational psychologists work with the problems of children and parents. The table also shows that professional groups not defined as psychologists can use psychology as a central part of their practice. Counsellors and psychotherapists working with children and parents, for instance, use humanistic and interpretivist psychologies, as might some educational and clinical psychologists. For other professional groups, such as language and communication therapists and teachers, psychology might form a small part of their knowledge base, even if it went unacknowledged.

This table presents a broad map of the current professional functions and institutional contexts relevant to the discussion in this chapter. I will start with a historical perspective on the changing relationship between psychology and education, including views on the relationship of psychology to teacher training and policy making. This leads on to an analysis of various critiques of educational psychology, followed by a section which discusses some current issues and concerns. Subsequent sections cover the changing position of the two branches of education psychology, the academic research-teaching and practitioner branches. The chapter concludes with a summary from which emerges a conception of psychology relevant to education and which connects the different branches of psychology in education.

Historical perspectives

Accounts of the origins of the emerging professional and institutional relationship between psychology and education come from different perspectives and often ask questions with different purposes. Some accounts come from professionals themselves, for example M. Sutherland (1988), Hearnshaw (1979), Tomlinson (1992). These are concerned either with paying homage to or dissecting the life and work of eminent psychologists, or with tracking what went wrong to draw lessons for future developments. Others come from professional historians, such as G. Sutherland (1984), and Wooldridge (1994), who are concerned with the application of mental measurement to selection and the development of the profession of education psychology. Some of this historical analysis represents a Marxist approach to science, society and inequality in education, for example Simon (1978).

Educational psychology was the original area of applied psychology, to use the term we currently use for a psychological approach used in a practical area. Here, we need to maintain the distinction between the two traditions of applied psychology, made by Schonpflug (1993): between the more recent application of basic science and psychology as part of practical areas like education, which have a longer history. It is in this context that Thomas (1996) reminds us that the application of psychology to education owes more to the work of university departments of education than to the psychology which emerged from the independent psychology departments. There was a long tradition of psychology as part of teacher training well before Cyril Burt got his London County Council post in 1913. The day training centres, which started in the last decade of the nineteenth century, played a key role in promoting psychology as part of the initial training of teachers. These day training centres later turned into the university departments and institutes of education. Though educational psychology existed before the training centres, it was the courses in elementary psychology taught in these centres, in accordance with government requirements, which strengthened the place of psychology in the initial training of teachers.

Belief in a grounding in psychology had its origins in the pedagogic traditions of continental Europe and Scotland. Thomas (1996) identifies this tradition as drawing on the work of Froebel, Pestalozzi and Herbart. There was also the influence from Scotland which is associated with Alexander Bain's book *Education as a Science*, originally published in 1879. This was a book which went into many editions and had a lasting influence on teacher training. Bain stressed the significance of psychology for education and the value of a scientific treatment of the art of education. As he explained at the start of the book:

> The scientific treatment of any art consists partly in applying the principles furnished by the several sciences involved, as chemistry laws to agriculture, and partly in enforcing, throughout the discussion, the utmost precision and rigour in the statement and proof of the various maxims or rules that make up the art.
>
> (Bain, 1922, p. 4)

Bain was professor of logic at Aberdeen University in the mid to late nineteenth century and was well known for two books on psychological topics. But there has been some disagreement about the lasting importance of his work. Simon (1981) portrays Bain's work as the dawn of a new era in educational thought. It was the start of professionalism for an occupation whose development, according to Simon, was marked by ignorance and which was in need of a theoretical basis for its craft. Simon sees in Bain's work an embryonic form of pedagogy which has been neglected in the English education system. But there were and are other views about the significance of Bain's work. Some of his contemporaries, the first professors of education in Scotland, Laurie and Meikeljohn (in the last quarter of the nineteenth century), disagreed most importantly about his view that psychology was the basic science of education, though they were strongly in favour of treating education as an academic study (Knox, 1962). Harrington (1989), in a recent historical study of Bain and his work, questions Simon's assessment of Bain's work. Though conceding that *Education as a Science* provided some stimulus for the reform of teaching methods, Harrington claims that there is no evidence that it offered the scientific underpinning sought by educators. Harrington's critique of Bain's famous work focuses on its lack of originality, its generality, vagueness and lack of empirical justification. He also points out that the idea of a science of education preceded Bain, as indicated by the quote from James Mill at the start of this chapter. Even Simon (1978) recognised the earlier origins of this idea in the eighteenth century and the early part of the nineteenth century in the work of Mill (1818) and Herbart (1802). Harrington notes that Bain had no experience of teaching children, and that he acknowledged in public that he was no authority on pedagogy.

These differences over the significance of Bain's work are interesting in that they relate to the central question of this book, the relationship between psychology and education. They show that the differences of view which are current now, a hundred years later, were around at the very inception of educational psychology. As mentioned in my second chapter, William James reminded teachers that education was an art and psychology a science, and that sciences cannot generate arts directly. James Sully (1892), a founder member of the British Psychological Society, also warned of misplaced trust in quasi-scientific theories, and of the fact that psychology was at an early stage and could provide no simple determinant of the curriculum or teaching methods. Like many others teaching psychology to teachers in initial training, Sully was by academic background a philosopher, being professor of mind and logic at University College, London around the end of the nineteenth century. Sully saw education as a field which derived its aims from philosophy: psychology gave the teacher knowledge of human nature, which could inform the teaching methods needed to achieve educational aims. He believed that this contribution went well beyond knowledge about cognition to include other aptitudes, the emotions and imagination.

When the British Psychological Society was founded in the early years of the twentieth century, there were three organisations interested in studying child development, or what has been called the Child Study movement (Wooldridge, 1994). It grew out of public concerns about the health and well-being of the British population from the mid nineteenth century. It was an interesting movement because it engaged the support of key figures in the development of psychology and educational psychology, including Sully, Winch, Ballard and Burt. Sutherland (1988) has noted that this movement might have threatened the psychological society, as it was also concerned with the kinds of knowledge and insights being sought from psychology. In 1919 the BPS formed three sections, including the Education Section. Whatever rivalry there was between these organisations did not last beyond the 1940s, when the Child Study group merged with the Education Section of the BPS. The formation of the Education Section is significant because it started the trend of talking about educational psychology as distinct from psychology in general or general psychology. Some BPS members regretted the move at the time, anticipating the separation and loss of contact that comes with specialisation. When the BPS increased the qualification requirement for membership, it did continue to accept associate members of Sections who were not full members. Sutherland (1988) interprets this as the start of the 'second-class' connotation which has been associated with the Education Section. A further development in the BPS was the establishment of the Committee of Professional Psychologists in 1943, from which arose the professional divisions, such as the current Division of Child and Educational Psychology.

The institutionalising process in psychology and educational psychology includes the appointment of staff, the design and teaching of courses, and not least the establishment of academic journals. The separation of the sections from the general part of the BPS was also marked by the running of both a journal for psychology and one for educational psychology. The *British Journal of Educational Psychology* established in 1931, picked up its focus on experimental education and knowledge of the learning process and learners from its predecessor, the *Journal of Experimental Pedagogy*, which was founded in 1911. This was itself the successor to the *Training College Record*, started in 1908. The links to the influence of the training colleges, noted above, are clear. When the training colleges became the university departments of education, educational psychology entered the mainstream of educational and psychological research in the 1920s and 1930s. The study of education as a university field came to be dominated by educational psychology. By the 1940s the majority of professors of education were psychologists. There was also a growth of research and higher degrees in these education departments, many of which were in educational psychology. For example, between 1918 and 1952, 55 per cent of higher degrees based on educational research were in educational psychology (Wiseman, 1952).

The appointment of Cyril Burt by the London County Council in 1913 made him a pioneer in applied psychology. He was responsible for examining children who were nominated for admission to special schools for the 'mentally retarded'. He extended the scope of his brief to include the distribution of 'backward children', the standardisation of various mental and scholastic tests and the determination of average and exceptional attainments. He soon came to the view that there was a difference between theoretical and applied work:

I have come to realise in a very concrete way that a psychologist who is doing educational work is really starting a new and independent science. Educational psychology is not merely a branch of applied psychology. Medicine is not merely applied physiology. The medical investigator has been found, by practical exigencies to build up an independent science of his own, of work not in the physiological laboratories, but in the hospital and by the bedside. Similarly, the educational investigator cannot merely carry over the conclusions of academic psychology into the classroom. He has to work out almost every problem afresh, profiting by, but not simply relying on, his previous psychological training. He has to make short cuts to practical conclusions, which for the time being leave theory or pure science far behind. Education is thus not a simple field for the illustration and application of what is already known; it is, as you say, a great field for fresh research.

(Burt, writing in 1914, quoted in Wooldridge, 1994, p. 87)

Burt was one of the most famous psychologists in his day, although he became infamous in the 1970s over allegations that he tampered with his data in relation to the genetic inheritance of intelligence (Gillie, 1978). It is clear that he saw the need for careful and precise research into educational attainments and the need for techniques to measure abilities. To this end he adapted the mental tests which had been devised by Binet in France. But he also saw the need to create a 'scientific profession of teaching', drawing on the systematic use of empirical methods and statistics, and like others in his day, he considered that it would be based on psychology. Burt is associated with the use of intelligence tests (which have come to be called IQ tests) and the measurement of mental abilities, otherwise known as psychometrics, which some psychologists still to this day consider to be the greatest practical contribution of psychology. From what I have already said, it is clear that these tests were firstly to be used in the area of special education, but they came to be used in larger-scale decisions about selecting all children for different kinds of schools. Once the techniques came into use in implementing important educational policies, they came inevitably to be tinged with the politics of education and schooling. Critics of the selective school system focused their criticisms on the evident weaknesses of the current tests. Those from the right and left who opposed the meritocracy of selection by ability questioned the validity and fairness of the tests. The fact that many of the psychologists interested in the measuring of individual differences were also associated with the eugenics movement, going back to Galton, only reinforced the attacks on the racist and elitist nature of the psychometric tradition. Along with this went theories about the largely inherited basis of individual differences which fuelled what has been one of the great debates about the implications of science for society in this century. This is the dominant tradition at the historical roots of educational psychology, from which many psychologists since the Second World War have tried to distance themselves. It has been outsiders to the educational psychology group whose accounts have focused on this part of the history, for example, Simon (1978) and Hargreaves (1978).

Margaret Sutherland (1988), in her insider account of the historical background to educational psychology, portrays it as the 'distracted handmaiden' to education. By this she means that educational psychology was able to provide the 'necessary insights into human nature' for education. She portrays the field in its early initial phase as having a clear purpose; but this was followed by an identity crisis. The crisis was provoked by critics who accused educational psychology of being concerned only with measurement and individual differences. Cast in this role as villains, educational psychologists came to be criticised for serving unworthy political and social causes. They even came to be attacked as heartless testers serving the interests of an elite, assessing children only to their disadvantage. Tomlinson (1992) provides another insider's historical account which focuses on the more recent demise of psychology as a component of initial teacher training. He uses the analogy of the industrial revolution in his historical explanation, the idea being that the pioneers, the educational psychologists, got stuck with outdated theories and methods. The clients in education became aware of these limitations and psychology came to be rejected. Though Tomlinson recognises this as only one strand of a more complex historical picture, his main emphasis, like Sutherland's, is on trying to show that psychology really was able to meet the needs of its clients. For Sutherland, psychology was distracted from its purposes by critics who ignored the wealth of educational psychology that did not focus on mental measurement. For Tomlinson, mainstream psychology began to grapple with the learning and teaching processes which really concerned education. His claim is that developments in cognitive models and complex information processing were missed by teacher educators and even some educational psychologists themselves (cf. Desforges, 1985).

Though these historical accounts are interesting, they come from educational psychologists in university departments of education who are mainly concerned with teacher education. They are confined to one area of educational psychology and do not take account of the other uses of educational psychology. Educational psychology was used in the special education system to identify children for placement in special schools. It was also used more publicly in the operation of the selective school system. It is in these areas that educational psychology had its more overt policy impact and drew widespread criticism. Simon (1978), for example, from a Marxist position, attacked the dominant educational psychology in both theory and practice:

> because it justifies the selective character of secondary and higher education in this country, because, on the basis of highly questionable statistical investigations and equally questionable theoretical propositions, it has asserted that the majority of children lack the necessary ability to profit from advanced education.
>
> (Simon, 1978, p. 126)

Since the Second World War critics, including many sociologists, have portrayed educational psychology as a pseudo-science, expressing the social aim, either of the profession or of a social class, to control the education system. Educational psychology came to be presented as the 'chief vehicle of technocratic legitimation of inequality during the twentieth century' (Esland, 1977), rather than making a positive contribution towards promoting a meritocracy, as Burt and educational psychologists saw it.

Of course, what was at issue here was more than the measuring of mental abilities with standard tests and whether this was a superficial method or not. What were at stake were ideological issues of meritocracy, the perceived threat from the lower classes and the social justice of the distribution of opportunities in society. This was an aspect of the struggle between progressive, conservative and reactionary movements. It was a struggle over the dominance of rival accounts of individual differences between the more and the less advantaged members of society. The significance and influence of different ideological positions was raised in my chapter 2. The history of the role of educational psychology is therefore closely bound up with these social and political matters. That is why the changing relationship between education and psychology has to be seen in this wider context. This is where Wooldridge's wide-ranging historical account of the origins and changes in the field of educational psychology is relevant (Wooldridge, 1994). He traces the early origins to three main sources. The first was the growing question of how to identify and classify children with difficulties and disabilities as the state school system assumed the responsibility for educating more children. This was an issue across European countries and in the USA, and included questions about what learning experience to provide, and how, for those who were 'mentally handicapped'. The second source, according to Wooldridge, was the interest shown by educationalists in putting teaching on a scientific basis. This was a longer-term project which went back to the eighteenth century (as discussed above), but with the growth of the education service and the challenges faced by educationalists, a scientific approach promised not only technical expertise but also enhanced professional status for school teachers. The third influence on the origins of educational psychology was the initial opposition within the academic world to a science of psychology. Psychology was taught by philosophers as part of philosophy courses and controlled by philosophy departments. Those interested in psychology had limited opportunities to teach and develop their interests. However, education and teacher training became an area where those interested in an empirical and scientific approach could develop their interests in psychological questions. This gave a boost to educational psychology.

From Wooldridge's historical perspective, rapid changes occurred in educational psychology after 1880. Before then, there was little empirically based knowledge about intellectual abilities and emotional development. Mental powers were not assessed in terms of how people actually performed on a range of different tasks. Measuring the size of skulls was still practised. Within 40 years, by the 1920s, educational psychologists had organised themselves into a professional community and had a recognised place in what was a hostile academic world. And their work had had a significant impact on the rapidly changing school system. Wooldridge argues that this professional community shared some important common beliefs up to about the time of the Second World War. This is not to ignore differences which existed among educational psychologists over matters such as the meaning

of intelligence and the different models of intelligence, nor forgetting different ways of using statistical methods such as factor analysis. But his point is
that there was a broad consensus about the needs of the child and the basis
for allocating positions in society. Psychology stood for an approach to education in which the curriculum and teaching methods were geared to the
developing needs of the child and not governed solely by the demands of the
academic system. The other common position amongst educational psychologists up to the 1940s was the meritocratic belief that education and
social systems needed to be reformed, so that positions were allocated by
abilities and not through social connections and patronage. The search for
the measurement of psychological dispositions and abilities was the search
for some independent technique, which would replace patronage and all its
associated abuses.

As noted by many critics of psychometrics, the early educational psychologists were influenced by the eugenics movement. Fears of racial degen-
eration and of the growth in the number of 'defectives' in society was
widespread amongst the intellectual classes in the nineteenth century. Psychologists in Britain and the USA were prominent in attempts to develop
policies and practices which would limit the reproduction of certain groups
of people, for example sterilisation. Cyril Burt, for instance, saw his work as
continuing the tradition of Francis Galton, a strong supporter of the eugenics movement. To quote Burt's appreciation of Galton's contribution to psychology, 'Eugenics, the art of breeding better men, imperatively demands
reliable measurement of human traits of body and mind, of their inter-
relations and of their modifications by environmental factors' (Burt, 1962,
p. 39).

Cattell, another psychologist well known during the middle period of the
twentieth century, was also a keen exponent of eugenic ideas and values. As
a socialist, he became convinced that there was a need for radical solutions to
contemporary social problems. In his *The fight for our national intelligence*
(1937), Cattell argues for a radical programme of eugenic reform to avert
social disaster. These two examples illustrate how psychometrics was seen as
supporting a system of scientific management of society as a way of planning
human resources, which required an expansion of state control.

One of Wooldridge's key historical points is that many educational psychologists combined a commitment to a child-centred approach to education with a belief in the biological basis of individual differences and
meritocratic selection. To many of those brought up after the Second World
War, this seems a strange association of ideas. Psychometrics, with its links
to eugenics and biology, and therefore to an unalterable basis for individual
differences, seems far from a child-centred approach, from what is considered
nowadays to be progressive. There has, however, been a tendency to focus
historically on the unpopular aspects of socio-biology: the idea that social
inequality is based on natural differences, the emphasis on racial deteriora-
tion and therefore on eugenic solutions. But there was also a connection

between biological and progressive positions. A belief that education should be based on the needs of children had to take account of factors outside current social and academic demands. This is why socio-biological ideas were influential in the progressive educational assumptions of that period. Psychometrics was also on the side of the progressive intelligentsia. It was common to find views amongst those on the political left which also supported the ideals of a society planned by the state, with the aid of scientific experts, aiming for national efficiency, including efficiency in the identification and use of human resources.

As mentioned above, educational psychology also had a significant impact on national and local policy making. For many social scientists the pinnacle of the application of their field has been its use in policy making. Similarly, for psychologists like Burt, their involvement in policy making was central to their professional vision and work. Of course, this affected how they worked and what they concentrated on. But it can be seen to be a major reason why psychometrics and psychology came to have negative political and educational connotations. Social policy, in fields like education, demands instant and practical solutions to policy problems, not the tentativeness and intellectual abstractions associated with theory building and testing over many years. So in the inter-war period psychology came to be driven by the requirement for practical techniques without the theoretical developments needed to guide the use of those techniques. It was therefore easy for educational psychologists to see their work as apolitical because they could not see beyond the technical issues. Many of these issues were bound up with mathematical analyses which were associated with psychology's scientific aspirations. But, in the process there was a tendency, as Wooldridge argues, for educational psychologists to lose sight of the social and political implications of how their tests were used to identify merit. By ignoring other aspects of merit they opened themselves to criticisms from others.

Critiques of educational psychology

Social critiques have linked educational psychology theories and techniques to the political interests of economic groupings such as the middle classes. From this perspective, educational psychology became the ideology of the capitalist status quo. Before discussing this view it is interesting to consider a historical analysis of this socially interested approach. Wooldridge reminds us that psychometrics was opposed from two distinct and opposing social directions. First, from a communitarian and egalitarian standpoint which questioned the very basis of a meritocracy on the grounds that it undermined communities by identifying and promoting individual social mobility so as to form elite groups. Secondly, from a socially conservative standpoint which favoured the values of social order and the hereditary classes. For the second group, psychometrics was a threat because it supported individual social mobility and the allocation of social positions through a detached technical system. Once IQ tests became an established part of the process of selection for secondary schools, they were also distrusted by many in the middle classes. When some children from the middle classes failed to get into grammar schools, this engendered doubts amongst parts of the middle classes about the selective system. Yet up to the 1950s the Labour Party had a meritocratic wing, which considered mental testing as supportive of justice and political change. For example, during the inter-war period even a socialist political thinker like Tawney could favour the measurement of ability as a fairer way of allocating educational places than the operation of the class system (Tawney, 1922). Tawney was later to revise his views on education, but it will surprise many to learn that someone with this socialist background was for a considerable period a supporter of Burt and the psychometric ideal.

Wooldridge uses his historical sources to argue that the psychometric movement did not express the interests of a social class (the simple Marxist argument) as much as the interests of various status groups. He identified these as scholarship winners from working-class backgrounds, middle-class professionals and the intellectual aristocracy. These groups had their own social interests in the benefits of mental measurement, but the point is that this was not, in Marxist terms, a simple social class matter. However, there has been another social critique of educational psychologists and their use of psychometrics, already mentioned in chapter 3, which focuses on their professional interests (for instance, Rose, 1985). It is that psychologists' theories and methods were designed to advance professional interests and enhance control over clients. However, there are difficulties with this interpretation. Though professional groups no doubt act in part from professional self-interests the historical evidence, as Wooldridge shows, does not fit this account. For example, psychometrists, acted against their own material interests by designing and disseminating standardised tests which could be used by non-psychologists. Though some tests are restricted to professional psychologists, even today this does not apply to many tests which are for use by teachers and others. Secondly, the interest in and connections with eugenics at the origins of educational psychology, unacceptable as they are, relate to the community and not to simple professional interests. Thirdly, educational psychologists have had a long-standing interest in identifying children with difficulties and disabilities with a view to providing appropriate education and training. Though some psychologists in both Europe and the USA were hard-line supporters of eugenic sterilisation programmes, this attitude was not shared by all psychologists. As I argued in chapter 3, there was a strong tradition of scientific psychology which underpinned progressive social policies. Even Cyril Burt was a keen supporter of social policies to eradicate the effects of social and economic disadvantage on the development of children from working-class backgrounds (Burt, 1937).

Wooldridge also identifies the sources of the more recent trends away from psychometrics and the meritocratic ideal. There were growing technical criticisms of the tests, doubts about their underlying theoretical basis and accounts of their abuses, even amongst psychologists. The very ideal of meritocracy also came under attack. Sociologists, after the Second World War, showed how the environment affects ability and achievement. This led to a resurgence of interest in environmentalism, which favoured the forces of social circumstances rather than inherited biological factors. Tests came to be seen as measuring social constructs which reflected the social values of dominant social groups. Poor performance in these tests came to be attributed to biasing factors in the social system and not to individual potential. As environmentalism rose with the growth of sociological accounts, so individualist and biologically based theories associated with psychology fell. This spells out more fully the background to the identity crisis in educational psychology described by Sutherland (1988), and with which we are still dealing. Part of this crisis was evident when practitioner psychologists themselves became critical of psychometrics and the individual focus of psychology, a topic which will be discussed more fully later in this chapter.

The post-Second World War critique of psychometrics and its ideal was also extended by political thinkers from a socialist position to raise doubts about the values of individualist social mobility and the kind of mechanistic and planned society dedicated to production and efficiency. This was in the tradition of communitarian socialism associated with William Morris from the nineteenth century, a socialist tradition which came to be revived at a time when the abuses of state socialism were emerging from the Soviet Union. The meritocratic ideal was incompatible with social values which favoured small-scale organisations, the weakening of the division of labour, greater decentralisation and the rebuilding of community relations. This was a more thoroughgoing egalitarianism which wanted to replace equality of opportunity with equality of reward. Meritocratic school selection came under criticism for its cost in terms of isolating those selected from their communities of origin and reinforcing the despair of those without merit who were not selected. This was most cogently expressed by the sociologist Michael Young in the 1950s, with his 'future history' of Britain up to the year 2033 (Young, 1958). Young portrayed a future society where those selected by measured ability formed the upper strata of society and those not selected formed the lower strata. This was shown to produce a hierarchical society where there was reduced social mobility. Thus the meritocratic ideal of equal opportunity led eventually to an unequal and elitist society. His point was that the consequences of a meritocratic society were the antithesis of socialist ideals of social solidarity and equality. These social ideals have been and continue to be the ones underlying the commitment to the common school for all children irrespective of ability; the community school which stands for social belonging, participation and equal respect for all.

One of Wooldridge's main points is that psychometric practices, though originally caught in the struggle between an intellectual aristocracy and a landed conservative elite, was associated initially with a technocratic socialism which valued opportunity, production and efficiency. But it later came into a conflict with a communitarian socialist tradition which valued social relations, equality and community. Wooldridge makes some very important historical points about the social and political context of applied psychology and how this context provides opportunities for psychology to be applied, but also how it sets psychology up for evaluation depending on dominant and prevailing social values. Psychologists in this account have a tendency to be naive about the wider social and political implications of their theoretical and practical work. When they have claimed to be technical experts and distanced themselves from the social and political uses of their work, they have served their paymasters at the cost of professional and scientific integrity. The political reputation of psychological measurement has changed more because of changing political needs than because of the conceptual and empirical validity of its theoretical and applied bases. Psychometrics had been favoured politically because it met a social need and because it expressed the dominant meritocratic ideals. When it started to fall into disrepute, the theoretical and practical apparatus came to be seen by many as pseudo-scientific, rather than in need of refinement and development. Over the last two decades some psychologists in education have retained a belief in the central value of psychological measurement and the individual focus, but if they have done so openly and confidently, they have been a minority.

The scandal over Burt's academic reputation has shown that the fortunes of psychometrics as the systematic measurement of human characteristics has had more to do with the changing political scene than with changes coming from within psychology. It is not my intention to discuss this matter in any detail, other than to make a few points relevant to the various critiques of educational psychology which I am considering. First, the accusations of scientific fraud over the methodology in Burt's twin studies arose at a sensitive social, educational and political period, particularly in the USA of the 1970s. Secondly, there was considerable media coverage of the matter which put psychology and psychologists under suspicion. The authoritative account of Burt by Hearnshaw (1979) supported the case against him, and many eminent psychologists accepted the charges. Burt's character was called into question with his flaws revealed for all to pity, in what could be seen as a bandwagon of fault finding. This led to, thirdly, the realisation that the case against him was not as solid as had been assumed in the 1970s. Around the early 1990s an environmentalist psychologist, Joynson, and a sociologist sceptical about comprehensive schools, Fletcher, produced independent books which showed the weaknesses in the case against Burt (Joynson, 1989; Fletcher, 1991). The outcome was a re-evaluation of Burt's reputation, though it was still hard to decide about the major charge against him: that he invented data on twins. This is a fascinating and revealing episode in the recent history of educational psychology which cannot be discussed at length here. But what it shows is the extent to which evaluations of psychology reflect the changing social and political context. It also illustrates how differences within psychology and among psychologists reflect wider ideological differences over the ideal society and relationships among individuals.

But the basic assumptions of applied psychology – that human characteristics can be measured accurately and that these measures can inform decision making about selection, training and scarce interventions – has always been ambiguous in relation to the interplay between progressive and conservative politics. Political and social interests did not fit neatly with the detailed assumptions of the psychometric model. As Wooldridge has pointed out, individual differences have been taken to be continuous, whether they are seen to be mainly of an inherited or an environmental origin. Even if differences are considered to be mainly inherited, the psychometric position does not accept qualitative differences between groups, whether of a social class, ethnic or gender nature. The model also assumes considerable overlap between individuals of different social groups even when their mean levels are different. Secondly, the results of psychometric research on learning and teaching have called into question the popular environmentalist belief that all children can reach a high standard if teaching is good enough. This follows irrespective of whether individual differences in current abilities are mainly of genetic or environmental origin, as it is the child's current entry abilities that influence learning outcomes. However, the assumption of continuous individual differences has not supported the idea that there is a simple clear division between the normal and the abnormal. Thirdly, and this is crucial for the relationship between an applied psychology like educational psychology and policy making, the connection between psychometric assumptions and the practice of selection in educational or any other sector of society is contingent. Measurement of human characteristics does not necessarily lead to social selection practices, just because historically psychology was in part developed and used for those purposes. Educational and psychological testing can be used, as it was by some LEAs, such as the Inner London Education Authority, in the 1970s, to identify a broad range of individual differences in comprehensive secondary schools.

Sociological and philosophical critiques

Wooldridge's analysis represents a historical assessment of the origins and development of educational psychology. His approach involves a careful empirical scrutiny of the social, political and professional issues, including the leading personalities involved. For him, educational psychology from its early origins represented a particular synthesis of Romanticism and utilitarianism. It was utilitarian in its emphasis on using practical techniques and quantification to maximise benefits for the majority of society. But it was also romantic in its opposition to traditional and authoritarian notions of what was to be learned and how. Education had to take account of the developing needs of the child; the intellect and emotions developed should be a major determinant of the educational process. This brought in the biological basis of psychological characteristics and needs, which were also given a role in understanding individual differences, even when there were major disagreements about the nature of inheritance. This perspective contrasts with a contemporary sociological analysis of the educational psychology, where the main focus of criticism is on the individualism of the field. I dealt with the social critique of psychology in general terms in the last chapter, but will consider a particular social critique of educational psychology in this one.

Ollsen (1993) bases his critique of educational psychology on some of the by now well-known criticisms of positivism in psychology, but argues that the main failing of educational psychology is its depiction of human beings in individualistic terms. He starts by setting out some of the key features of positivism as a philosophy of science as applied to psychology, which I discussed in chapter 3. Here he refers to the belief that empirical data is theory free and that research is value free. He also refers to the authority of empirical data for accepting or rejecting a theory, to the search for generalisations, to the unity of methods across the social and physical sciences and to the assumption that complex phenomena can be analysed by reduction into their separate elements. These assumptions have been called 'methodological individualism' when applied to social phenomena. He then sets out some of the recent philosophical criticisms of positivism and empiricism, which I outlined in the last chapter. Though he refers to the growth of social and historical analyses of the development of science associated with Kuhn and others, he hardly deals with the major questions of relativism and realism. Nor does he examine the pragmatist positions, outlined in chapter 3, which try to relate subject and object in understanding the process of knowing. He allies his critique with Habermas's rejection of positivism in terms of the three different social interests which structure knowledge, which I discussed in chapter 2. Here Ollsen identifies much of educational psychology in its scientific tradition as representing what Habermas called the technical interest. This is the knowledge interest which aims for prediction and control; it underlies the concept of the educational psychologist as a specialist and expert who solves social and personal problems with the authority which comes from a detached and objective basis. Ollsen then reminds us that there are other social interests which structure knowledge. One is concerned with social life as communicative action and interpretation – the practical interest – while the other is concerned with promoting the values of autonomy and freedom – the emancipatory interest. In a similar way to the argument in my chapter 2, he points to other kinds of psychology within this broader conception of knowledge. However, although he concedes that knowledge based on the technical interest can be important in industry, production and the health sector, he does not acknowledge this when applied to education. This is a curious distinction, as the practical and emancipatory interests are as relevant to the former sectors as the technical interest is to education.

However, for Ollsen it is psychology's individualism which is a more serious problem. From a sociological perspective, he contends that the contemporary crisis for psychology is its continued focus on the individual. He attacks what he considers to be the continuing assumption that the reality is the individual. He contrasts this with the sociologies of Marx and Durkheim which both, though from different perspectives, took society to be independent of individuals and the individual to be socially and historically constructed. What Ollsen does is follow the usual presentation of a conflict between psychology and sociology over whether the individual or the social has priority in terms of what really exists. He then argues that the priority of the individual has been favoured in political theory since the Enlightenment in the form of individualism. He then associates this with a mean possessive form of egoism, as I discussed in chapter 3, rather than with a responsible pro-social form of individualism. Political thinking from Hobbes till the twentieth century, according to Ollsen, has been characterised by a model of the individual as 'pre-figuring' society and with assumptions that society will be fulfilled and secure to the extent that individuals are fulfilled and secure. The impact of this individualism on psychology was that 'Psychology took the individual as a unitary actor and the primary object of investigation. It was a science of the single case abstracted from culture' (Ollsen, 1993, p. 164).

He then treats most of the different schools of mainstream psychology as fitting this model of a culturally abstracted science of the individual, including cognitive, developmental and behavioural psychologies. His is the argument we met in the last chapter: that these psychologies are unable to explain the social nature of development and functioning. At this stage in his critique, however, Ollsen makes the important point that psychology is unable to conceptualise the relationship between the individual and social phenomena, because it does not deal with philosophical questions about the nature of knowledge and what exists. This is a relevant point, but it is one thing to realise the critical and significant role of broader theorising, it is another to do so in a way which opts for an over-socialised epistemology and ontology. Ollsen also refers to the important debate within sociology about the relative focus on structure or agency, and then accuses psychology about being macro-blind, that is, blind to social systems and the collective nature of society which shapes individuals. But he does not present a position which includes the relative contribution of social structure and agents, nor does he distinguish between social and individual agencies. Agency can be attributed to an institution, like a school, or to an elected assembly, like a legislature. These may influence, but are a different level of agency from the personal agency of individuals. As agency can be attributed to several different levels including the individual person, there is no reason for an either–or between the social and the individual. That such a dichotomy is false was argued in the last chapter, and it can also be seen in the context of the connections between the individual and biological levels of analysis.

Ollsen illustrates a common sociological critique of applied psychologies like educational psychology: that educational problems are individualised rather than being seen in social and institutional terms. This is the view that what arises from structural features of society can be explained in terms of individual psychological characteristics. For instance, deficiencies in personality or abilities can be invoked as explanations for low attainment or behavioural difficulties. Interventions can then be focused on fixing the individuals. This over-psychological approach has been and in some situations continues to be practised by psychologists both in theoretical and practitioner settings. But such an over-extension of the individual level of analysis and intervention has much in common with the over-extension of a social level of analysis and intervention. What I am arguing for in this book is for a clearer conceptual framework which connects the different and interrelated levels of analysis. What we need are disciplinary frameworks which do not define themselves in opposition to, but as connected with and complementary, to frameworks which apply to different levels of analysis.

Schwieso (1993), in his reply as a psychologist to Ollsen, recognises that the latter's critique implies that educational psychology is a waste of time and, even worse, a cover for oppressive interest groups. Schwieso makes several important points, some of which I will draw on in this section. The first point is that Ollsen tends to over-estimate the significance and impact of educational psychology in education and society generally. In the UK, there are only about 2000 practising educational psychologists in LEA service (Maliphant, 1997). As for psychology in teacher training, this has been weakened by recent reforms in teacher training (Wilkinson, 1992), something which I will examine in more detail later in this chapter. Psychology has continued over the years to be a major source of quantitative research methods in education research, though not their only source. But it has lost its theoretical dominance in sociology, curriculum studies (Nisbet, 1983) and, more recently, the field of school effectiveness and improvement. A second point made by Schwieso is that, as I outlined above in the historical section of this chapter, there is a tendency to ignore or overlook historical evidence about the 'science' of education, the origins of psychology and educational psychology and their connections. A psychological interest in education with scientific aspirations was present in teacher training well before the establishment of academic departments of psychology. Thirdly, Ollsen's argument about the weaknesses of positivism in science in general and as applied to psychology seems to imply that any psychology linked to positivist assumptions is seriously undermined. Yet even if positivism is an inadequate epistemological framework for science, this does not require the rejection of findings made in the name of science, as shown by the continued acceptance of much nineteenth-century physical science supposedly done within a positivist framework. In any case, as Schwieso argues, much mainstream psychology reflects non-positivist frameworks, such as Piaget's development theory. As some commentators on psychology have noted, psychology is theoretically diverse, with many rival theories. Psychology has been taken as pre-paradigmatic in the sense that there is, as yet, no established theoretical framework, though with maturity it will develop one, an idea discussed in the last chapter. Alternatively, the diversity may not be a matter of historical development of the discipline, but may reflect something about the nature of the subject matter.

Schwieso also makes some pertinent points in reply to Ollsen's criticism of excessive individualism in educational psychology. He reminds us that psychology's focus is on individuals by definition, as it is psychology which deals with analyses towards the individual end of the individual–social continuum of human phenomena. He also makes the point that the independence of the social in sociological analysis implies that the social exists separately from any particular individual. But this does not necessarily mean that the social exists separately from any individual. In other words, discrimination is not something that exists in some mysterious social realm, it is shown in the beliefs and actions of individuals. Also, because psychologists work or theorise about individuals, this does not require that they explain phenomena or problems only in terms of internal child factors. As in the points which I made above about working at different levels of analysis, Schwieso is keen to remind us of the connections and movement between these levels. In this vein, he notes that though educational psychologists can invoke interpersonal, institutional and societal factors and processes, this does not rule out individual factors, as some psychologists tend to imply (for example, Thomas, 1985). In conclusion, Schwieso acknowledges that despite the weaknesses in his argument, Ollsen makes some important general points relevant to educational psychology. One is that psychologists need to take account of the social context. This also extends to taking account of the goals of the institutions they serve and how these match their own professional goals. Schwieso also notes that there is a social account of the general growth of applied psychology in industrialised societies that sees it neither as the result of professional self-interest nor as simply sustaining capitalist socio-economic interests. This sees the general growth of applied psychology as part of the impetus to organise society and to optimise human resources and their development according to rational principles (Rose, 1990). This is an account with clear similarities to Wooldridge's historical perspective on the origins of educational psychology, discussed above.

This debate between Ollsen and Schwieso has been one of the most searching and rigorous interchanges between a psychologist and a sociologist in recent times. It is interesting that as it drew to an end Ollsen raised the question of whether educational psychologists had a form of expertise not on offer from educational sociologists. Behind this question was the issue of why there are practising educational psychologists but no practising educational sociologists. Ollsen accounted for this difference in terms of the development of a service which was grounded on historically based discourses which falsely assumed the priority of the individual over the social. Schwieso by contrast saw this position as a distraction from the more obvious fact that learning just happens to take place at an individual level. What is interesting about the tail end of this debate is that it reveals some of the rivalries between psychology and sociology in education, which are evoked by the fact that psychology has an applied practitioner base within education and other systems.

Educational psychology has also been subjected to a sustained critique from David Hargreaves, a well-known (and considered by some to be a controversial) figure in education. Over the years, Hargreaves has been identified more with socio-psychological and sociological perspectives on education than with psychological ones, although his undergraduate studies were in experimental psychology (Hargreaves, 1986). He argued twenty years ago that the proper study of educational psychology was education and what went on in schools and classrooms (Hargreaves, 1978). Here he was questioning whether educational psychology, in the form of its contribution to LEA services, teacher training and educational research, was sufficiently tentative and humble about its benefits. This was at a time when psychologists themselves were having such doubts. Hargreaves identified one of the reasons for these doubts as disquiet about the traditional psychological conception of intelligence and the continuing debates about its nature-or-nurture origins. He contrasted the original educational psychology belief that mental measurement contributed to an emergent meritocracy with the growing critique from sociologists and others that it was unscientific and expressed discriminatory social interests. But what is most interesting about Hargreaves's early critique is that he identifies the differing goals of research and theoretical psychologists and practising applied psychologists. Though IQ tests arose from policy and practice needs, the constructs they assessed were theorised and subjected to empirical grounding as part of a more basic psychology. A tension builds up here between the tentative and provisional nature of the constructs and measurement models, and the confidence with which practitioners present the measurement tools as solutions to pressing service needs. Also, as Hargreaves argued, once the application becomes accepted and widely used, it becomes entrenched within a new industry which serves its use. His point is that most of the criticisms of IQ testing focused on how testing was designed, done and then used, not on the principle of psychometrics or testing. But these attacks on the practice are then unjustifiably taken to undermine the whole enterprise, including its principle. Here Hargreaves identifies a cycle of events which runs as follows:

1 Original ideas and instruments are developed by psychologists.
2 Over-zealous educational psychologists apply these prematurely and make exaggerated claims.
3 Teachers receive these ideas in an attenuated form, as they become distorted and abused.
4 Abuses become subject to criticism.
5 Original enterprise is denigrated.

Not only can the fate of psychometric measurement of intelligence be understood in terms of this cycle: so can many other developments in the area. But
Hargreaves's point is the critical one that it is the whole system of applying
and using developments which has to be reviewed. It is easy to blame
psychologists for educational irresponsibility, but they are subject to demands from educationalists. What is at issue here is the tension in the work
of educational psychologists between the caution required by scientific standards and the hard decisions about pressing problems being demanded from
practitioners. Hargreaves is identifying one of the key dilemmas for applied
psychologists who aim to be scientific practitioners. It is a tension which can
become especially acute when there are strong ideological struggles over the
values guiding educational policy and practice.

Hargreaves was also right to point out that the pressures on applied
psychologists in education who try to serve two masters should affect psychologists in psychology departments, not just those working in education.
Here he made some insightful comments about the relatively low status of
applied and practising psychologists in comparison with pure or basic psychologists and their consequent lack of confidence. This confidence point
relates to some of Sutherland's comments about an identity crisis, discussed
above. Psychology departments should have given the applied psychologists
the esteem they deserved, according to Hargreaves. As for educational
psychologists, they needed to review their practice and their professional
identities. Hargreaves supported these views with some keen insights into
educational psychology practices related to their dilemmas about goals. On
this basis he recommended that educational psychologists should take risks,
be creative and inventive and not adhere slavishly to the patterns of 'pure'
psychology. He was encouraging educational psychologists to make links
with the interpretive psychologies of Rogers and Kelly. It is interesting in
hindsight to note that educational psychologists have broadened their psychological focus over the last twenty years in both practitioner and taught
educational psychology. This is the context in which Hargreaves was urging
educational psychologists to look at what was going on in schools and
classrooms and reminding them that teachers found popular educational
writers, like John Holt (1964), more interesting and useful than their formal
texts and theories. Though Hargreaves was perceived by many educational
psychologists at the time as unfairly critical, he was reminding them that
they needed confidence to promote a two-way interchange between applied
and basic psychology.

About ten years later Hargreaves returned to the question of psychology
and education in his Vernon-Wall lecture to the Education Section of the
BPS (Hargreaves, 1986). Although there had been some clear moves towards
looking at the processes of teaching and learning in schools, Hargreaves
continued to argue that psychological insights in teaching and learning were
limited because educational psychologists were not playful enough about
this serious matter. His attack had become even more critical, for example,

in his astonishment that psychologists were only beginning to accept the importance of social context, when anyone involved in education would have been aware of this. Hargreaves picked up his point from the 1970s that important psychological insights were to be gained from outside established psychology, quoting John Holt again and commenting that academics in his experience felt threatened by this. In identifying several areas where educational psychologists have been immune to innovative work and not responded to the challenges presented by important issues in education, such as race and gender, he claimed that educational psychology was locked in its past: 'it suffers from chronic necrophilia' (p. 17). In accusing educational psychologists of lacking the courage and self-confidence to engage with education, Hargreaves has been a stimulant, even if an irritating one, to many of them. It is interesting that Hargreaves has more recently been a vocal supporter of the need for evidence-based teaching as part of a wider critique of educational research (Hargreaves, 1996). It is possible to discern some continuity in his themes over the three decades from the 1970s; but the fact that his current critique is focused on educational research and not on educational psychology may reflect the declining role of psychology in the study of the processes of teaching and learning. I will return to this issue in the next chapter.

Having discussed some key critiques from a social perspective I want to end this section with an analysis of an important critique from a philosophical perspective (White, 1988). Based on a philosophical analysis of the intentional nature of psychological phenomena, which I outlined in chapter 3, White has argued that educational psychology, with its interest in learning, memory, thought, motivation and emotion, requires a hermeneutic or interpretive mode of inquiry, not a causal scientific one. He welcomes the moves towards an interpretive model in psychology more generally, and in educational psychology as exemplified in the work of Francis (1984). But he still identified a strong causal scientific commitment in Francis and other contemporary treatments of educational psychology. Here he analysed Tomlinson's position, one which was itself well informed by a philosophical background (Tomlinson, 1981). Tomlinson portrayed two broad approaches to teaching which he wanted to avoid. One was what he called naive technology, in which a positive view was taken of psychology as providing the practitioner with proven procedures or techniques. These techniques derived from understanding the teaching situation in terms of the formal concepts of psychology. I discussed this type of technological approach in chapter 2. The other approach, as characterised by Tomlinson, was arrogant amateurism. It rejected the belief that actions can be analysed and studied systematically. It had romantic associations in its assumption that education was about unique individuals, emotions and intuitions. Tomlinson proposed that we steer between these extreme positions by adopting an open, critical approach which drew on both systematic theory and common sense. White's point was that although Tomlinson might appear to advocate co-existence between common

sense and science-based theory, causal science was very much more important for him than common sense. Tomlinson uses the familiar argument,
discussed in chapter 2, that psychology is a young science, and his use of
George Kelly's account of common sense as a kind of lay science, placed,
according to White, a greater value on the systematic methods of scientific
inquiry than on common sense.

White's case was that it is possible to avoid the clouded and stereotypical
views of common sense by adopting a hermeneutic mode of inquiry, which is
empirical but does not seek empirically based causal generalisations or laws.
This would avoid, to use Tomlinson's terms, an arrogant amateurism in
professional teaching practice. But White does not see how causal generalisations can be justified in psychology, owing to the intentional nature of
many psychological phenomena. He used the philosophical analysis outlined
in the last chapter to show that there are no brute or intersubjectively given
data on psychological phenomena on which to ground such generalisations.
He realised that this argument threatened the very foundation of educational
psychology as an applied science. He also understood why, for reasons of
professional status, psychologists might hold on to the causal scientific model;
but he believed that for many psychologists it was about their commitment
to and the value they attached to rationality, practical realism and rooting
out dogma and distortion. He also defended his position against those who
claimed that he did not understand scientific generalisations. Finally, he
refuted attempts to demonstrate that there are important empirical generalisations in causal scientific psychology, by explaining that these statements
merely asserted what is true through the meaning of terms. He gave the
example of the generalisation 'practice informed by feedback tends to lead to
improved performance', and suggests that the meaning of the term 'feedback' includes the intention to improve performance, and therefore the connection is built into the generalisation. He could also have made this point
in other terms, by saying that if a teacher's comment or response during
student practice at a task did not lead to improved performance, then it
would not be counted as feedback.

White is applying a general view of psychology to educational psychology, which I discussed in the previous two chapters in general terms; it
needs to be addressed here in more detail. It is interesting that he makes the
same point as Smedslund about generalisations in mainstream scientific psychology, without making reference to this wider work and its implications
(see chapter 3). Though he went some way to understanding the difference
between those committed to a causal science and those promoting an interpretive psychology, he dismissed the causal generalisation model as dogma
without appreciating that it can be made to work. As I explained in the last
chapter, the different elements of causal generalisations can be treated in
practice as discretely identifiable and then investigated for their possible
relationship. I used the example of self-efficacy and persistence, but it can

also be shown with the example used by White, feedback and improved performance. Applying this causal model does raise doubts about the validity of assessment; for example, whether what is identified in concrete empirical terms as feedback is really what we mean by feedback. This is because we usually identify some action as feedback if it has the effect of improving performance during practice. But we cannot do this if we are trying to establish a relationship between feedback and improved performance. Underlying White's position and Smedslund's psychologic is the assumption that causal connections are built into the meaning of everyday psychological terms. The implication is therefore that they need not be discovered empirically, but revealed by elaborating their meaning and connections, which is the aim of Smedslund's psychologic. So if White's position is to be developed, then it needs to connect with Smedslund's concept of psychology.

The interpretivist conception of psychology advocated by philosophers like White does reserve a place for empirical study. This is in the investigation of the particulars of a person in her or his context with the aim of identifying relevant intentions, beliefs, emotions and actions. Predictions can then be made by applying relevant statements from the conceptual framework implicit in everyday psychological language to these concrete particulars. From this it follows that when there are problems in prediction, there is a need for more concrete knowledge about the particular person and situation, rather than a need to discover hidden causal generalisations. There is also a place in this conception for empirical work to evaluate the outcomes of different procedures and actions. But the function of empirical inquiry in this model is to apply our everyday knowledge of psychology and its implications to particular situations. When put in these terms an interpretive educational psychology involves empirical inquiry and goes well beyond, though it is continuous with, common-sense psychological assumptions. These ideas have connections with the discursive psychology promoted by Harre (1995), which I discussed in the last chapter. But once the model is developed along these lines, it should be clear that there is much in common between a causal explanatory version and this psychologic version of interpretive psychology. The popular depiction of difference, in terms of mechanism versus meaning or prediction and control versus understanding, becomes superficial because causal relations, understanding and prediction are common to both models. What can be contrasted is more basic: should causal relations be discovered through empirical and experimental methods or identified in the meaning of everyday psychological terms? Empirical inquiry is also common to both models, but is nomothetic (seeking generalisations) in the causal explanatory model and idiographic (descriptive of individual cases) in the interpretive one. Seeking generalisations about causes and effects requires collecting samples and subjecting them to comparable measurement formats, thus calling for quantification. Seeking to describe the beliefs, intentions and actions of an individual in context requires intensive single-case exploration of the agent's perspectives and actions, thus calling for qualitative accounts including that of the agent. Predictions can be made by applying the relevant psychologic statements to these qualitative accounts.

I doubt whether the psychologic approach to the study of psychological phenomena will be found persuasive by mainstream psychologists and educational psychologists who are socialised into the causal scientific model and committed to maintaining their professional identities. But it is important for all psychologists to consider a project like the psychologic one, as it represents an alternative which goes beyond psychology as a descriptive field. It offers the prospect of prediction based on empirical evidence from the individual case and the explicated psychology built into our natural language, which has more affinity to the classical causal scientist model than the descriptive study of interpretations and perspectives. This is what emerges when we follow through a philosophical critique of the causal scientific model. By its very nature it delves more deeply than the sociological critiques because it focuses on the nature of the phenomena subject to inquiry and draws implications about the processes and products of inquiry. The sociological critiques work from an allied field of inquiry and focus more on the nature of the relationship between the social and individual levels of analysis. Both kinds of critique highlight the extent to which the scientific nature of educational psychology relates as much to its uses and abuses by psychologists in their expert role as to the kind of inquiry and knowledge it generates. Though these critiques help shape conceptions about the nature of educational psychology, they leave us in a state of unresolved uncertainty. As I discussed in the last chapter, they leave us having to tolerate a coexistence between different models of educational psychology. We become more aware of the interests and social contexts which shape and structure what we call psychological knowledge and understanding.

Current issues for educational psychologists

In the previous section I analysed some key critiques of educational psychology from sociological and philosophical perspectives. I drew on outside views of psychology, but brought in psychologists' views in response. This section presents a more inside perspective on recent issues in educational psychology. I will discuss two related issues. The first is the distinction between different kinds of psychology related to theoretical and practitioner psychology, something which I have dealt with at several places in this and the previous chapters. The second issue involves some contemporary views about the difficulties and ways forward for educational psychology advocated by educational psychologists.

Psychology is one of the social sciences which has developed both as a scientific-theoretical endeavour and as a professional practitioner field. This is an important feature, especially as there are many more practitioners than academic psychologists in this and many other countries, such as the USA.

For psychology this has raised questions and led to debates about the nature of the respective functions and contributions of these different specialisms, how they relate to each other and outwards to other allied academic fields, services and professionals. The dominant kind of orientation within psychology, and between psychology and practical fields like education, has been from theory to practice. This direction is clearly marked by the language of application and applied psychology. There is a growing belief that this has been one of the problems in the relationship between education and psychology, but it is interesting to consider how there can be difficulties even within the traditional kind of relationship. In an interesting view outlined over twenty years ago, Hilgard (1970) argued that although the findings of psychological research on learning should influence educational practices, it was necessary to avoid too sharp a distinction between pure and applied research. He did this by breaking up the pure–applied distinction into six steps according to their relevance to the educational enterprise. Three of the steps are put into the pure end of the continuum and the other three into the applied end. Hilgard understands pure science to be guided by interests without any direct relevance to practical needs or problems. This does not mean that the psychologist has no practical interests, only that the questions are addressed without any short-term or practical end in view. The three steps within this pure range are:

1   research on learning, not directly relevant;
2   research on learning with relevant topics and subjects;
3   research on school-related learning with relevant topics and subjects.

Steps 2 and 3 could be seen to represent pure research done by academic educational psychologists. Hilgard considers that the third step falls on the border of the pure and applied continuum because its prime goal is to understand the process of learning, not how to teach the subject matter, but it is close to research on techniques of teaching. This forms the bridge to the three steps within the applied range of the continuum concerned with techniques, their development and dissemination. The three steps within this range are:

4   research into techniques in special conditions (e.g. laboratory class);
5   trials in normal or regular settings;
6   design, adoption and dissemination of techniques.

Hilgard's analysis has continuing relevance, not only because it shows how distinctions can be made between different kinds of research and development work, but because his framework allows us to identify where links in the relationship can break down. He maintained that too much research even by academic educational psychologists was in the pure range, and therefore not educationally relevant. He also claimed that there was a tendency to jump to step 6 in the applied range without enough patient research and development at steps 4 and 5. There are some clear similarities between Hilgard's continuum and Hargreaves's cycle discussed above. Hilgard as a psychologist gives a more detailed overview of the steps towards increasing relevance for practice, but they both identify the over-hasty movement towards application and dissemination.

The tensions between pure science and applied practice were brought into focus by the Burt scandal in the 1970s. May Davidson, in a presidential address to the BPS on this debate (Davidson, 1977), presented some useful ideas from her position as a professional educational and clinical psychologist. Her way forward was to suggest that we agree on the value of knowledge which has been systematically acquired and explored, but do not foreclose on exclusive definitions of what counts as systematic. For example, she advised that we should not exclude the systematic disciplines of a field like psychoanalysis. Secondly, she suggested several distinctions: between the scientist, to be found in universities, the applied scientist, to be found in universities, units and research centres, and practising psychologists employed in public or private services. The scientist, from this analysis, seeks knowledge about how things work. The applied scientist uses this knowledge in scientific ways to find out what interventions work. She or he contributes to the use of this knowledge, but is less likely to contribute to theoretical knowledge itself. The practitioner uses the best available knowledge to help clients deal with practical needs and problems. This requires that practice be based on knowing the best available techniques, but also knowing when there is no reliable knowledge about techniques. Davidson was putting forward a conception of specialisation for these three kinds of roles. Her point was that in practice psychologists tend not to engage in all three kinds of specialisms and that sticking to a particular specialism is all right if the connections to the others are maintained. There needs to be a sharing of specialist experience and knowledge and a sympathy for the responsibilities and demands placed on the other specialisms.

Even with its recognition of different forms of systematic inquiry, Davidson's scheme is modelled too strongly on the science-to-technology model of applied psychology. It does not take on fully her own eclectic view about the legitimacy of different ways of generating basic knowledge. Much theoretical knowledge derives from theorising about the outcomes of using certain techniques, some well established, others perhaps novel. Educational psychologists with an interest in theory might also be interested in 'home grown' theory, which is generated from research in schools and classrooms, not in detached or simulated settings (Francis, 1995). Practising educational psychologists also point out that they do not only use applied educational psychology, but also draw on others' disciplines and fields to find knowledge and strategies relevant to a current educational problem or need (Lindsay, 1988). The problem with the science-to-technology model or pure–applied version of psychology is that it assumes that science takes place in artificially contrived settings where experimental work can take place. This model is associated exclusively with the experimental model of science. If theoretical knowledge in psychology can be generated through different kinds of inquiry, including experimental methods, then it is unhelpful to consider basic theoretical knowledge as pure.

This is where Middleton and Edwards (1985) make a strong case for abandoning the distinction between pure and applied psychology. They argue against establishing a dichotomy or rigid separation between 'pure' and 'applied', but also against the use of the term 'pure' to describe theoretical knowledge in psychology. They argue, along with Davidson and many others, that this separation undermines any defence of psychology as a relevant and applicable discipline. They also argue that some areas of 'pure' research have also centred on real-life contexts, the supposed base for applied research. They therefore urge that the pure–applied distinction be replaced by a theory–needs-driven distinction. Theoretically driven research focuses on theoretical questions and issues which may be of a general or open-ended nature, without any particular immediate need or problem in mind. Its data base might come from simulated, detached or real-life settings. Needs-driven research is more problem-focused and is concerned with outcomes in real-life contexts. Middleton and Edwards also point out that 'pure' has connotations of cleanliness, normality and goodness, which by contrast implies that applied work is inferior and abnormal. They contend that the notion of applied psychology can be misleading and, following suggestions from psychologists such as Belbin (1979), that a distinction should be made between applied and applicable psychology. The term 'applied' retains the implication that it derives techniques for practice from theoretical research. 'Applicable' research is about methods and issues which arise from the needs of practising psychologists. Applicable psychology focuses directly on the issues and concerns of practitioners. This relates to what I called practitioner psychology or psychology-in-practice in chapter 3.

When focusing on the relationship between academic educational psychology and practitioner educational psychology, it may be assumed that there is a coherent basic psychology outside this. This can arise because general undergraduate textbooks of psychology, and the courses they support, present it as being a coherent discipline. It is even evident in the various models presented by Francis (1995) of the relationships between psychology, educational psychology and education. They reflect an erroneous belief that things that are really different are of the same kind. What can be taken as psychology is not a coherent common core of basic theoretical knowledge: it consists of various branches or areas which can be defined in quite different terms. For example:

- areas of psychological functioning, as in cognitive psychology;
- individual differences, as in personality psychology;
- life periods, as in developmental psychology;

- the interface with allied levels of analysis, as in physiological or social psychology;
- areas of applications, as in clinical, educational or forensic psychology;
- theoretical and value-based models, as in feminist psychology.

Bodies of theory and research focused on particular topics such as cognitive theories of emotions and motivation can be seen as part of social, developmental and clinical psychology. A topic like learning to read and spell can be studied within developmental psychology, cognitive psychology or educational psychology. These different branches might also have different research orientations, some being more experimental, like cognitive psychology, while others are more survey-based, like personality psychology. There is no common core of theoretical knowledge in psychology, but different overlapping areas using a range of different research methods: this is another reason for not talking in terms of 'pure' psychology. It is more accurate to talk of general psychology when referring to the different bodies of theoretical psychology. The term 'general' emphasises that the concepts, principles and theoretical relationships are set in general terms which can be used in different practical contexts or age ranges. This point can be illustrated with Bandura's theory of self-efficacy (Bandura, 1977). Though derived from research in the field of clinical psychology concerned with the treatment of phobias, it was given a formulation as a general theory in terms which could be used in different contexts and age groups. It was then applied to the field of educational psychology (Norwich, 1986; Schunk, 1990), health and industrial psychology.

It is clear from the above discussion that there has been no simple application of psychology by practising educational psychologists. But this model is also too limiting for the relationship between psychology and its use by teachers, a point which was made by Schwieso et al. (1992). Following the same lines of argument as I did in chapter 2, they question whether psychological knowledge can be simply applied by teachers to deal with practical teaching matters. They see this as relevant to the role of psychology in initial teacher training. Their main point is that the science-to-technology model has been over-used even in the hard sciences and engineering. Technical advances were made by artisans as the practical need arose, by trial and error. It is interesting to see in this context how the word 'experiment' has two distinct meanings: trial and error with a practical technical goal, and the control of variables in a scientific experiment to make a causal inference, aiming at a theoretical goal. Schwieso et al.'s point is that understanding whether some procedure or technique works is more important to practitioners than why it works. Only when a theory can lead to specific predictions can techniques be derived: that is, when we know the conditions which will lead to something happening, or know the consequences of carrying out some action. The problem for the relationship between psychology and education is that the diversity of theoretical models so confounds matters that there is doubt about the possibility of making predictions, let alone predictions that are specific and accurate enough to base practice on. For these commentators, this calls for careful analysis of ways in which psychology and education contribute to each other. Research and theory from psychology can, for example, inform ideas about effective teaching practices for children with specific learning difficulties. Psychologists working in education have done and can do research in areas where education and psychology overlap, for example in classroom management, teaching reading and curriculum match. This is not just research done by researchers with psychology backgrounds, but research which draws on psychological concepts and methods. Like many other contemporary commentators, Schwieso et al. conclude by calling for a two-way relationship between psychology and education, with phenomena dealt with in education research being fed back into general psychological research and theory. Central topics within education, such as class management, behaviour change and motivation, are too important to be ignored within the broad field of psychology.

This discussion has already led into some contemporary educational psychologists' views about the difficulties and ways forward for educational psychology, the second theme of this section. Tomlinson's (1981) proposition about steering between arrogant amateurism and naive technology by adopting an open-critical stance has been outlined. But to characterise the 'folk pedagogy' of teachers, as Bruner (1996) calls it, meaning their implicit theories and ideas about teaching and learning, as arrogant amateurism could be to be-little and underestimate them. There is a need to distinguish between personal anecdotal, trendy and perhaps biased conceptions about teaching and learning and those conceptions which arise from teacher reflection and analysis of practice or explicit traditions which may have origins in philosophical and social theories about the aims of education. Psychologists who aim to bring theoretical insights from psychology to bear on the professional beliefs and skills of teachers need to have a fuller understanding of the social, ideological, personal and practical underpinnings of these beliefs or folk pedagogies. Kyriacou, in his textbook on effective teaching in schools (1986), also discussed the disappointing fact that psychology has been unable to make a useful contribution to effective teaching. He points out what is too easily ignored by all educational psychologists: that teachers' concerns are with practicality and effectiveness, not with understanding the research and theoretical bases of psychology. Kyriacou takes this to imply that there is no point in introducing teachers to the theoretical and research base. Teachers need broad principles which they can be helped to use to evaluate their craft knowledge of teaching and learning. The purpose of psychology is therefore to sharpen their craft knowledge. He introduces three models for thinking about teaching. Model 1 is at a surface level of analysis and is concerned with the amount of time involved in learning and the quality of instruction. This kind of analysis derives from educational research on factors which optimise learning, such as the amount of actively engaged time for learning and the content and structure of the learning tasks provided. The second model involves a psychological level of analysis. Here the focus is on the psychological conditions necessary for engagement in learning. From amongst the many psychological concepts and principles he identifies three broad conditions necessary for learning:

1   attention to learning;
2   receptiveness to learning (including motives and willingness);
3   appropriateness of learning experience (taking account of learner's knowledge and skills).

The third model is at a pedagogical level of analysis and is based on how teachers themselves think about their teaching. It is the kind of analysis which expert teachers and teacher educators use with new entrants to teaching. Kyriacou's point is that this is the level of analysis with which psychologists need to engage if they are to provide teachers with resources to better understand and develop their teaching.

Tomlinson (1992), as discussed in a previous section, believes that part of what went wrong in the relationship between psychology and education was that educational psychologists involved in teacher education got stuck with outdated ideas and approaches. This happened while psychologists interested in cognitive and developmental psychology were grappling with the processes of learning relevant to teaching and learning. Yet some versions of psychology, such as the behavioural and humanistic theories of Rogers and Kelly, were being used actively in some areas of teacher training. For example, behavioural psychology had a major impact on the teaching of children with special educational needs, and humanistic ideas and practices on pastoral care teaching. Tomlinson notes that what teachers were given in these cases were procedures for meeting practical goals which derived from psychology. Along with the practical procedures, teachers were given some theoretical knowledge, but usually of a fairly rudimentary nature, just enough for supporting the practices. This had the clear disadvantage that they became familiar with only one kind of theory and had little flexibility to evaluate the theory or its scope of use.

This kind of proceduralism, potent as it is for teachers, can lead to the narrowness which has been called a mindless technology (Norwich et al., 1977) and Tomlinson earlier referred to as naive technology. Tomlinson also makes some very important comments on the relationship between psychology and education. Psychology in its various areas and theoretical models provides a wide network of resources for education which can illuminate and directly influence practice. But this calls for *a critically open* stance, from which all sources are seen as fallible and likely to be limited. Tomlinson advises that these resources be evaluated critically for their internal coherence, for evidence of their validity and for relevance to practical concerns. Much as I support the spirit of critical openness for its tolerance and opposition to narrow and exclusive psychologies, it does not resolve the educationalists' and practitioners' question of what ideas and techniques they should adopt from psychology given the pressing practical needs in education. One of the main points in this book is that this is a continuing problem in the relationship between psychology and education which cannot be resolved in a simple and definitive way. It is a fundamental problem concerned with the foundations and nature of social sciences like psychology, and it needs at least to be understood for what it is. It is a problem that should not be ignored or overlooked by psychologists in education in their need to demonstrate to themselves and others that they have useful contributions to make.

There are different ways of making sense and coping with this problem. One is to close down on a purist conception of psychology by adopting a particular theoretical model about psychology and assuming that this one model can provide psychology's contribution to the relationship with education. One version of this response is to opt for a constructivist kind of psychology and present this as a way of reconstructing psychology for education. Salmon (1995), for example, presents the Personal Construct Psychology of George Kelly as a single and exclusive psychology of education. Though this psychology, which is based on personal learning, has much to offer education with its focus on personal constructs and practical and creative methods of exploring them with explicit and systematic techniques, it is still only one amongst many other psychologies. It is presented by Salmon and others, such as Ravenette (1988), as having a basis in humanistic progressive values, as discussed in chapter 2. This forms part of its appeal to educationalists who are positively inclined to these social and personal values. But while one can have an interest in and use this kind of psychology, it does not address questions in education which arise from other educational models and concerns, such as technical aspects of subject-specific teaching.

Another version of this single-minded response comes from a diametrically opposite tradition in psychology, that of radical behaviourism (Skinner, 1984). He suggested that applied behaviour analysis could be used to resolve the key problems in American education and no doubt in other countries too. As I argued in chapter 2, this is a facile approach because it ignores the fact that education is as much about the ends of learning as the means and techniques for attaining those ends. Radical behaviourism can be relevant to certain ends, particularly those concerned with training certain educational skills, but it cannot exclude educational concerns deriving from other educational ends concerned with developing personal autonomy, for example. This is for exactly the same reason as a humanistic psychology such as Kelly's Construct Psychology cannot exclude educational concerns about teaching techniques.

Yet another response to the difficulties of coping with model diversity within both psychology and education is to opt for a purist philosophical conception of psychology. This is what psychologists do who opt for a social-constructionist position about science in opposition to what they call positivism. This does not foreclose on a particular psychological approach, as it can include various psychologies which can be broadly included within this framework, including Construct Psychology, Symbolic Interactionism and neo-Vygotskian theories. Burden (1992), for example, argues that one of the main reasons for psychology's failure to offer more to education are the double standards amongst many psychologists. He argues that on the one hand, they claim to be scientists laying claim to objectivity as the basis for being experts, while on the other they advocate psychological theories which are incompatible with such scientific objectivity. According to him, this leads to confusion and cynicism amongst teachers. Burden's approach is to abandon a positivist model of science in favour of a social constructionism which recognises the value systems underpinning psychology and rejects the 'positivist baggage', as he calls it. It is an approach which arises from assumptions behind the work of practising educational psychologists and their training. He also makes the important point, which I will discuss more fully in a later section, that practising psychologists for over twenty years have been involved in using psychological approaches based on interactional and socially oriented models. But, as I argued in chapter 3, there are risks and difficulties in defining social constructionism as opposed to realism without becoming stuck in a relativism which undermines any systematic inquiry. Those who advocate social constructionism need to be careful not to propose false dichotomies when justifying an epistemological basis for psychology. They might also find that in focusing on the significance of the environment in learning, they find themselves wanting to make statements about the environment, not just as someone's perspective but as 'something' to be analysed and modified. This is what we find Burden doing in his very interesting work on classroom learning environments (Burden and Hornby, 1989). Here the learning environment is assessed in quantitative terms using structured pupil self-report inventories. The point is that there is an inconsistency between making general criticisms about positivist scientific methodology and then adopting realist assumptions and methods associated with positivism. Self-report methods may reveal personal perspectives, but Burden is using them here to represent intersubjective classroom phenomena in quantitative terms.

Another way of making sense and coping with the educationalist's problem of what psychological ideas and techniques to adopt is to turn away from psychology and expect home-grown ideas and research in education to provide the way forward. This would leave it to teacher educators and subject and phase methods specialists within education to address practice questions without psychology input. This is largely the current context of policy and practice in initial teacher education, where psychology and psychologists have a very minor role and the emphasis on practical teaching techniques and subject knowledge has squeezed out a psychological input. Smith (1992), working along similar lines to the one in this chapter, has set out a very clear scheme for the scope of psychology in education, which he uses to resist the separation of psychology from education. There are four steps, as follows:

1   Select an area of education which is ready for improvement.
2   Adopt a preferred psychology perspective as a theoretical base which can offer techniques.
3   Design the techniques for educational intervention using the psychology base.
4   Evaluate empirically to see whether the outcomes work better than alternatives.

Smith recognises that there are many obstacles to putting this sequence into operation, most of which have been discussed in previous chapters. Step 1 involves a question of values, while step 2, as I have argued above, suffers from pluralism or diversity, there being little agreement on the preferred perspective. In the third step, psychologists have tended to cast teachers in a technician role and have not always spelled out general prescriptions in the detail required for practice. In the fourth step, evaluation may show that the interventions are no better than alternatives. Smith's view is that it is not possible to show that psychology cannot contribute to education. It might be argued, starting at step 4, above, that no psychology-informed interventions have been shown to work better than alternatives. But, as Smith points out, this may be true of some specific interventions, but it does not necessarily apply to all specific interventions. To reject the principle of a psychological contribution we would need to find consistent failure of all interventions. Experience shows that some interventions have worked. On this basis, Smith concludes that although educational problems go well beyond the scope of psychology, most importantly, some have a psychological dimension and the contribution of psychology can be understood and justified in this way. But there are further aspects to the constraints which Smith identifies in the relationship between education and psychology. Not only is there a plurality of psychological approaches, which makes selection open to other influences including judgements about human well-being and about epistemology, but also evaluating the outcome of interventions depends on the educational goals of those interventions; and as there are multiple goals and their relative importance is disputed, evaluation itself becomes open to uncertainty. This is one way of understanding why the goal of effectiveness in education is itself problematic without greater value and goal clarification, something which I will return to in the last chapter.

The current position of educational psychology in academic settings

As indicated in table 3, psychologists in universities with an interest in education are mainly in psychology and education departments. They share common academic responsibilities for teaching and research, but there are important differences between education departments and psychology departments. In psychology departments the focus is on psychology as a broad discipline, often including general and applied psychology. Teaching is directed at undergraduates studying psychology and post-graduates at master's and doctoral levels. There may be some training in applied psychology for practising psychologists, which may include professional educational psychology. Psychology relevant to education would probably be found in the professional training course and in teaching and research concerned with developmental psychology and perhaps some aspects of clinical psychology related to children and young people. By contrast, in education departments or schools, the ethos will be more focused on the practice of education. These departments will be strongly involved in undergraduate courses in education, which support initial teacher training through BEd and BA courses, and in post-graduate training of graduates for teaching via the PGCE. There will also be higher degrees, master's and doctoral, for teachers or those involved in some other aspects of education. Psychologists in education departments will be involved in teaching the professional studies part of initial training courses, though some may teach psychology as part of the education modules of mixed-subject undergraduate degrees. They will also be involved in teaching modules at master's level. In some cases these may be specialised psychology and education courses, in others they may be modules in a master's programme. Some of the specialised educational psychology master's courses act as BPS-recognised conversion courses for teachers seeking a qualification for training to become practising educational psychologists. Teachers can also enter practising educational psychology by doing a psychology degree through the Open University or some other part-time study route. There is also training of practising educational psychologists in some education departments and schools.

The picture is complex and shows areas of overlap and difference between the work in psychology and education departments. Amongst the wider group of psychologists who work in education, there are two main sub-groups, the practising educational psychologists and the research-teaching psychologists. Most of those in the practitioner group will be employed by LEAs, but there are some practitioner psychologists who have moved into research and teaching roles. Some will be involved in the initial and in-service training of practising educational psychologists, but there are others who will be involved in teaching and research work in special educational needs and wider areas of psychology. This latter group merge into the traditional group of psychologists who have taught educational psychology in initial and in-service courses. They are psychologists who may have moved from psychology to education departments, or psychologists who started as teachers and have become graduate psychologists, without any practical psychologist experience. These intersecting entry routes for practising and research-teaching educational psychologists are important, for there is a tendency for the differences to be over-emphasised. I will return to that point later in this section.

What is remarkable about the erosion of the influence of psychology in departments and schools of education is that it tends to be considered by academic psychologists in the narrow context of teacher education. Burden (1992) has commented that practising educational psychologists have been developing ways of working with teachers in practical contexts. It is not that research and teaching educational psychologists are unaware that they are not connecting with their practitioner colleagues (see, for example, Francis, 1995). It could be that this is yet another instance of the divisions between theory and practice, between basic and applied psychology, being played out within what could be considered an applied or specialised area of psychology. As I discussed in the historical sections, this relates to the continuing ethos in psychology of the superiority of pure versus applied psychology. It is unlikely to be simply that research-teaching educational psychologists have become so preoccupied with the erosion of their contribution to teacher training and education that they cannot broaden their sights.

That there are serious questions for research-teaching psychologists in education departments is without question. During the 1980s the government increased the time spent by trainees under the supervision of teachers in schools, in what was called school-based training. There has also been a move to increase the training focus on curriculum subjects and on teaching the relevant content, with the effect that there has been less time for psychology input. For example, from the mid-1980s the secondary PGCE at the London Institute of Education, the largest course of its kind in the country, ceased to offer a psychology foundation option. Any psychology content became part of the professional studies part of the course, which also included aspects drawn from history, philosophy, curriculum studies and sociology. The emphasis was also on making these professional studies more professionally relevant, and so whatever psychological ideas and techniques were included tended to come under some other service-related topics, such as pastoral care or classroom management. This move arose partly from the growth of these other areas of educational studies relative to educational psychology, which came to be seen as either too theoretical or associated with psychometrics and discriminatory practices in education. It can also be seen to arise from the renewed government interest in education over the last two decades and the growing cross-political-party sense that all was not well with the education system, especially in England and Wales. There was a sense that teachers needed more and better practically oriented initial preparation and in-service training. The Conservative Government began to specify a more competence-based programme of initial training through the Council for the Accreditation of Teacher Education (CATE), which was the precursor of the current Teacher Training Agency (TTA). The political rhetoric which justified this move contained criticism of educational theory and associated it with left-wing ideas which were seen as contrary to the needs of society and teachers and pupils in schools. Since then the demands of the National Curriculum and the inspection of teacher training courses have required further tightening of the teacher training curriculum. We have now reached the stage where the TTA has finalised the required teacher training curriculum for all phases of compulsory schooling.

The move towards a greater focus on curriculum subjects, especially at secondary level, meant that admission to PGCE courses placed greater stress on the subject qualifications of applicants. This raised concerns about the admission of psychology graduates to PGCE courses. When the government was pressed on the matter, there were assurances that there was no reason in principle why psychology would no longer be an acceptable subject for entry to PGCE. This left it up to individual training courses to decide whether psychology graduates had appropriate content in their degrees for admission. The government was not prepared to clarify the access question in more detail. When a survey was done of course admission practices in 1990, it was found that courses for primary teachers would consider psychology graduates, but that they were reluctant to make this policy explicit (Wilkinson, 1992). Nevertheless, some primary courses did reject psychology graduates. For secondary teachers, the picture was that graduate psychology applicants had to show how their qualifications equipped them to teach one of the subject areas. This increasingly sharp definition of what was required to become a teacher could be easily criticised from a psychologist's perspective because it restricted the simple movement from psychology to education. But from a teacher educator's perspective, this was part of making teaching a more professional occupation. Part of the concern for psychologists was that reducing the number of psychology graduates entering teaching limited the number of psychologists who could then train as practising educational psychologists. It is worth noting that this tightening of admission to PGCE courses did not lead to a rigid system of rejecting all psychology graduates. The requirement that practising educational psychologists should also be trained and experienced teachers is itself an issue in the training of practitioners, something which I will return to in the next section.

Concern about the role of psychology and psychologists was actively expressed in the mid-1980s within the BPS Education Section, as shown in an interesting volume edited by Hazel Francis (Francis, 1985). This included a wide range of discussions which re-asserted the value of psychology in teacher training from many points of view. But most of the contributions failed to locate the issue in the wider social and institutional context of teacher training and teachers' working lives in schools (Norwich, 1985). In the early 1990s the British Psychological Society (BPS) through its Education Section began to pursue the issue further. A special conference was called by the Education Section and the Group of Teachers of Psychology at which psychologists from all parts of the BPS came together to discuss the contribution of psychology to teacher training and education. Many interesting and provocative papers were presented, but the intended publication never appeared. This would have shown the extent to which those present, many of them leaders in the field of psychology and educational psychology, were still preoccupied with the nature of psychology and the science-to-technology model, and had little appreciation of training from the perspective of teacher trainers and educators, let alone teachers themselves.

The BPS supported various areas of action, including a discussion paper identifying how modern psychology could and should be used in the service of education and a survey of psychology input to initial training courses. In 1992 the BPS submitted a document to CATE (Tomlinson et al., 1993) which expressed concern that teachers in initial training were losing access to psychological work at a time when the 'research base has yielded increasing recognition of its applied uses' (p. 1). It argued that teaching was the promotion of learning and necessarily involved psychological aspects. This meant, it was stressed, that 'relevant and well-grounded psychological insights would therefore promote the effectiveness of teaching and teacher preparation' (p. 3). Though the document rested on the assumption that psychological aspects are central to pedagogy, this was not seen to exclude other aspects and levels of analysis. The case was based on the assumption that teachers need to have some pedagogical understanding in their professional knowledge. They do not need an abstract body of knowledge, but knowledge which informs their teaching and their learning from their teaching. This is where the document draws on Tomlinson's notion of critical openness, discussed above. Teachers, it was then argued, need to 'ground their professional knowledge rigorously in evidence and analysis, otherwise they will be prey to mere fashion and assumption' (p. 4). The document did not say how this was best achieved in the organisation of initial teacher training and education. But the contention was that interdisciplinary teams were needed, which would include those with 'appropriate grounding in recent psychology'.

The model of teaching competence was defined in a three-level approach:

level 1   broad analysis of essential components of teaching and therefore pedagogy;

level 2   designation of broad psychological aspects of components identified at level 1;

level 3   more specific educational and psychological sub-areas and concepts constitutive of an understanding at level 2.

Each level of the model is specified and related to the preceding one. The basic analysis of teaching is in terms of seven broad aspects, concerned with: intended learning outcomes, learning activities and experiences, internal and external influences on action, learner variations as individuals and groups, teaching strategies, matching, and assessment. Under each of these seven broad aspects, psychological content is specified. For example, at level 1 of the third aspect, internal and external influences on actions, the following content is identified:

- nature of motivational processes both value and habit based, personal and social;
- social communication and group processes;
- effects of school organisation and climate.

The proposal is that it is level 3 components which should feature in the specification of teacher competences. This is because they reveal the complexity that exists within teaching and because they relate to various different aspects of teaching at level 1, the basic pedagogic description of teaching, and are therefore transferable. To illustrate this for the same aspect of teaching, internal and external influences on action, level 3 includes:

- views and forms of human motivation (this relates to another aspect at level 3 concerned with intended learning outcomes, amongst which are included attitudes and values);
- effects of motivation, emotion and stress on skill learning and knowledge acquisition;
- self and social motivation in the classroom;
- group dynamics and the influence of expectancy effects;
- formation of attitudes, balancing of intrinsic and extrinsic motivation;
- verbal and non-verbal communication;
- attribution and expectancy effects, episodes and social definition.

Although there might be queries about specific elements of this scheme, it reflects a sophisticated analysis of a broadly based psychological understanding relating to pedagogic knowledge and skills. But it fell on deaf ears in the government agency and seemingly had little impact on teacher educators more generally. This needs to be understood in terms of the pressures on teacher training, concerning both finance and accountability. The inclusion of level 3 specifications would compete with the core of the teacher preparation programme, which focuses on curriculum subject content and acquiring practical teaching skills in schools, unless there was a major increase in preparation time. It would require employing more psychologists and bringing them together with other teacher trainers and subject specialists. This kind of scheme goes well beyond the current system whereby psychological aspects are included, perhaps not labelled as such, in the professional studies part of the course. In this part of the course they are separate from what trainees learn about their teaching subject area and from their classroom teaching practice. This puts psychological aspects in the theoretical part of the course, their traditional place, and does not promote the practical application of this psychological understanding. The case for interdisciplinary teams was also not specified in detail. There is a difference between including psychologists and (say) sociologists with teachers in a training team, and building in some system of training whereby psychologists are working with teachers on teaching practice to support practically applicable understanding. The latter requires a more radical review of teacher training.

Wilkinson (1993), based on a survey of 53 UK initial training courses covering nursery to further education, including mainly BEd and PGCE courses, found that psychological aspects were integrated with other disciplines and in some cases these integrated parts had some psychological options. Psychology was more visible in specialised units in nursery and primary than in secondary courses. With more time on the BEd courses, there was more time for psychological aspects. Though caution was advised in accepting the collected figures about contact time, these were very low, especially on the PGCE, where for example the mean number of hours was 16 over what was more than a 30-week course. Wilkinson also found that about half of the professional studies tutors were teaching psychology-related content, while only 40 per cent of them had a minimal psychology qualification. It was hardly surprising that 60 per cent of the course directors considered the provision of psychological aspects to be unsatisfactory. It is in this context that teaching and research psychologists in university education departments have good reason to be worried about their contribution and even redundancy. Francis (1996) raised the question whether psychologists should rethink their role in teacher education. This would involve moving away from treating psychology as a body of knowledge to be applied towards treating it as a field of research and tutorial support for trainees. Francis argued that the teaching of psychology in initial teacher preparation has been traditionally theoretical and separate from the preparation which goes on in schools. Trends in other countries can be taken to support this position. She is critical of educational psychology as something to be applied from general psychology, and favours grounding psychology in educational practice (Francis, 1995). In her 1995 talk she presented this not as an either–or, but as a development on two fronts. However, in her more recent 1996 paper she seemed to be moving more towards the idea that educational psychology offers not fields for application but fields for development, in this case meaning that psychologists should be involved in the professional development of teachers.

Francis was arguing for the psychologist's role to be that of teacher developer. not provider of theory to be applied to practice by teachers, which she claimed had been shown over many years to be unsatisfactory. She suggested two main areas of contribution. First, psychology can help teachers treat practical educational questions as open to empirical investigation; and secondly, this should be done in a way that promotes sensitivity to individual learner needs. It is an interesting version of the contribution of psychology to teacher preparation in that it focuses on what underlies the values associated with psychology as a systematic empirical study rather than on specific content related to the nature of teaching. It is a view which relates to the model of educational psychology she sketched in her 1995 talk, what she calls working in education. It is a model which presents educational psychology as being in a two-way relationship with psychology on one side and education on the other. Educational psychology is cast as developing its own theory and research, drawing on psychology, and testing this in education.

But the relationship is closer to education, as there is also a commitment to work with teachers in their preparation. By placing psychologists directly in the supervision of teaching practice, she is highlighting a critical question for psychology in education. But it is a suggestion which, by playing down the contribution of psychological understanding to professional teaching knowledge and skills, loosens the legitimacy of its involvement. Teacher educators and tutors from other allied disciplines, such as curriculum studies, school effectiveness and sociology, could also claim to be able to offer an approach which treats practical questions as open to empirical investigation. Psychology has never had the sole claim to an empirical orientation, especially so now with the greater establishment of educational research as a field in its own right. Though psychologists might have some claim to a particular interest in individual learners and learning, sensitivity to individual needs is also a concern of those committed to progressive ideas in education.

It has been widely noted that the prime determinant of the fate of psychology in teacher preparation has been the systematic government policy over the 1980s to reduce its influence. However, Wilkinson's survey, discussed above, suggests that this had not happened in the early 1990s as effectively as the political rhetoric might have implied. Gammage (1996) in his response to Francis's views contends that the problematic position of psychology owes more to the 'deliberate erosion of independence of thought in teacher education' (p. 6) than to inappropriate psychology teaching or a problem in the relation between theory and practice. Gammage is making an important point about the effects of adopting short-term instrumentalist views about education, which is compatible with the need to reconsider how psychology is taught in teacher training and education. Fontana (1996), in his reply to Francis, makes a point which I made above, that the contribution of psychology to teachers goes well beyond enhancing their teaching practice. It has relevance to their wider understanding of children and their general well-being and development outside schools. It is also relevant to teachers' own professional and personal development. In his response, Tomlinson (1996) points out that the failure of psychology in teacher preparation was not only because it was taught as an abstract body of knowledge, but because much of its content was irrelevant. But his most important point is that by promoting a process contribution, Francis is overdrawing the distinction between psychology as a field for application and as a field for development. Along with Fontana, Tomlinson suggests that process requires some content; as far as psychology's specific contribution is concerned, this means some theories about teaching and learning, irrespective of whether these come from home-grown educational psychology theory or imported theory from psychology more generally.

This discussion about the contribution of psychology to teacher preparation shows that research-teaching educational psychologists in university departments and schools of education are concerned with much the same problems and issues as their practitioner colleagues working in LEA services.

Both are concerned with how to bring psychology as an empirically based process of inquiry and as a theory-based field to bear on the practical needs of teachers. Research-teaching psychologists like Francis and Tomlinson do so in relation to initial teacher preparation and in-service higher degrees, while their practitioner colleagues do so in relation to service-based in-service training and consultation. The two groups also differ in that practitioners tend to specialise (though not exclusively) in teaching and learning related to special educational needs, while those focusing on initial training relate to the full range of learners and learning. However, there is no hard distinction between the 20 to 30 per cent of children with special educational needs (falling within the SEN Code of Practice) and the generality of children. The contribution of psychology to initial training and in-service higher degrees is also relevant to SEN (see the BPS CATE document discussed above), which for many teachers in initial training is a topic of considerable relevance and personal interest. My point is that there are strong interconnections between the issues facing research and teaching and practising educational psychologists and many lessons to be learned and shared between these branches of educational psychology. The work of Francis (1989), which supports teachers in developing their perspectives on learning and its application to special educational needs, is just such an example of sharing and interchange.

The fact that there are few connections between practising and research and teaching educational psychologists arises from and is perpetuated by the weak links between the two parts of the BPS which represent these groups, the Division of Educational and Child Psychology and the Education Section respectively. Some psychologists are members of the Section and the Division, but they will be practising psychologists, because membership of the Division requires professional training. Many research-teaching educational psychologists are not qualified professional psychologists, though there are some. The professional qualification sets up a barrier between these two groups, which is also reinforced by the fact that research and teaching psychologists see their academic research specialisation as their distinguishing feature. The position of the Education Section has also been affected by the growth of developmental psychology as one of the major areas of research and theory in psychology over the last two decades, and its representation within the Developmental Section. There are psychologists who are members of both the Developmental and Education Sections, but the rise of the Developmental Section means that the focus for much basic research and theory about children and young people lies outside the Education Section. There are also developmental psychologists whose work is applied, and though this may be in relation to health or social welfare needs, it also relates to educational needs. So there is an overlap of interests between research-teaching educational psychologists and applied developmental psychologists. Some psychologists might see themselves as developmental and educational psychologists, but there are differences in professional tradition, as shown in journals, conference orientations and even master's course programmes. Educational psychology has more focus on educational ideas, needs and institutions, whether this is for school learning or adult learning. Applied developmental psychology has more focus on the child's functioning and development beyond what is included in an academic school curriculum. Its concerns include development as it relates to wider needs and services across institutions other than schools.

This network of overlapping connections extends also into the relationship between research in educational psychology and educational research more widely. The British Educational Research Association (BERA) has become established as the organisation which represents educational researchers covering many different aspects of research in and about education. It covers curriculum studies, sociology and policy studies in education, school effectiveness and improvement, assessment and evaluation studies, special needs education, gender and ethnic studies in education, as well as approaches associated more with teachers as researchers. Amongst these is psychological studies, which is just one amongst many aspects of educational research. Seen in this light the traditional aspiration of psychology to provide the foundation discipline for education and educational research has been completely eclipsed. There are too many other competing disciplinary positions as well as critics of the traditional scientific mode in educational psychology. Nevertheless, there are members of the Education Section of the BPS who are active in BERA, but, as with the BPS sections and divisions, there are significant professional cultural differences between the Education Section and BERA. However, though the growth of education research and its professional structures may have taken away from psychology any hope of leading educational research, this does not mean that psychology and psychologists do not retain a significant position in educational research and university departments of education.

The influence of psychology when broadly defined has not been, and is not now, solely through the direct work of research and teaching and practising educational psychologists or applied developmental psychologists. It is also through educationalists and educational researchers who have either learned psychology as part of their studies of education on higher degree courses or have been psychologists earlier in their careers. It is also through teacher educators who in their initial and in-service teaching incorporate aspects of psychology relevant to their specialist areas in education. One well-known area is Personal and Social Education where symbolic interactionist social psychological and humanistic psychology ideas and practices have been taken up and used (for example, Watkins and Wagner, 1987). There are also examples in science and mathematics education (Noss and Hoyles, 1996; Ogborn et al., 1996), assessment and evaluation (for example, Gipps, 1994) and school improvement (Watkins et al., 1996; McGilchrest, Myers and Reed, 1997). In these and other cases reference is made to psychological theories developed by psychologists related to some area of functioning, whether it is motivation for learning (e.g. Dweck, 1986), a particular kind of learning theory (e.g. Biggs and Moore, 1993) or a theory about different conceptions of the scope of human abilities (Gardner, 1993). The point is that even if psychologists are not consulted directly, their works are a major resource for these diverse areas of education. This is another way of saying, along with Tomlinson (1996), that with or without psychologists and educational psychologists, some kind of psychology will be used in education theorising or taught in the initial and in-service training and education of teachers. And in some cases, educationalists develop their own psychological ideas and their implications without relating these to psychologists' thinking about the field (e.g. ideas relating self-esteem and expectation on pupils' motivation in Barber, 1996).

One way to make sense of how psychologists have diversified their interests in education and related to educationalists is to consider three typologies of educational researchers:

A. Background training and qualifications:
    has a psychology qualification recognised by BPS
    has an education qualification (e.g. diploma or master's) with a psychology component
    has some other subject qualification with an education component.
B. Current professional identity:
    is an active psychologist
    is an active psychologist and educationalist
    is an educationalist and lapsed psychologist
    is an educationalist (non-psychologist).
C. Areas of education specialism (examples):
    behaviour management
    assessment
    school effectiveness
    special needs/inclusive education
    literacy teaching.

Certain patterns can be identified using these dimensions. Contributors to the growth of education research areas have included researchers with psychology training whose psychology identity has been replaced by their education specialism. They may present themselves as specialists in some area of education, such as assessment, special needs or school effectiveness. Quantitative education research methods may have been drawn from psychology, though they are now being developed within educational research in their own right and are taught as part of higher degrees in education at master's and doctoral levels by non-psychologists. What is involved in this process of diversifying is partly a move away from the psychological level of analysis to other levels, from the micro- to the macro-social. But it can also be a move away from an understanding–explaining mode to a design–

evaluation mode. However, some psychologists in education, while diversifying their interests into specialist education areas, still retain their psychology identity and active involvement. For example, they may be specialists in
personal and social education or special educational needs while still retaining an active interest and identity in educational psychology. Another interesting pattern is for educational researchers with educational qualifications
to move into research and theory of a psychological nature. Their psychology
may come from components of their educational studies, but they may not
have a psychology identity, even though they may be as actively involved in
psychological research as BPS psychologists. What we have, therefore, is a
movement out of and into psychology.

This analysis calls for some clarification of what features define a psychological approach or study. First, as was argued in chapter 3, the psychological is concerned with analysis of those human phenomena which are towards
the individual end of the individual–social continuum of analysis. Secondly,
it has been argued that psychology can be given different analytic treatments
and can include both causal scientific and interpretive models. If this is
accepted, then different methods of inquiry are implied, all of which have
some systematic empirical element. Thirdly, it has been argued that there
can be an applied aspect to psychology concerned with practical needs.
What defines procedures and techniques as psychological is that they derive
from psychological understanding. Analysing these three strands together
shows that one is also found in other analytic fields in the social sciences, the
kind of analytic treatment (causal or interpretive); and another, the applied-
practical, is found in a field like education. This leaves, as the core, the broad
range of levels of analyses at the individual end of the social–individual
continuum. This analysis of the psychological implies that not all academics
with psychology backgrounds in university education departments practise
psychology. It shows that some non-psychologists (formally defined in professional terms) do practise psychology and that psychological studies can in
principle apply across the range of specialist areas in education. This framework will also be useful to make sense of the work of practising or professional educational psychology and psychologists in the education service.

The position of professional educational psychologists

As discussed above, professional educational psychology goes back to Cyril
Burt's work in London schools which involved not only the examination
of individual children, but also large-scale surveys of the range of abilities
and achievements and policy advice for the London County Council. His
appointment was followed slowly by others around the country, with more
limited roles. Psychologists were also involved through the therapeutic influence of psychoanalysis and the child study movement in helping individual children. They became members of child guidance teams which received
referrals and formed links with schools. At the early stages, professional

psychologists were trained for work across health and educational services; the separation in training became established as the respective groupings grew in size. The main increase in numbers of educational psychologists was after 1945: they grew from 140 in 1955 to over 1000 in 1980 (Wedell, 1982). The great shortage led to the Summerfield Committee, which examined the situation and made recommendations (Summerfield Report, 1968), including a system of post-graduate training and a ratio of one psychologist per 10,000 school children. The demand for educational psychology services and for psychology teaching in initial teacher preparation came from government policy and legislative changes. Demand increased as LEAs took over responsibility for the education of children with severe intellectual disabilities from social services in 1970. The Department of Education also placed educational psychologists at the centre of decision making about special education provision when, in Circular 2/75, it specified that the provision decision was mainly an educational one. The effect was to thrust psychologists into the lead role which had been contested between medical officers and psychologists. Currently there are about 2000 full-time educational psychologists in LEA service in the UK (Maliphant, 1997).

Until the 1970s educational psychologists relied heavily on individual psychometric assessment and on investigating the child removed from the setting where the problem arose (Lindsay, 1991). However, a survey of practice carried out in 1977 found an emerging trend towards investigating the child in the problem setting and towards more preventive work and a wider sets of clients, including primary care agents and systems (Wedell, 1982). Wedell outlined a matrix of work which related to the type of work (prevention, investigation and intervention or monitoring and evaluation) and to different clients (children, primary care agents or systems). The survey showed examples of work in each of the nine kinds implied by the matrix. Wedell attributed the move towards preventive and indirect work in part to a move away from within-child models of problem causation to more interactive causal accounts. The re-examination of educational psychology practice was led by new entrants to the profession in a political and educational context increasingly sceptical about the individual-child focus (Gillham, 1978). The reconstructing movement, which started in the 1970s, expressed dissatisfaction with traditional practice and wished to provide services with greater effectiveness through preventive rather than remedial work and through early screening and in-service training. This move away from the individual focus was seen to express a more educational and less clinical approach, assessing and intervening in the setting where the problems arose and in terms of educational aims. Gillham saw that this professional re-focusing would lead to overlap and potential problems with the work of LEA education inspectors and advisors, where in the past educational psychologists had acted in rivalry with medical officers. He noted a shift in practice (also shown in Wedell's survey) which meant that educational psychologists would tend to become community and school psychologists. This was a shift towards avoiding the individual referral of cases, as it was seen to set up impossible expectations of remediation. However, in advocating this shift Gillham was not denying the need for a clinical perspective, only that this was for a very small minority whose difficulties were evident across different social situations. Though he was not explicit about what proportion of work this would cover, Gillham and others working from this new perspective were clear that the learning and behaviour problems of most children lay in the interaction between themselves and adults in both school and home. These changes also led to the eventual development of educational psychology services with direct links to schools and other agencies, separate from child guidance.

There were different degrees of becoming a 'reconstructed' educational psychologist. For some, it was a matter of broadening their focus to more contexts and to other levels of assessment, while not letting go of the individual level. This seemed to be the implication of the Wedell matrix and the tradition followed by educational psychologists like Lindsay (1988). For others the reconstruction was a more purist commitment to a systems or ecological approach which took the focus off the individual. Thomas (1985) wondered what had happened to the reconstructing movement, as he noticed that many psychologists were finding new ways of working with individuals in classrooms and not confronting the issues and difficulties at the institutional level. Thomas was pointing to the introduction of behavioural approaches both in the management of behaviour and in the design of teaching by objectives. This was a major move which gave professional educational psychologists a curriculum-based alternative to psychometric assessment techniques. It was a theoretical move which at a stroke switched the level of analysis from the individual's abilities and dispositions to the level of action and behaviour in context (Norwich, 1990). It also enabled psychologists to identify alterable variables without the need to identify characteristics, like intelligence, which were assumed to be enduring and less open to intervention. This fitted with the renewed interest in effective intervention practices. But though the behavioural move involved interactions between behaviour and environment, it was still mostly at the individual level of analysis. And, as Thomas rightly noticed, this was not compatible with the alternative implied by a more radical reconstructing position.

Behind the move of professional educational psychologists towards adopting a more socialised model was the wider critique of psychology as based on positivist, scientistic and individualistic assumptions (Claxton et al., 1985). These were discussed in chapter 3, where I argued that there were problems with a radical social constructionist model of psychology. Individuals are shaped by social contexts, but this does not mean that there is an indivisible link between the person and the context. Though there are interconnections between different levels of analysis, this does not mean that there is no distinct individual level of analysis. This seems to be the basic weakness of systemic or ecological models in professional psychology. For example, a systemic model assumes that the child is part of the class-group system and this is part of the school system and so up the embedded hierarchy of systems. But while the micro-to-macro social systems could be subjected to analysis in terms of the interaction of their parts within the wider environment, this analysis was not allowed for the child as a system. The point is that a rigorous systemic model would include the individual as a distinct but related level of analysis amongst other levels. This anti-individual version of systemic thinking arose from its adoption as a counter to the excessive and unconnected individual focus of psychology. It can be attributed to the lack of cross-disciplinary links, interdisciplinary rivalries in the social sciences and value differences, rather than being inherent in the field of a connected psychology. Aspects of this anti-individual version of professional psychology can be found, for example, in the historical survey of changing psychology practice by Sutton and McPherson (1981). These psychologists suggested that there had been a change in the knowledge base from the intrapersonal to the extrapersonal. They contended that for many psychologists psychological practice had connotations of individualisation indicating narrow, even reactionary, reductionist interpretations of human affairs (p. 167). The abandoning of psychometric tests and the emergence of intervention skills vis-à-vis clients and client groups was portrayed as presenting a conception of a more socialised vision for professional psychologists. This kind of account, however, can be seen as a prescription along certain theoretical and value lines, rather than an accurate account of the changing and sometimes confusing mixture of practices in educational psychology.

The picture of educational psychology services coming from more formal evaluations has been fairly positive. In 1990 inspectors from HMI visited a third of services and reviewed practice (DES, 1990). As with previous studies, they found that overall most time was spent on assessment, advice and treatment. Only about one-fifth of time overall was spent on in-service training work. The overall quality of work was judged as 'good' with some work 'particularly perceptive and insightful'. Working relationships between teachers and psychologists were also judged as 'good'. There were criticisms of service management and relationships within LEAs. The variation in the ratio of psychologists to pupils was noted, raising the continuing issue of under-staffing. Some of the service difficulties were also shown in another study of service users' views in Sheffield (Lindsay et al., 1990). Head teachers of different kinds of schools tended to see the educational psychology service as of a reasonable quality, but considered that service availability was a significant problem. This was attributed to suppression of posts, early retirement and increased statutory assessment and statementing work.

Despite these kinds of positive evaluations, there has been and continues to be some dissatisfaction about the work of educational psychologists, amongst not only teachers and education officers, but also psychologists themselves. Not only are there not enough to cover the rising number of requests for statutory assessment (advice needed for LEA decisions about whether to issue a statement of SEN), but there is some concern amongst officers that psychologists are too independent. This is the issue of who is the client of the educational psychologist. Though employed by the LEA to serve their interests, educational psychologists also have professional responsibility for the interests of children and parents. This makes for a split allegiance which underlies some very pressing professional dilemmas, especially when the resources for educational provision are limited (Gregory, 1993; Lindsay, 1995). But the concern can run deeper. There has been a historical concern that the educational psychologist worked on a 'test and run' basis, with little time to get involved with teachers, parents and children. Where there has been better staffing and the adoption of new practices, this detachment has been reduced. But with the impact of the educational restructuring since the 1988 Education Reform Act, there have been increased pressures to narrow the focus of work onto statutory assessment for statementing. For example, the Association of Educational Psychologists reported a rise of 500 per cent in the number of statements of SEN over the decade, alongside a growth of 50 per cent in the number of psychologists' posts (AEP, 1995). The AEP represents the concerns of educational psychologists that their wider role and contribution have been reduced because of these demands. But concerns are also expressed about the psychologists' reports: that they tend to be descriptive, with little insight or diagnosis, depend too much on other peoples' views and offer guidance in generalised rather than specific terms. Users of educational psychology services are also sensitive to the differences among individual psychologists and different services in their assessment practices. Assessments which are done in 'real contexts' can be read as overly optimistic and general and not adding much to what teachers can provide. Assessments which are overly based on tests might be regarded as suspect for their cultural and class bias (Wood, 1997).

The call comes for a re-examination of what educational psychologists do, their experience, independence from LEAs, knowledge, what they do to help others and their difference from clinical psychologists. For some psychologists this comes over as an unfair and over-generalised attack which ignores the wider context of their particular role and contribution. However, critiques of educational psychologists come from psychologists themselves, even if they are not practising educational psychologists, but rather their trainers, or academic psychologists acting as commentators. Gale (1993) has argued that educational psychology needs a major revolution in its approach to problems in education and must 'grasp the nettle of reform' (p. 17). Gale has a very welcome breadth and optimism in his perspective which does not get stuck in the division between practitioner and research educational psychology. He argues that psychology as a field will assume many of the functions previously provided by religion, insofar as it deals with understanding human affairs and helping people with their personal and other problems. His approach is to urge professional psychology to realise that it cannot be value-free and avoid taking moral stands. Gale is making a very important point about the moral dimension in the work of the professional psychologist in the scientist-practitioner role.

His vision of psychology is that it seeks to understand human experience and behaviour and seeks to enhance human well-being, potential and prosperity in general based on this understanding (Gale, 1997). In my judgement, this is a very important conception as it recognises the dual but interconnected aspects of psychology. He identifies the link between them through a psychology practice which is based on a systematic understanding, so giving applied and practitioner psychology a unique contribution amongst other fields also focused on human well-being, such as teaching. However, Gale's position can be criticised for being too focused on the practice side of the science–practice duality and for not addressing questions about the nature of science and the place of values in this part of psychology. His references to positivism may resonate with misgivings felt by practitioners, but it does not resolve the question of the balance between epistemic and human well-being values, discussed in chapter 2. His position also tends to be excessively psychology-centric, which might be acceptable to psychologists who warm to his calls for greater unity and optimism. But calls for educational psychology 'to make clear statements about the aims and purposes of education' on the grounds that 'such aims can be logically derived from the basic moral premise of psychology' (Gale, 1993, p. 18), will without doubt turn off other key participants in education. As I discussed in chapter 2, any contribution to a practical field like education from an explanatory or interpretive science has to be located within and led by an educational conception of aims and goals. This is not to deny that psychological theories can and do influence ideas about aims. Aims require a conceptual and value analysis of what education is about. Value judgements may be influenced by facts, though they cannot be deduced from them. But value judgements are needed which involve philosophical analyses and are informed by theories about social processes and goals – the prime interest of colleagues in the wider social sciences. That Gale's conception of psychology does not respect explicitly the specialisations and contributions of other social scientists is clear from his call for a systems-based analysis which goes beyond the child and the classroom:

> Effective interventions are likely therefore to be at the level of management policy, organisational cognitions and organisational change . . . Intervention focused on the child is at best a palliative . . . Intervention at the level of the organisation is more cost-effective and carries with it the means of helping the school to help itself.
>
> (Gale, 1993, pp. 18 and 19)

This resembles the position associated with the school effectiveness and school improvement area in education. Gale and others who advocate an organisational systems approach to educational psychology can justify this with reference to the tradition of organisational psychology, which deals with issues of ethos, organisation review and change. This field of applied psychology has had a considerable influence on management and through that into educational management. But management and educational management themselves also draw on their own theory and research and on sociological analyses which relate the organisation to wider social structural and economic factors. It becomes tenuous to base educational psychology on a level of analysis at the limits of what is usually understood to be the focus of the psychological, the intra- and interpersonal. It may well be that intervention is most powerful beyond the personal and micro-social levels, but then psychologists need to switch their field of specialisation (as some have) to organisational psychology, management or school effectiveness and improvement. When it is argued that psychology seeks to enhance human experience and self-esteem, as Gale argues, we need to remember that this means at personal and interpersonal levels. Of course, this is connected with the aims of enhancing well-being more widely through interventions by institutions, communities and states.

However, when we consider what systems educational psychologists would do, according to Gale it is more in keeping with a modest role, using the skills and knowledge associated with counselling and organisational, occupational and clinical psychology. But this also involves a broadening which calls into question the adequacy of the training of educational psychologists and raises questions about the separateness of training from other areas of applied psychology. Gale sets this analysis of educational psychology in the wider context of applied psychologies which have been employed by different services. Patterns of training have been different, reflecting the briefs which have been set in these different work settings. Educational psychologists are alone among professional psychologists in having to be first trained and work as members of another professional group, teachers. Gale envisages that educational psychologists could be based in schools and therefore provide the practical experience needed for graduate psychologists going on to train as professional educational psychologists. He sees this as the alternative to prior training and experience as a teacher. I will return to this point shortly.

Gale's argument is that there need to be greater commonalities between the different fields of applied psychology, through joint conferences and common training and further professional development, which would enable easier transfer between applied specialisms. He sets out a core of applied psychology skills which cover five broad areas:

1   beliefs, aims and values;
2   psychological science;

3 humanistic commitments;
4 *modus operandi*;
5 professional obligations.

There is little doubt that there is a strong case for some commonality, but these broad areas need to be judged not only in terms of whether they serve the current and new specialisms within applied psychology: they also need to provide a basis for identifying the core contribution of psychologists compared with other allied professional groups. When applied to professional educational psychologists, there is likely to be some detailed elaboration to the common skills deriving from the education field. This elaboration needs to be such that they are not all covered by teachers, whether advisory or special needs teachers. Four of the above five areas would be shared by teachers to some degree, and they relate to common professional skills associated with those working in human services generally. But the fifth area of psychological science is particular to professional psychologists, especially the analysing of complex problems in terms of different models of the person. This version of the common and unique contribution of professional educational psychologists resembles the analysis presented at the end of the last section of this chapter. What connects research and practitioner educational psychology is the focus on developing and using the systematic understanding of phenomena at the individual end of the social–individual continuum.

Though an increased commonality with clinical psychology would perpetuate the strong historical links between educational psychologists and the field of special educational needs, commonalities with other applied areas such as occupational, organisational and health psychology would expand what they can offer the education service more generally. This has been a long-standing issue for professional educational psychologists, who have seen their contribution to the education system as being narrower and less effective than it should or could be (Maliphant, 1994, 1997). A broadening would mean working beyond the statutory assessment required before an LEA decides whether to issue a statement of SEN for an individual child. It also means an involvement in preventive work at individual, class and systems levels, which has become an established part of educational psychologists' work. This work is recognised under current government guidelines, on the assumption that psychologists and other support services are involved in stages prior to statutory assessment (stage 3) and even consult with schools over children at stages 1 and 2.

It is widely believed in the education service that educational psychologists' competence is confined to SEN children (Lunt and Farrell, 1994; Maliphant, 1994; Lunt, 1998), a view which reflects the routine service they provide. Yet, as Maliphant (1994) suggests, the move towards greater accountability and effectiveness in the service, including target setting for schools, creates the need for increased empirical and quantification data handling skills. Psychologists are seen as familiar with these areas and able to contribute their methodological skills to these developments. This argument reflects a more general line taken about educational psychologists when role difficulties are analysed. Areas for broadening and revitalising work are linked either to some aspect of their prior training and experience or to skills of other applied psychologists. But it is often not shown that educational psychologists actually have the required skills. They are assumed rightly to have the ability to learn to undertake that kind of work. But the point is that without appropriate training, professional educational psychologists are probably not equipped to fill these broader roles, given their existing training and work roles. And, as Lunt and Farrell (1994) explain, educational psychologists have a specific task in statutory assessment which is enshrined in legislation. From the LEA perspective, it is the key to decision making about whether LEAs will protect the additional and special provision for pupils with significant difficulties in learning. This provides job security, but at the expense of a restricted role, a problem which is particularly acute in times of growing demands for statutory assessment.

The need for a radical rethink about the training needs of professional educational psychologists has also been at issue recently (Lunt, 1993; Lunt and Farrell, 1994; Maliphant, 1994; Gale, 1997). This has focused, as discussed above, on the question of a generic applied psychology training, the length of training needed and whether initial training and experience in teaching is required. Teacher training and experience is not required in Scotland or other European countries. Longer training is the pattern in these countries. Maliphant (1994), for example, suggests that prior practical experience can be gained through extended placements in education and social services. The fact that the training system has come under criticism reflects the wider difficulties faced by professional educational psychology in its current educational service role and the relatively low value placed on it by government and LEAs. It needs to be remembered that psychology is the smallest of several professional groups in the educational service – there are about 2000 psychologists compared to some 396,000 teachers (Maliphant, 1997). But what has also been worrying has been the question of the meaningfulness and status of psychology in the training of professional educational psychologists. Lunt (1996) has shown examples of training courses where trainees have found it hard to make practical sense of how they should use psychology in practice. She attributes this partly to trainees losing touch with their psychology in the teaching period between their initial psychology studies and their professional course. But this assumes that their undergraduate studies were relevant in the first place. Burden (1992) has questioned whether these degrees can guide teachers in any meaningful way in their practice, given their predominantly positivist orientations. It can also mean that the short one-year preparation course has to help trainees relearn their psychology and learn relevant skills for LEA service work. Gale (1997) responds to this issue by calling for changes to the undergraduate psychology degree so that students can relate psychological knowledge and understanding to real problems in practical settings. Here again is the question, discussed in the last section, of how teachers in initial training can understand and use psychology meaningfully in a practical setting.

It is clear from this discussion that the issue at the heart of these matters is the core contribution of professional educational psychologists to the education service. On this depends the focus and kind of training needed and the relationships between psychologists and their clients – the LEAs, schools, teachers, parents and children – on one hand, and allied professions, on the other. To what extent can the demands made by the service be modified to enable psychologists to take broader roles which extend beyond individual assessment work to preventive work, group work and work beyond SEN? Does an interest in systems level work derive from an ideological avoidance of the individual focus or from widening the base of individual work?

My line of argument in this book is that individual work is a core part of professional psychology work, because that is what doing psychology is about, in contrast to doing something else. But this means individual work which connects the individual to her or his relationships and social context, and to the wider systems which affect her or his well-being. This does not mean choosing between individual or systems work. Nor is it about working either within SEN or with educational needs and problems beyond SEN. Psychological analysis starts with the individual person, not as an isolated individual out of context, but in a context which could lead to interventions at several levels, including systems approaches. This is a position which has been well argued by Dessent (1992), an educational psychologist turned education officer, who supports a broader role for professional educational psychologists beyond SEN and accepts the need to reduce the need for individual casework through policy and provision planning. Like others, Dessent recognises the historical role of psychologists in the assessment process of 'defining specialness' and its contemporary extension of 'defining resource worthiness'. He makes the point that while the special education system operates in its current form, it will require this function and the demand for individual work will continue. But like others, he reminds us of potential and actual boundary disputes which arise between psychologists and advisory teachers, advisors and inspectors over SEN provision, curriculum and teaching matters. These can become more serious when psychologists detach themselves from individual work and view their core contribution within the domains of special educational and wider educational advisory work. Like Maliphant (1994), Dessent also sees a wider role for educational psychologists arising from the growth of accountability and monitoring systems which require empirical and methodologically sound data. He also questions to what extent psychologists really want to 'give psychology away', as this would threaten their occupational security. Though this has been and is being done to some extent by developing training programmes and resource systems for teachers and others, in the core area of individual assessment many psychologists still hold on to the closed psychological tests. A legitimate case can be made for certain assessment procedures being confined to those with a degree of skill and understanding which cannot be achieved in a short training programme. But this kind of justification for the restricted use of certain tests needs to be argued in detail, if the required standard of training is taken to be the long entry procedure for becoming a professional psychologist. As Dessent notes, educational psychologists have made few attempts to establish alternative ways to define specialness which do not need direct psychologist input.

Dessent's case for individual work is fully conversant with the current received wisdom that professional educational psychology can be more effective if it works at the organisational level. There are also practical issues concerned with coping with the demands of individual cases and its low status compared to advisory and development work focused on schools and larger systems. But to give up the individual focus is to lose access to important evidence about how the education system works. Psychologists have this unique opportunity to connect the individual and the system, and to do so, according to Dessent, with a breadth and impartiality unavailable to others in the education system. The psychological concern is with all children across different areas of difficulties and ages, taking account of their wider social and emotional functioning in diverse contexts. Professional educational psychologists also present the 'educational voice' within the multidisciplinary world of special needs and disability. Dessent goes so far as to assert that, if educational psychologists did not exist, then the educational system would need to develop a similar kind of professional role. What is interesting about Dessent's argument is that it comes from a psychologist turned education officer, for whom the LEA need for generic individual focused professional assessors is paramount. This is evident when he states that the major client for professional educational psychologists 'has been and is always likely to be the LEA' (p. 47). Many of the role and identity problems of professional educational psychologists come from the tensions between what those who manage the education service are required to do and what psychologists feel able to offer the service. This is not just a simple case of needing to publicise or market a wider set of professional capabilities. It is also more importantly about the way in which the education service is legislated for, organised and managed through LEAs, and also the wider culture of teachers' work in schools and teachers' attitudes towards working with allied professional groups.

Underlying these issues is the important question whether individual children with learning difficulties need a psychological assessment, made by a professional educational psychologist, before an LEA can decide whether to issue a statement of SEN. Perhaps what the LEAs need is advice about which individual children need significant additional provision in the form of a modified and individualised curriculum focus and teaching methods. What is psychological about this, which cannot be provided as educational advice?

I have argued over the last decade that we need to distinguish between the contribution *by* professional educational psychologists and their contribution *as* educational psychologists (Norwich, 1988). Some of the contribution comes from psychologists as psychologists, but much does not and is more accurately seen as special education advisor work focused on individual children. This arises because the work of professional educational psychologists is strongly determined by the service needs of LEAs in relation to special educational legislation and the organisation and demands of special education provision in LEAs and schools. As Dessent has argued, the statementing system requires LEAs to procure assessments of individual children, which will inform decision making about special educational provision. Whether LEAs use professional educational psychologists or some other professionals, they need to have assessments which are external to the school where the problems arise. It would also be economical for them to have professionals who can cover the range of difficulties in learning and take a broad perspective. But they also need professional assessors who have a broad knowledge of curriculum and teaching adaptations. The question is therefore whether external generalist assessment of childrens' special educational needs is the same as psychological assessment. Many psychologists may come with years of experience to provide a major contribution to the SEN identification task, but this does not resolve the wider issue of principle: is this what psychological assessment is about? It could be that these questions need to be asked about the regulations governing the LEA operation of the statutory assessment system. Though the role of professional educational psychologists was raised in the recent Green Paper on SEN (DfEE, 1997), it did not make the more basic links between the psychologist's role and the operation of the identification system. We await the findings of the working group set up by the government to look at the future role and training of educational psychologists (DfEE, 1998a).

Nor did the Green Paper consider some of the basic principles underlying the statutory identification system and consider alternative ways of identifying individual needs for children with SEN and protecting provision for them. The driving impetus came more from the wish to extend the principle of raising education standards to children with SEN, promoting inclusion and dealing with concerns about the rise in the number of statements of SEN. There have nevertheless been changes following the SEN Code of Practice 1993, which improved the administration of the statutory assessment procedures, including the introduction of some general criteria for initiating statutory assessment. However, there is still no renewed justification for statements as legal protection for additional resource allocation and as specific educational programmes for individual pupils. Nor has there been the clarity needed about how to deal with the gap between identified needs and available provision, a problem which continues to be acute in view of the pressures on educational funding. There are understandable government concerns about rising SEN expenditure, but these have been met by proposals

on reducing the number of statements, without rigorous analysis. What is
needed is a more radical review of purposes and procedures, especially to
decide whether full statutory assessment is needed in all cases when the LEA
decides to determine special education provision for an individual pupil.
One option is that the full multi-disciplinary statutory assessment procedures might be used only under two conditions: first, in rare cases of severe
and complex difficulties (much less than the current 3 per cent or the
previous 2 per cent of all pupils), and secondly, when parents are initially in
disagreement with the LEA about special provision. This would introduce a
more flexible system whereby there would be more continuity in the movement of individual children between special education provision determined
by schools and that determined by the LEAs. This is relevant to the current
situation whereby over half of all those with statements are already provided
for in mainstream schools. Movement between ordinary and special schools
could be more like movement between primary and secondary schools.
Special provision would be monitored by LEAs or some other agency, and
systems of individual review would be maintained. But parents who are
content with special provision would not have to undergo the full statutory
assessment procedures, unless their children's difficulties fell into the categories of 'severe and complex difficulties'. These categories would need to be
well defined themselves, but parents who were not satisfied with special
education provision (determined by the mainstream school) and the LEA's
position on additional provision could invoke the full statutory procedure.
This would give parents access to the statutory procedures and in the final
stage allow them appeal to SEN tribunals. Care would be needed to ensure
that parents were given full briefing about their rights and support to use
this option.

Such a system could be designed to release professional educational psychologists from much of their statutory assessment, while ensuring they
retain a core function in LEA decisions about the contentious and severe or
complex cases. But even here this might be a conditional contribution determined by the decision of a multi-disciplinary panel which included a psychologist. Psychologists might no longer be involved in routine assessments
of children with sensory and motor difficulties. LEAs would retain the use of
specialist teacher assessments here. Nor would psychologists be involved
routinely in moderate learning difficulties and the milder emotional and
behaviour difficulties, which produce the majority of statements for SEN.
Wood (1994) has also argued that psychologists have not put forward a co-
ordinated response to the current issues of identifying children through
statutory assessment. He suggests that with the national move towards speci-
fying criteria for when to issue statements of SEN, the professional educational
psychologist's role might become narrowed and diminished. Wood suggests
that psychologists should become involved in actively changing the legal
system set up in the 1981 Education Act, the one still currently in operation,
and begin to develop alternative frameworks. Though it is not appropriate

to go into the details of such changes here, there are some important points to be made. The key one is that it is only when professional psychologists engage in a basic analysis of the service system which determines their work contributions that they are able to consider realistic ways forward for promoting a broadly based psychological contribution to the education service. This kind of change in the system would link up with the calls for greater links with other areas of applied psychology and the debate about whether prior teacher training and experience were needed.

Were psychologists to negotiate a more focused role in the statutory individual SEN identification system, this would not necessarily mean that they would make more limited use of psychometrics. As Burden (1994) has pointed out, international surveys show that the role of the psychometrician continues to be central to the work of many school psychologists. The reasons he gives are the continuing need for classification across many countries arising from the need to allocate resources for SEN, and the belief that tests help identify children's strengths and difficulties. That psychometric tests continue to be used by professional educational psychologists in this country was evident in the recent survey by Lokke et al. (1997) of just under half of all educational psychology services. These services reported substantial use of psychometric techniques and an increase in use following the 1993 Education Act and the introduction of the Code of Practice. This is an interesting situation, as there have been moves away from psychometrics as a central part of the training of professional educational psychologists. Trickey (1993) claimed that training courses either gave a token input, cut out psychometrics completely or limited coverage because of course time limitations. Course orientations differ but Trickey's account fits with the view that courses have tried to give a professional lead towards broader, more interventionist, social and systemic approaches. Trickey agrees with a strong strand of professional opinion in practitioner educational psychology that avoids focusing on individual ability and disposition, especially in its quantified version. But it is also important to see these psychological assessment issues in the context of the position of the Division of Educational and Child Psychology (DECP) training committee of the BPS (which oversees the recognition of the training courses). This committee defines competencies in terms which include understanding the principles and rationale of normative psychometric tests and their skilled use (DECP, 1994). The joint guidance from the Association of Educational Psychologists (AEP, as the professional association) and the DECP about statutory advice to LEAs is also important in this context. The psychological in 'psychological advice' is defined as being based on a scientific methodology, but also expressing an interactional and holistic view of the problem. The reporting of only psychometric testing is rejected as it focuses on the child and not the interactions between child and environment. But similarly, accounts in terms only of the context or environment are not accepted as 'psychological' because they leave out what the child brings to the situation.

It follows from the preceding discussion and analysis that psychological assessment needs to go further than descriptions of children's difficulties in context to include understanding how these might come about. I have argued for seeing this as focusing on both the individual and the social context or environment. This is not an either—or issue, nor is it one that implies that standardised and quantified assessment techniques are only relevant to child factors. This is a point made by Frederickson et al. (1991), who also argue persuasively for a renewal of psychological assessment which includes asking 'why?' and 'how?'. They remind psychologists that what is distinctive about their contribution lies in the 'ability to generate a very broad range of hypotheses when attempting to find explanations for a particular child's difficulties' (p. 21). This retains the core role of practising psychologists as providing relevant knowledge about particular practical problems drawing on psychological knowledge and investigative skills. It implies not only that professional educational psychologists have to become better versed in hypothesis generation, but also that they need to draw on a wide range of domains for this, including motivation, social skills, self-esteem and interactions with others at home and school. But this also calls for psychological assessments to explore the specific aspects of these domains and go well beyond general references to problems in self-esteem or social skills. It depends, however, on practising psychologists having knowledge and understanding of basic areas of cognitive, developmental, social and ecological psychology.

The use of measurement in psychological assessment in the form of standardised psychometric tests continues to have narrow and misleading associations. Measurement is of performance, not competence which is inferred from performance. Measurement need not be only of cognitive constructs, but can be of emotional, motivational and personality constructs as well as environmental factors. The distinction between performance, current competence and innate competence has long been made by educational psychologists (Kaufman, 1979), yet the circumstances of professional psychology practice have managed to obscure this distinction in the way that psychometric tests have been used and interpreted. IQ type tests are measures of performance, which may not represent current competence. Their construction for some social groups and their use with other groups and in circumstances which might obscure competence has been the main source of valid criticisms. Psychologists have also debated throughout this century, and not just since the recent theory of multiple intelligences, whether abilities are best understood as multiple or unitary (Gardner, 1993). The pressures from the service have inclined towards a unitary concept as it is more economical to assess and involves less complexity. Unitary concepts of abilities also reflect dominant ideas about the school curriculum rather than broader curriculum values. But psychometrics cannot be confined to the systematic and quantified measurement of cognitive performances: it can be applied to other domains, including motivational and emotional aspects of functioning and home and school environmental factors. To recognise this is not to present this mode as the only type of systematic empirical inquiry. The limitations of psychometrics need to be understood: for example, that it is based on generalised constructs which might not apply across contexts and different individuals.

Following the logic of the case I made in the last chapter for seeing connections between different models of psychology, we can identify false dichotomies in representing certain kinds of psychological assessment as incompatible with psychometric approaches. Curriculum-based assessments, drawing on behavioural psychology, have been presented as alternatives to psychometric-based assessments (Cline, 1992), as have dynamic assessment methods which avoid quantification (Feuerstein, 1979). Stringer et al. (1997), for example, have also stated that dynamic assessment does not fit with scientific models and by implication psychometrics. Yet this presents dynamic assessment in limited terms, as it represents what is really a model of teaching-based assessment as an approach to quantification of assessment. For example, there is a European and American tradition of dynamic assessment which measures the gains following standard teaching inputs (Budoff et al., 1971; Guthke and Wingenfeld, 1992).

This limited portrayal of dynamic assessment may make it more appealing to professional educational psychologists who are looking for a practical approach which is neither curriculum based (and so not exclusive to psychologists), nor IQ psychometric (with historical links to discriminatory practices). But it is a false portrayal of assessment dichotomies – dynamic versus static, active intervention to promote learning versus assumed typical limits. The purpose of some dynamic assessments is to predict future learning rates and levels: they are intended as one-off performance tests of ability. Theoretical fads and technical fashions are no substitute for thoroughgoing analyses and evaluations of specific practices, plus an understanding of the more general principles which guide these practices and their scope and potential for development. Professional educational psychologists need to find their bearings from a rigorous analysis of the demands made on them and the risks they are exposed to in their position as scientist practitioners.

From the analysis in this section of the role of professional educational psychologists, it is clear that the contribution is not a simple problem-solving one. Problem solving is what all professionals do in whatever field they specialise. It cannot provide any justifiable basis for professional psychology input in education compared to that of teachers, including SEN specialists, on one hand, and educational researchers, advisors and consultants, on the other. It is common for professional educational psychologists to identify the various stages of problem-solving cycles in terms of 'identify, assess, plan action and evaluate'. Miller (1991), for example, has identified such a problem-solving sequence as the basis for professional psychologists applying their various areas of knowledge and skills to referred problems. These include social, cognitive, developmental and biological psychological knowledge and understanding in addition to research and inquiry methods. He also includes a formulation stage, which asks how the problem comes about, after the assessment and before the action planning stages. But unlike Frederickson et al. (1991), Miller does not place special emphasis on this analytic stage, although he does recognise that everybody is a problem solver and that teachers are the key problem solvers in the education service.

I would contend that unless professional educational psychologists do come to resemble other practising applied psychologists, such as clinical psychologists, in taking on responsibility for working directly with clients through the problem solving sequence, their predominant contribution will be in the formulation stage. This is where they can provide an added perspective on how the problem has come about. This is something which allied professionals cannot be expected to do, as they do not have the professional educational psychologist's external and generalist perspective. Nor can allied professionals be expected to use creatively a knowledge base and understanding of the processes and contexts of learning, as professionaal educational psychologists can. This view resembles Dessent's (1992) recognition of the centrality of individual cases to professional educational psychologists' work and the connecting of the individual to the system in such work. It also fits with Burden's (1994) call for professional educational psychologists to become applied educational psychologists, who can help teachers, learners and their families understand and apply the lessons from a broadly based interaction psychology. Burden also asserts that this is most likely to be effective when psychologists are not constrained by economic and political pressures and gatekeeper functions for special education provision. This, as argued in the previous section, would require better interconnections between the two branches of educational psychology, research-teaching and professional educational psychology (Burden, 1992). Such calls have also been made in other countries, as by Knoff and Batsche (1991) in the USA, who have also proposed greater integration there between school psychology, the practitioner branch, with educational psychology, the research-teaching branch.

Summary and concluding comments

In this concluding section I will pull together the various lines of argument in order to address the question whether psychology has a unique and worthwhile contribution to make to education practices, teacher training, educational theory and research. In discussing whether psychology has been given away already, I recognised that psychologists have an occupational interest in holding on to some parts of psychology: a total giveaway would threaten their security in either university or service settings. A historical analysis indicates that psychology has made a substantial, even if somewhat politically controversial, contribution to promoting systematic empirical inquiry into educational issues and the values of addressing the learning needs of all individuals, not just those with special educational needs. In this respect, it would be accurate to say that some of the important contributions from psychology have already been made and taken up and built into education and educational research. However, this does not mean that psychology no longer has a continuing contribution, just one that needs to be adaptive to the changing circumstances within education and to co-ordinate with and respect the contributions of specialist areas of education and their research endeavours. The analysis also raised important questions about the nature and relationships between specialisations within a broad psychology field; between areas of basic and applied developmental and other areas of psychology in university departments of psychology; and between psychology in university education departments and LEA psychology services. It was also pointed out that psychology is used in education not just by those with overt psychology identities, but also by educationalists in ways that often go unacknowledged. Overlaps between the functions of different professional groups and their fields of study are a predominant feature of the interrelationship between psychology and education. For example, psychologists across university psychology and education departments have an interest in applied and practitioner psychology, even if there are overall differences in focus and ethos in these settings. In practitioner psychology, both clinical and educational psychologists work with the problems of children and families.

The historical perspective revealed that the contemporary debates and issues about the role of psychology in providing a scientific base for education and teaching have been around for about a hundred years, ever since psychology became established as an independent academic field. One of the origins of educational psychology was the developing interest in a science of education, which promised increased technical competence and enhanced professional status for teachers. Another was the service need to find better ways of identifying and helping those with difficulties and disabilities. A third was that education provided an area for developing psychology when it was not academically accepted in universities. The historical perspective also showed the role of the eugenics movement in the formation of psychology and educational psychology and how evaluations of psychometrics can be seen too easily from the narrow perspective of our contemporary social and political preoccupations. Post-war critiques of psychometrics for its racist and elitist conceptions and uses can also be shown to reflect continuing social and political struggles as much as the nature of the psychometric project of theorising and measuring human characteristics. Educational psychologists themselves have taken the historical view that psychology had become stuck or has been misrepresented. It is understandable that psychology has continued to be presented by insiders as able to meet the needs of its clients. It has been argued that critics have focused excessively on mental measurement, while ignoring other key contributions. But a broader historical perspective shows that educational psychology was closely bound up with social and political matters. What was at issue was more than measuring abilities. It was as much about the value of meritocracy as the basis for social organisation and the allocation of valued social opportunities.

One historical interpretation is that by the Second World War many educational psychologists had come to share a broad set of opinions despite certain differences about the nature of abilities and technical matters. One opinion was that curriculum and teaching should be geared to the needs of the child rather than governed by academic authority and convention. Another was the meritocratic belief that social positions should be allocated by abilities and not through social connections. In this interpretation educational psychology in the early part of this century was a synthesis of romantic and utilitarian positions. But there have been continuing tensions within the role of the educational psychologist as a scientist-practitioner, between being tentative and systematic on one hand, and the need to respond to the practical need for techniques and solutions on the other. This presented pitfalls for educational psychologists who, when driven by policy-making requirements for assessment techniques, developed them without the theoretical and empirical base needed to guide their use. Psychologists, in their wish to influence policy, were also prone to lose sight of the social and political implications of how tests identified merit. The established use of psychometrics in a changing political climate exposed testing to the criticism that the tests and their use were in the service of dominant social-class interests. The historical evidence might not have supported this class-based account, but nevertheless the use of psychometrics did represent the interests of certain status groups in society. So, as the recognition of environmental influences on educational attainments grew with sociological accounts, the belief in individualist and biologically based theories associated against psychology declined. Psychometrics was launched in support of the earlier struggles of the intellectual aristocracy with the landed aristocracy. But its early associations with technocratic socialism brought it into the later struggle with a more communitarian socialism after 1945.

This historical analysis shows how the social and political context provides opportunities but also constraints for applying psychology in education. A certain political naivety was evident amongst psychologists about the way in which psychology came to be evaluated in terms of changing social and political values. The political reputation of psychological measurement depended more on changing political needs than on the empirical validity of the theoretical and technical base. So, when psychometrics was favoured, this was mainly because it supported and served meritocratic ideals. When its reputation fell, it came to be seen as pseudo-scientific rather than needing refinement and development. Changing responses to the Burt scandal from the 1970s to the 1990s also show the impact of the political scene. Applied psychologies such as educational psychology have had and continue to have an ambiguous position in relation to the interplay between progressive and conservative politics in education. The assumption that human characteristics can be measured has been and can be taken to support quite different political and social values and ideals.

Other critiques of educational psychology focused not only on its alleged scientific basis but also on its individualism. This is where sociological critiques identified that much of psychology had problems in conceptualising the links between the individual and the social. Psychology's need to address theorising from philosophy and sociology has been well pointed out by sociologists. But this does not justify an excessively social epistemology and ontology. There has been no need to opt for an either—or conception of the individual versus the social. We need disciplinary frameworks which define themselves as having a connected and complementary relationship, not as in opposition with each other. It has also been argued that criticisms of positivism in educational psychology have ignored the early history of the field and the range of epistemological frameworks found in psychology. Critics of educational psychology need to be reminded that psychology has no established theoretical framework and model of inquiry, but several rival ones.

I also addressed the philosophical critique based on the view that psychological phenomena are holistic and intentional and need interpretive modes of inquiry, not causal scientific ones. It is a critique which also applies to versions of educational psychology which acknowledge the role of the common-sense psychology of teachers in their teaching. But from the interpretive viewpoint even these educational psychologies still give priority to scientific theories. I argued that such critiques are often misunderstood by those professionally socialised in the causal scientific mode. Proponents of interpretivist models can themselves also ignore the fact that the causal model can be made to work, even if it raises doubts about the originality of the generalisations and the validity of their use in concrete situations. There was, I argued, more in common between causal and interpretivist models than often portrayed, as causal connections are built into the meaning of everyday psychology terms. So both could be used for predictive purposes. The difference is in the purpose of empirical inquiry – whether it is nomothetic (experimental inquiry to establish causal generalisations) or idiographic (case studies to identify perspectives and their implications based on everyday psychological understandings). As I argued in chapter 3, these kinds of philosophical analysis show that psychology and educational psychology do not have a well-established theoretical model. We therefore need to work with these different models and promote a constructive co-existence between them.

I then considered some current issues about the relationships between the different parts of psychology that bear on the relationship with education. That the dominant partner in the relationship has been psychology is evident from the language of application. We talk of applying psychology to education, not education to psychology. Yet it has been noted that we cannot draw too sharp a distinction between basic and applied psychology. There is a gradation of research studies from those with theoretical to those with practice aims. Some work is on the boundaries between understanding learning in context and identifying teaching techniques. Some useful distinctions have also been drawn between psychology as a basic science, as an applied science and as a professional practice. Most psychologists do not undertake all three kinds of psychology, they specialise in one or perhaps two of them. This degree of specialisation is useful because psychologists work in different settings in services with different goals. But each kind of psychology and role needs to be connected to the others, with a sharing of knowledge and techniques and mutual respect for other specialist contributions. In this context, the risks of overusing the science-to-technology model of applied psychology need to be appreciated. Educational psychologists have also developed home-grown theories in education contexts. It is this development which has called into question a tight distinction between pure and applied psychology, where 'pure' has connotations of coming from outside the educational context, from the experimental laboratory. This is where the pure–applied distinction should be replaced by the distinction between theory-driven and needs-driven psychology. This latter distinction also avoids the risk of assuming that there is a coherent basic psychology outside educational psychology. The conclusion from this line of analysis was that there is no simple application of psychology by practitioners, whether for psychology practitioners or for teachers.

One of the main features of educational psychology has been its tendency to characterise the folk pedagogy of teachers as anecdotal and amateurish. This has been part of the justification for bringing the theoretical insights from psychology to bear on the professional beliefs and skills of teachers. I have argued that educational psychologists need a fuller understanding of the origins and bases for these beliefs or folk pedagogies. This is important if the aim is for psychology to sharpen teachers' craft knowledge. It also implies that teachers need to be familiar with the broad principles of psychology rather than its research base. But it has been pointed out that there is another risk, of psychology being used to promote the mindless use of procedures or techniques relevant to practical educational goals. This calls for a critically open stance in which psychology provides a network of resources for education which can illuminate and directly influence practice. But teachers need to be able to evaluate these resources for their internal coherence, validity and practical relevance. The problem here is that there is no simple way of selecting between different ideas and techniques. This is the major issue which I have raised in this book, and it is associated with the diverse nature of psychology. My contention is that this uncertainty needs to be addressed and confronted rather than ignored or overlooked. Avoidance is tempting in an anxious eagerness to demonstrate to oneself and others that psychologists can make a useful contribution.

There have been several ways of responding to this uncertainty. One has been to close down on a purist or exclusive theory in psychology. Some proponents of personal-construct psychology and applied behaviour analysis use this approach. A second way is to opt for a purist philosophical conception of a social science like psychology, such as applying a social constructionist framework to psychology. Though this provides a greater theoretical breadth, proponents find themselves making assumptions which contradict the epistemology. For example, they may want to make statements about the environment not just as someone's perspective, but as something to be analysed and modified. A third way of responding to the uncertainty is to turn away from psychology as offering anything worthwhile to education. Home-grown ideas and techniques from within education are expected to provide the way forward. The recent government approach to theory in initial teacher preparation characterises this kind of response. This response can also express the position described in chapter 2, of practitioners who avoid overt theory, only to act out assumptions associated with discredited theories from the past. As I have been arguing, this separation can be resisted, but only in a way that recognises that education goes well beyond the scope of psychology, although it has a psychological dimension.

What has been notable about the psychologists' response to the reduction of psychology in initial teacher preparation has been its narrow perspective and lack of connections to the perspectives of practising educational psychologists. This probably reflects the institutional divisions between the theoretical and practical branches of educational psychology. But it also shows psychologists overlooking the wider social and institutional context of training and teachers' working conditions. The BPS proposals for teacher preparation were too extensive to be practically incorporated with other training requirements for curriculum subject content and practical teaching skills in schools. One response from educational psychologists to this situation has been to doubt the value of psychology as applied to teaching. It has been proposed rather as a field for research support for trainee teachers. This would involve psychologists in helping teachers develop ways of approaching practical questions as open to empirical inquiry while promoting sensitivity to individual learner needs. The major problem with this response is that it undermines the unique contribution of psychology, because teacher educators and other education tutors themselves can promote these ends. Though a psychological-process contribution would be valuable, it needs to be supplemented by content.

To understand the position of educational psychologists specialising in research and teaching in university education departments, one needs to consider their relationships with developmental and other psychologists, on one hand, and educationalists and educational researchers on the other. The rise of developmental psychology with its own BPS section means that it overlaps with educational psychology, and this has shifted the focus of much educationally relevant research away from what has traditionally been educational psychology. But the relationship between educationally relevant psychology and educational research is of greater significance. Psychological studies form one amongst many specialist areas and approaches to educational research within the British Education Research Association. The growth of educational research and its professional institutions has taken away from psychology any remaining hope of leading educational research. However, I have argued that this change will not prevent psychology from retaining a significant position and contribution in educational research. But psychology's influence in education does not always come through psychologists directly. It also comes from educational researchers who have a professional background in psychology or who have studied psychology as part of education courses. It also comes from the different kinds of texts produced by psychologists, which are a major resource in diverse areas of education. With or without psychologists' direct input or even reference to their work, psychology will be used in teacher training and education and psychological ideas will be developed by educationalists themselves. There have also been some revealing patterns of professional identity and work amongst psychologists and educationalists within university departments of education. There are educational researchers with psychology training who have replaced their psychology with an educationalist identity. There are research and teaching educational psychologists who have diversified their interests away from psychological levels of analysis to more social levels and from understanding–explaining modes to design–evaluation modes. There are also educational researchers who move into research and theory of a psychological kind. So the movement has been both out of and into psychology in education departments, as it has been in professional educational psychology. Teachers become professional educational psychologists and professional educational psychologists become advisors, inspectors and education officers.

Professional educational psychology has undergone a re-examination since the 1970s with the growth in numbers and the changed political and social context of education. There are different forms of reconstructed educational psychology. One involved a broadening of focus to more contexts and levels of work while retaining an individual focus. Another was a more purist commitment to systems-level work and a move away from the individual focus. The problem with the purist version was that in its anti-individualist focus it was more rhetorical than real. Its weakness was also in adopting systems-based thinking, while denying the logic of treating individuals as themselves systems within higher-level systems. I have argued that there are risks in expanding psychology into areas which are the specialisms of educationalists and other social scientists. There is a temptation for psychologists to be drawn into levels of analysis outside the intra- and interpersonal because this is where some perceive the more powerful interventions to be. If this is how psychologists feel, then switching specialism is relevant, either into educational management or school effectiveness and improvement.

Certain issues have continued since the beginning of the profession. The split between allegiance to the LEA as client or to parents and children as clients is common to professionals employed by agencies like LEAs. Other issues reflect the uncertainties of the practitioner role in terms of defining client needs and deciding on appropriate practices. These differences reflect different psychological assumptions, which arise especially as tensions over assessment practices. There are also long-standing issues about broadening the role of educational psychology outside the field of special educational needs. Alongside this is the issue of having a distinctive contribution in relation to allied professionals. All these issues have raised questions about the length and nature of training and the need for training links with other areas of applied psychology.

At the root of these professional issues for practising educational psychologists is the dilemma about their statutory contribution to statutory assessment in the LEA decision making about special educational needs. Put simply, if they give up the statutory assessment role, they lose tenure; if they stay with it, they limit their psychological contribution. This raises the question of the core contribution of professional educational psychologists. I have argued that individual work is a core contribution, but that such work be seen as connected to the interpersonal and social context. This is not an either–or between individual and system or context. Nor is it an either–or between working within SEN or working beyond with other areas of need. Professional educational psychologists need to address their role in statutory assessment. I have argued that to do this they need to be involved in examining the wider policy and practice issues in the SEN system and the assessment it needs. This is about the LEAs' need for external generalist assessment of individual need when making decisions about the allocation of additional provision. Here we can distinguish between educational assessment work which happens to be done by practitioner psychologists and psychological assessment carried out by practitioner psychologists. One way forward is to consider the more limited and conditional use by LEAs of full multi-disciplinary assessments. This could be arranged to release psychologists while protecting some statutory role. But for psychologists to provide assessments, whether for statutory assessment or for other work which is distinctively psychological, there needs to be clarity about what makes an educational assessment psychological. I have argued that such assessment needs to be more than descriptive of a child's difficulties, strengths and contexts. It needs to provide some further understanding about how problems came about. This requires analysis in terms of individual and social context within a wide focus that includes dispositions, abilities and processes both within and between people and draws on analyses from a broadly based psychology. Providing such psychological understanding means specific analyses not, for example, generalities in terms of concepts like self-esteem and social skills. This would include a broader notion of psychometrics, not limited to measuring abilities, and would involve measuring other domains and social contextual factors and processes. The interpretation of such quantitative methods would ultimately be determined by qualitative judgements based on interpretive investigative methods. This is a position which is sceptical of fads and fashions, and sees the future of professional educational psychology as dependent on grasping the nettle of statutory assessment.

The psychology which emerges from the discussion in this chapter is one which seeks to understand human experience and actions and to enhance well-being based on this understanding. It is a dual and connected conception which links basic theoretical with applied practitioner psychology. It gives practising psychologists a distinctive practice role relative to allied service professionals such as teachers, based on systematic psychological knowledge and understanding. However, it cannot give practitioners a unique practice because there are different models of psychology, and some of these form the basis of psychoanalytic and interpretivist therapeutic practices. But it does link academic research and teaching and practising educational psychologists, since both forms of educational psychology involve working with teaching and other practitioners.

This conception of psychology relates it to other social science specialisms and to specialisms within education. Psychology's concern with enhancing human experience and well-being centres around the intrapersonal and interpersonal levels, because its focus is towards the individual end of the individual–social continuum of human phenomena. The challenges of maintaining a scientist-practitioner role and balancing the tensions of being tentative and practically decisive are not to be underestimated. Over-hasty applications and unfulfilled promises have pervaded the history of educational psychology over the last century. These are challenges which unite both academic and practising educational psychologists in the preparation and further professional development of teachers in the university courses, and in working with and advising teachers, parents and LEAs in psychological services. Building better links between psychologists involved in education is a pressing need, especially in times of a renewed political interest in education, and when simple technological solutions are sought. These are times when the tensions between theory-science and practice are at their greatest.

5 Conclusion

A future based on recognising dilemmas and connective specialisation

The characteristics of dilemmas are revealed as fundamentally born out of a culture which produces more than one possible ideal world . . . social beings are confronted by and deal with dilemmatic situations as a condition of their humanity.

Billig et al. (1988, p. 163)

Introduction

The overall aim of this book has been to explore and develop a better understanding of the relationships between psychology and education as two separate but interdependent and interconnected fields. In the introductory chapter I set out the key educational issues with which we are confronted in the current social context. This involved examining the significance of social and political values and practices for the relationship between education and psychology. In the second chapter I considered the relationship from the perspective of education and education theory. In that chapter I set out some central points, such as the differences between theory in education and theory as social science knowledge. I also argued against exclusive positions in favour of more complex connected positions, such as a science of the art of teaching. In the third chapter I considered the relationship, starting with an examination of the nature of psychology. Here the main emphasis was on the divided nature of psychology, split in part by different models of the person and what is involved in knowing. In the fourth chapter I examined the relationship in terms of the origins and development of educational psychology, as a field with research and teaching and professional practitioner areas. Some of the current issues and problems were examined in this chapter in terms of what they meant for the future of the relationship between psychology and education.

In this concluding chapter I start with a summary of the key points made in the three main chapters. Other sources will also be used to develop some of these points. In particular, I will consider two social analyses, one of the social functions of pedagogic practices linked to different psychological models, the other of the social and cognitive basis of academic disciplines as tribal cultures. This leads into a further examination of the underlying core issue, across both psychology and education and other social sciences, of how to reconcile the different epistemological assumptions in the human sciences.

Summarising and developing the main points from previous chapters

Chapter 2

In chapter 2 I looked at the diversity of educational theories and asked whether education needs and can sustain a scientific basis. Behind these issues is a realisation that we have come to expect much from education in helping us solve our social and personal problems and in giving us confidence to face future global threats and risks. The line I have taken in this book, and began to demonstrate in chapter 2, was that to seek simple causes to educational problems itself presupposes a particular technical perspective on education. One of my main points has been that our concerns have led us to look for and propose simple technical solutions. What we need is a more basic analysis which looks at the nature of education theory and its relationship with practice. If there are technical solutions, they will have to be set within this broader and more basic analysis. Any such analysis will start with the nature of education as a practical activity and of educational theory as practical knowledge. In making this point I have been aware of the strong ethos of practicality amongst teachers which arises partly from the nature of the educational task, but also from the pressures and often demanding conditions under which they work. From this it follows that there is an important difference between the practical knowledge required by education and the explanatory or interpretive knowledge generated by the social sciences. Educational knowledge is prescriptive, unlike psychological knowledge, which is explanatory or interpretive. Educational knowledge is about what is taught and why, about how and when it is taught and why, and about its expected and actual learning outcomes. This kind of practical knowledge has been influenced by social science knowledge, but it can be developed without a foundation in the social sciences or philosophy. This means that a social science such as psychology is not a foundation discipline to education, but a contributory discipline which acts as a critical resource and guide for educational theory. I argued that it also means that psychological knowledge can be applied to education only in the context of some formulated educational theory. There is no place in education for the simple mechanical application of rules of action derived from psychology. Any action rules need to be evaluated in the context of an educational analysis of goals, methods and assessment procedures.

However, I also discussed in the second chapter the diverse and conflicting kinds of educational theory, relating to different foci and expressing different social and political values – about the content of learning, the social aims of education, the personal aims of learning and techniques of teaching. There are different but related ways of representing these diverse educational theories, which can be taken to support the judgement that they do not represent pure and coherent positions. A dialogic framework was proposed as revealing the pretences of different positions that are presented as coherent and pure. Conceptions of education are often presented falsely as containing no contradictory elements. For example, child-centred theory contains some aspects of imposition by authority, and teacher-centred theory has elements of learner activity. Curricula based on different forms and fields of knowledge do assume that these fields have some bearing on what is socially useful. Curricula which are geared to preparing learners for what is relevant and useful do not ignore what is known to be true. Similarly, education which promotes egalitarian and inclusive principles has to consider not only common educational needs, but also individual needs which require some degree of differentiation between learners. In the reverse, education geared to meeting individual needs cannot make sense of individuality outside the context of common needs. The underlying principles of educational theories are therefore connected with each other: utility and knowledge, autonomy and control, equality and individuality. But these connections do not make the principles fully compatible with each other. There are clearly tensions between these principles: the more learner autonomy, the less teacher control; the more equality, the less individuality. These tensions present dilemmas about the balance between these different but connected principles underlying education (Berlak and Berlak, 1981; Judge, 1981; Clark et al., 1997). There is an inescapable *ideological impurity* in education, which arises from these connections and tensions between multiple values (Berlin, 1990; Norwich, 1993, 1995). Such connectedness is in the nature of this and other human fields. It is better confronted and dealt with than responded to in the false purism of either a technological, inclusive or a romantic individualist conception of education. From this perspective, educational theories which assert a disconnected coherence and purism can be seen to represent a conceptual response to the connections and tensions between value principles, to these underlying value dilemmas. Though this framework helps us make sense of education theories and practices, it does leave open a range of different resolutions of the underlying value dilemmas. It is within this range that there are grounds for continuing debate and struggle over the balance and emphasis between these different value principles. This is a framework which locates education within a continuing historical argumentative dialogue at different levels: political, institutional and personal. It is a dialogue which goes through periods of acute differences and periods of finding common ground, and it is a dialogue which is influenced by changing social and economic conditions. But it is a framework which keeps reminding us that any dominant conception of education represents a working balance between the underlying multiple values which fit contemporary social and economic conditions. Thus the present dominance of the conception of education in terms of technical and procedural effectiveness also represents a working balance, which should not be treated as capable of solving fully our educational ills. As I have argued in chapter 2 and throughout the book, constructive ways forward will not be simple technical solutions, they will require understanding of the nature of the problems.

I also argued in chapter 2 that although education and psychology are distinct fields, conceptions of education cannot avoid making assumptions about the nature of learning and the learning–teaching interaction. This is the conceptual link which connects education to what I have called meta-psychological assumptions. These are assumptions about the nature of the person and were shown to relate to different psychological models and theories. It is in this sense that education should be regarded as a connective specialisation, with connections to fields like psychology and sociology. 'Connective specialisation' refers to the inherent connections and interdependence between different specialisms (Young, 1995). It represents a fundamental approach to the social realm which ties together the contrary tendencies towards specialisation and differentiation, on one hand, and integration on the other. It is a concept with strong similarities to Koestler's idea of holons, units of analysis of biological and social systems which represent the dual aspect of being *parts* of larger wholes while also *wholes* in themselves (Koestler, 1972). Connective specialisation has this duality, a duality which, I have argued, is found in education as theory and practice.

The argument in chapter 2 presented education not only as a specialist field in connection with social sciences but as having internal and connected duality as well. Teaching is not simply either an art or an applied science. I argued that an analysis of the concept of teaching showed that it was both a task and an achievement. Objectives in education were about mastery (teaching as an applied science) and about expressiveness (teaching as an art). There is a tension between these conceptions, but they are both built into our concepts of teaching and we need to balance them so that one does not rule out the other. This means that purist conceptions of teaching which deny any contribution from applied social-science based rules of action, or deny the value of spontaneity and creativity in teaching, are to be avoided. The tendency to adopt exclusive positions leads to the unjustified dominance of one or other conception of teaching. There is scope for different attitudes to the balance between the creative and technical aspects of teaching, and it is within this scope that there is room for constructive debate about how technical and artistic elements interrelate. But this depends on recognising the diverse nature of teaching, which limits what can be expected of the technical mode as well as the artistic one. The tendencies to excessive polarisation and false dichotomies have to be resisted. At present, these can be seen in the recent criticism that education research does not provide the knowledge about effective teaching techniques required to improve classroom practices (Hargreaves, 1996; DfEE, 1998b (Hillage Report); Tooley and Darley, 1998).

The current dominance of technical models of teaching arises, as commentators have pointed out (e.g. Winch, 1997), from the wider expectations and demands placed on the education service. These influences and the interested response of many educationalists need to be seen in the context of the long-standing debate about whether teaching can have a scientific basis. Connections to the past are also needed here when considering reservations about the possibility of generating empirically based generalisations and about the significance of social and historical influences on the social sciences. I argued in chapter 2 against the tendency to exclusiveness and purity in these debates about the scientific basis of the art of teaching. It is possible to be positive about a scientific basis for teaching which is moderated and directed by clearly formulated educational theorising. This would avoid the purism of objectivism, subjectivism and social constructionism. It would recognise the interconnections between the particular and the general and between what is humanly constructed and what is given. A similar line of argument was pursued in resistance to the exclusive dichotomy between technical rationality and reflection-in-action in understanding the professional knowledge of educators. The concept of a practical argument was suggested as a useful way of considering teaching as active and deliberative, which connected beliefs based on intuition, on direct experience and on generalisations from systematic empirical research. So, in chapter 2, I introduced the themes of connective specialisation, false dichotomies, the avoidance of exclusive and false purism and the balance needed in coping with value dilemmas. Dichotomies, such as between practical and theoretical knowledge, teaching as task and achievement, or idiographic and nomothetic science, were presented as useful in drawing attention to important differences. But when positions are adopted which either implicitly or explicitly do not recognise the value in and connection of elements in opposed positions, we end up with distorted and contradictory concepts of education. Education needs theory which includes value judgements, conceptualisation and empirical elements. It should not be subject to excessive focus on any of these aspects. Its need for psychology arises from its core concerns, but it is not a need for the dominance of psychology as a science for education. Whatever contribution psychology makes to education is also one of many contributions from allied fields. Its links with education provide it with a constant reminder of its place amongst the network of connected social sciences relevant to education.

Chapter 3

In chapter 3 I examined the nature of psychology and explored how this bore on its relationship with education. The two main features of psychology which are analysed in this book are its theoretical nature and its status as a basic theoretical and applied field. In the third chapter the main focus was on the first and overriding question of whether psychology as a study of humanity is a causal science or an interpretive field. Just as there are diverse and opposing concepts of education, so psychology is a diverse and divided field. The continuing question for psychology is how we can be true to notions of our humanity and human values and to a coherent concept of a science of this humanity. In examining the theoretical diversity in the field, I argued that we cannot make simple distinctions between mechanistic causal theories and constructivist and holist ones. Theories differ in their episte-mological assumptions (objectivist–constructivist), assumptions about the connection of the person to social context (individual–social), degree of analysis possible (elementarist–holist) and the person's position in different orders (natural causal–moral orders). In illustrating these differences I also pointed to the connections between psychology and value judgements at the founda-tion of the field of study. A distinction was made between epistemological values and well-being values. The first set relates to what Habermas called knowledge-constitutive interests, and were presented simply in terms of participant compared to spectator perspectives on the study of humanity. These are connected perspectives, as the objects of psychology – ourselves as human beings – are also the subjects with intentionality. There is no per-spective on humanity as a spectator which does not involve someone as a participant. The second set of well-being values were presented simply in terms of progressive compared to conservative social and political values. These values are connected, as both need to assume that there are conditions which affect and set limits to change; they differ in how much change is considered possible and in attitudes to change. I drew attention to these underlying value dimensions because I wanted to show that progressive values are not necessarily associated with participant epistemologies. Causal science from a spectator perspective has been and can be used to improve human conditions and empower, if causal mechanisms are identified and used in partnership between spectator and participant.

Though the question of educational psychology as an applied psychology was addressed in chapter 4, I discussed in chapter 3 how different psychologies arose in different kinds of settings. The goals and demands of the institu-tional contexts decide what psychology is generated, what is relevant to meeting individual needs in different settings for practising psychologists, and what maintains academic credentials for academic psychologists. It was observed that the tradition of humanistic and interpretive psychologies arose from practitioners working in counselling and psychotherapeutic settings outside university departments of psychology. The contemporary idea that applied psychology derives from basic academic psychology was shown to be inconsistent with a broader historical analysis of psychological study in the Western intellectual tradition. There was a pragmatic tradition of psycho-logical ideas and techniques within different practical disciplines well before the emergence of psychology as a distinct academic field about a century ago. More was said about this tradition and its impact on the development of educational psychology in chapter 4.

For most of the rest of chapter 3 I set out the argument for a co-existence between interpretivist and causal models in psychology. I did this by noting the connections between the principles of human agency and of causal determinism. When pressed into purist forms, they are opposed principles, but when limits are set to both sets of principles they can be seen to depend on each other. Causal mechanisms can give rise to human agency if we follow the Darwinian logic developed by Dennett and others, but it is an agency operating within certain constraints. From the other side, we assume some human agency in the search for causal mechanisms in science and their use in practice. But criticisms of the causal scientific model have also focused on the individualism of psychology from a social constructionist position. The individual person is represented as being indivisibly linked to the social context and therefore needing to be studied in terms of wider social and historical processes. These critiques, which include much of feminist psychology, appeal by highlighting the social uses and abuses of knowledge generated in the name of psychology. These abuses have adversely affected the interests of those who have been subjected to social disadvantages and oppressive conditions. But I argued that commitment to a psychology which is based on progressive social and political values does not imply that the individual person has to be regarded as wholly a social creation. A strong social model leaves proponents with no grounds on which to assume an individual's personal continuity across contexts, and this makes it difficult to base personal agency. It also fails to distinguish between micro- and macro-social phenomena, between group and interpersonal levels and the institutional and state levels of analysis. But the critiques of individualism in psychology also accuse it of identifying psychology with a narrow and brutish kind of egoism. I argued that this criticism is a misreading of those psychologies and their explicit value positions. These humanistic psychologies favour a form of socially responsible individualism and are clearly opposed to egotism.

Philosophical analysis is required in any serious discussion of education and psychology and their relationships. To examine critiques of psychology for its scientism and individualism, it is necessary to consider ideas about what kind of science psychology is. In addressing different ideas about psychology as a science, I followed those who see no opposition between social constructionism and a form of realism. This is not a belief in an external reality based on absolute foundations, nor does it keep out values and interests from the field. It is a belief that if we are to make sense of communication and knowledge, we must assume an external reality, which is something we cope with, rather than something we copy into our knowledge. Well-being values are central to a field like psychology, but so are epistemological values concerned with generating knowledge and understanding in terms of the values of openness and critical evaluation. This pragmatic philosophical stance can also be connected with biological evolutionary models of the mind. I discussed recent Darwinian ideas about how the brain could evolve to operate with language and come to benefit from the collective wisdom of culture. They also illustrate the embodied nature of mind and how psychology links both ways, with biology and the wider social sciences.

The third chapter concluded with a discussion of several themes related to different kinds of explanations. That psychology connects with other fields reinforces the idea that explanations in the human sciences extend beyond psychology and require interdisciplinary perspectives. This has especial relevance to the relationship between psychology and education: the point arises from an examination which starts with psychology, not just one that starts with education, like the one I used in the previous chapter. Psychology has been discussed in this book as being composed itself of a set of sub-specialisms, a family of related but different sciences with different tasks. Experimental psychology is essentially theoretical in its search for causal mechanisms. Applied and practitioner psychologies seek interpretations building on everyday assumptions of intentionality. Both kinds of approaches are needed in my view.

Another important theme is the negative influence of the Cartesian dualist heritage in psychology, which has disconnected the psychological from the public and observable realm. I considered the argument that by connecting the mental with social behaviour, it would be possible to develop a science of the personal based on meanings and behaviour in a social context. But in the end we come back to the core issue of the dispute between the two epistemologies, the classical scientific and the interpretive, something which arises in all fields which study human action, not just in psychology and education. Taylor (1985), referring to the correlators and the interpreters, proposes a place for both in a diversified field like psychology, but states that the trouble comes from the 'limitless imperialism of the correlators' (Taylor, 1985, p. 129). His proposal, outlined in my chapter 3, is for the correlators to specialise in the psycho-physical boundaries, and for the interpreters to specialise in the area of motivated behaviour, what he calls the area of performance. Taylor also suggested that the area of competence, concerned with the structure and competencies and capacities, could be subjected to empirical treatment by the correlators. This form of co-existence was criticised by White (1988), who favoured a division between interpreters and correlators in terms of whether the phenomena were intentional or not. If the way forward for psychology is through some form of co-existence, then there is no simple way of resolving these tensions. Tolerance and a capability to understand and empathise with the rationale of these different traditions are needed, as Bruner (1996) has recommended. I will return to the co-existence issue later in this concluding chapter, but it is important to note at this point that co-existence does reduce the dominance of an imperialist and purist belief in causal science. This recognises that a mode of understanding which objectifies human realities, in order to generate understanding which enables prediction and therefore control, has its limits because it has to make place for another mode of understanding. In its worst forms such causal science can become what has been called scientism, which can be applied in manipulative ways to serve the short-term political and social interests of power elites.

The core issue of the knowledge aims of psychology runs through all its divisions. The threats to psychology as a coherent discipline arise from the growth of multi-disciplinary fields, like cultural studies and the cognitive and neuro-sciences, which draw out those psychologists and parts of psychology across the epistemological divide. The prospect of a coherent psychology uniting emotional, social, biological and developmental aspects depends on a methodological integration of experimental, quantitative and interpretive qualitative methods. And, as argued in chapter 3, this depends on working out an epistemological co-existence which can be fruitful for the different areas of psychology. Such a methodological integration is also important for bridging the gap between basic theoretical and applied practitioner psychology. It is unlikely, especially in the present circumstances of the funding of universities and research in the social sciences, that psychology can thrive if it is isolated from practical problems and needs in everyday life. In this sense, I argued that bias either by the users of psychology or by psychologists may advance the field by introducing new topics and questions and engendering debates. But this bias can become a serious threat if the inquiry disciplines of the field are not supported by the funding base or psychologists are unable to maintain their competence and commitment to these disciplines when subjected to external social influences. Thus basic psychology depends on applied and practitioner psychology, in education and other spheres of practical activity. When dealing with practical needs and problems, psychology is therefore connected to other fields. The conclusion to this line of argument is that psychology is a broad and diverse specialisation which is connected with education, amongst its many areas of connection. Chapter 2 showed the connective specialisation from the education standpoint, chapter 3 from the psychology standpoint.

Chapter 4

In chapter 4 I examined the contribution of psychology to education in its various forms from a historical perspective and in the current circumstances. Psychology has had a substantial and at times controversial impact. I suggested that its positive contributions have been as much in promoting general approaches as in applying specific knowledge and techniques. These are the values and techniques of empirical inquiry into educational issues and the value of addressing the learning needs of individuals, not just of those with special educational needs. From this I concluded that a major contribution has already been made by psychology which is now built into education and education research. Psychology continues to contribute, but needs to be more adaptable to changed circumstances and co-ordinated with other specialisms in the social sciences and education. We also need to remember that psychology is itself made up of various specialisations located in different settings and with different roles. Chapter 4 also set out how these different groups overlap in their functions.

Historical analysis shows that there is continuity over time in the central debates about the relationship between psychology and education. The question of a scientific base for education, for example, has been around for over a century, and was one of the sources of the development of educational psychology. The continuing tensions in the role of scientist-practitioner have also presented repeated pitfalls for educational psychologists, most notably in the development and use of psychometrics in the education service. The commitment to being tentative and empirical has been undermined by pressures to respond to the practical needs of policy makers and practitioners. Psychologists have been prone to urge practice that goes beyond what theory and empirical evidence can support, and to lose sight of the social and political use of their work. But the historical perspective also shows how the social and political context provides opportunities at one stage which can become constraints at another. Psychometrics, for example, was developed as part of the rise of the intellectual aristocracy over the landed aristocracy. But in becoming part of a technocratic approach to meritocracy it later came to be opposed by a communitarian socialist tradition. The political reputation of psychological measurement, I argued, depended more on changing political needs than on the principles of its theoretical and technical base. Psychometrics was favoured when it served meritocratic ideals, but when these ideals became suspect, psychometrics came to be seen as pseudo-scientific, rather than needing to be further developed. The dominance of political agendas is clear in the way that psychometrics came to be identified with certain specific kinds of ability measurement rather than a more general project of measurement in educational psychology. It is only in its narrow IQ testing-hereditarian interpretation that it has had conservative political associations. I also argued that in its wider project of measuring human characteristics, psychometrics had a more ambiguous position in relation to social and political values.

Critiques of educational psychology follow a similar form and content to those of psychology generally, which were discussed in chapter 3. I addressed two key kinds of critique in chapter 4, the best known being the social critique that educational psychology has been dominated by excessive individualism. Following the line of argument from chapter 3 I acknowledged that psychology tended to be disconnected from the social, but explained that this did not justify ignoring the individual levels of analysis, nor a total rejection of a causal explanatory model. In suggesting that this is not an either–or situation, I argued that we need disciplinary frameworks which can be interconnected and complementary. To have this we need to be aware that psychology is diverse and has theories which differ in terms of their classic science–interpretivist epistemology and in terms of their atomist–holist assumptions about the individual's relation to the social. Holistic intepretivist psychological theories are more easily connected to sociology which have similar assumptions; the same applies to reductionist causal psychological and sociological theories.

That psychology has been the dominant partner in the relationship with education is evident from the language of application: we talk of applying psychology to education, not the other way round. But there is no sharp distinction between basic and applied psychology. The distinction is better seen in terms of a continuum where some research enhances understanding of learning in context and can help identify techniques of teaching. There is also a useful (but again not a sharp) distinction between psychology as basic science, as applied science and as professional practice. This is a distinction which aids the clarification of the respective and interconnected roles of different specialisations within psychology. It helps to reinforce the importance of mutual respect between the different specialist psychological contributions and is compatible with an awareness of excessive expectations of the science-to-technology model of applied psychology.

I also discussed in chapter 4 the tendency within educational psychology to characterise the professional knowledge of teachers as anecdotal and amateurish. If the aim is for psychology to sharpen teachers' craft knowledge, then I argued that it is important for educational psychologists to have a fuller understanding of the origins and bases of these beliefs or folk pedagogies. This is important because these folk pedagogies sometimes incorporate prior psychological conceptions and models in modified and often simplified forms. But the most serious risk which arises from this process is that psychology may promote a mindless use of procedures and techniques relevant to practical goals. This relates to the science–practice tension already discussed. It is a risk which requires a critical and open attitude by teachers and practitioner psychologists to psychology and its use in practice. As the title of the present book indicates, the trouble is that there is uncertainty about how to evaluate different ideas and techniques and select between them. This arises from the diverse nature of psychology and poses the major challenge in the relationship between psychology and education: how to work with this uncertainty. This is a problem not only for the users and potential users of psychology, but also for applied and basic psychologists themselves. However, education is also a diverse field, with its diversity paralleling that of psychology. At least this means that the relationships between the fields can be coherent between educational theories and psychological conceptions which share similar epistemological and ontological assumptions. Recognising this, however, should make us alert to the risk that education may draw on psychology and select between its different theoretical positions. My contention is that we need to confront the uncertainties about both fields and work with them in an open and constructively critical way. We need to avoid the temptation to overlook uncertainty in our anxious eagerness to prove our worth to ourselves and others.

I also argued in chapter 4 that psychologists in education, both research and teaching and practising professional psychologists, whether they see themselves as educational psychologists or not, ought to realise how much they have in common. They share the goal of teaching the value of psychology for teachers in the practical contexts of their teaching. For education psychologists in academic settings this is initial training, and higher degrees concerned with further professional education and training; for professional educational psychologists, it is in-service training and consultation work. The position of psychologists in university departments of education also needs to be understood in terms of relationships with psychologists in university departments of psychology and educationalists and educational researchers in their own departments. I suggested that the growth of educational research has diminished the lead role of psychology in educational research. But it does not, I contended, mean that psychology does not have a significant and distinctive position. This view is based on the direct work of psychologists, the psychological work of educationalists and the impact of psychological texts on educationalists and teachers. I concluded that with or without direct educational psychologist input or even reference to their written work, psychological ideas will be used in teacher training and education and be developed by educationalists themselves. The history of education indicates this, as does contemporary observation of education.

Professional educational psychology has grown over the last half century and in the process has undergone a re-examination of its aims and kinds of psychological provision. These changes reflected the falling reputation of psychometrics and individual case work. In discussing these trends I noted the risks of expanding psychology into areas which are the specialism of educationalists and other social scientists. This was associated with the temptation to be drawn into levels of analysis and kinds of work where more powerful interventions were perceived to lie. I suggested that if this is how individual psychologists felt, then switching into management or school effectiveness and improvement work was appropriate. However, there are long-standing issues for professional educational psychologists: should they accept a multiple allegiance – to LEA and to parents and children – take a wider role than in special educational needs, make a distinctive contribution relative to other allied professionals? My view is that the central current issue is the dilemma about the statutory contribution to assessment when LEAs decide whether or not to issue a statement of SEN. Following the views developed in previous chapters, I argued that though individual work is a core part of practice, it has to be connected to interpersonal and social contexts, and does not preclude systems work. But to do justice to this range of work and to have appropriate training for it, professional educational psychologists need to be released from some of their input to statutory assessment. This requires an involvement in re-examining SEN policy and practice and the system of identifying pupils with SEN. Ways of retaining the security which comes from a statutory contribution, while having a more limited and conditional input, need to be considered. To justify even this kind of contribution professional educational psychologists have to be clearer about what is distinctively 'psychological' in their assessments. I argued that such assessment is more than descriptive of a child's strengths and difficulties and contexts. It has to provide understanding about how the problems came about – an understanding that can inform decisions about intervention.

The kind of educational psychology that is presented in this book is one which connects the research-teaching with the professional-practitioner branches. This reflects the duality and connectedness in a broader conception of psychology as a basic theoretical and applied practitioner field. Professional psychology derives its distinctive role compared to other practitioner fields from basing practice on systematic and explicit psychological knowledge and understanding. However, it does not give a unique practice, because psychology is diverse, and some forms of psychology form the basis of the practice of allied professional groups. This conception of educational psychology relates it to other areas of psychology, to other social sciences and to various specialisms within education. It is a conception which does not underestimate the challenge and difficulties of maintaining a scientist-practitioner role whether in the fields of individual work, consultation work, teacher training, educational research and development or policy advice.

Social perspectives on the relationship between psychology and education

In this section I will outline and discuss briefly two different social accounts, relevant to the psychology–education relationship, which provide some insights into some of the key themes of this book. They are both relevant to my pulling together of the arguments in the previous chapters. The first account is Bernstein's sociological analysis of the social relations involved in pedagogic practices (Bernstein, 1990; cf. Broadfoot and Pollard, 1997). This account arises from his wider interest in pedagogic practices as part of cultural reproduction and the relationships between pedagogies and different social conditions. Bernstein's analysis is relevant to the discussion in chapter 2 about different kinds of educational theories. These theories represent differences over the focus in designing the curriculum and teaching: should it be subject knowledge, social relevance or the learner? For Bernstein, cultural reproduction depends on the pedagogic relation between transmitters (teachers) and acquirers (learners), what he calls the process of relay, which is distinguished from the content of what is relayed. In focusing on the rules of pedagogic relations, Bernstein identifies three rules concerned with (1) hierarchy, (2) sequencing of teaching, and (3) criteria. The hierarchical rule reflects the rules of social order that there is an asymmetry between transmitter and acquirer, with the transmitter dominant. The hierarchical rule can be explicit or implicit – in which case it is harder to detect, as the power of the transmitter is concealed, being focused on the context of acquisition rather than the acquirer. Sequencing rules are about what precedes what in the transmission process. They imply rules about pacing and timing and about expected acquisition. They too can be explicit or implicit. Explicit rules regulate development in terms of age levels with the learner aware of them; implicit sequencing rules are known to the transmitter and are drawn from a range of developmental psychology theories. These theories, such as Piaget's stage theory, assume an active child who functions largely outside particular social contexts. Such psychological theories are critical of the transmitter as an imposer of meanings, so that 'domination' is replaced by the notion of 'facilitation'. Such theories therefore involve an implicit hierarchical rule as well. The third set of rules is about what counts as legitimate communication between transmitters and acquirers. They too can be explicit or implicit.

On the basis of these three rules Bernstein distinguishes between *visible pedagogies* when the rules are explicit and *invisible pedagogies* when the rules are implicit. In visible pedagogies, practice is evident, with the focus on performance judged against explicit criteria. It is product-oriented and identifies differences among children. By contrast, in invisible pedagogies, the practice is not visible to the acquirer: the focus is on procedures internal to the acquirer and procedures which are common to all. What is acquired is therefore some internal competence, so that individual differences arise in how these competences are realised in performance, depending on situational factors. Visible pedagogies are therefore concerned with explicit transmission and performance, invisible pedagogies with acquisition and competence. Bernstein uses this framework to account for three broad kinds of pedagogic practice, what he calls the progressive, the conservative and the radical. Radical pedagogies are those where the focus is on political change between social groups, as expressed by educationalists like Freire (1973). In conservative and progressive pedagogies, change is focused on the individual, but they differ in terms of the visibility of pedagogy. In progressive pedagogies, the pedagogy is invisible, while in conservative pedagogies it is visible. Progressive pedagogies draw on what in chapter 2 I called 'organismic psychology theories' (those assuming inherent activity, holism, discontinuity). Conservative pedagogies draw on what I called 'mechanistic psychology theories' (those assuming external causation, atomism, continuity). Organismic theories such as Piaget's are developmentally staged and assume the person's inherent activity; mechanistic theories such as behaviourist and cognitive-behaviourist theories assume causal chains linking antecedents to predictable consequences.

The point of this sociological analysis is to show how social and economic factors affect the effective understanding and use of these different pedagogic types, and how these different pedagogies have different consequences for children's ability to use them. Bernstein argues, for example, that though visible pedagogies can reproduce different achievement from different social groups, this is not necessarily so. It is possible to relax the sequencing and pacing rules, though at greater cost and effort in school management and teacher training. However, he also argues that more disadvantaged social groups find invisible pedagogies more difficult to read and control. Visible pedagogies are also experienced more in the middle classes employed in the economic and business fields, while invisible pedagogies are experienced more in the middle classes working in human service agencies, such as education.

There are several points that arise from this analysis which relate to points made earlier in this book. The first is the degree of similarity between this sociological analysis of pedagogic practices and the analysis of different curricula models by curriculum theorists. Visible pedagogies, with their explicit rules of hierarchy, sequencing and criteria, relate to transmission models either of the knowledge-centred or society-centred type, while invisible pedagogies relate to elicitation or facilitation models of a learner-centred type. Secondly, there are similarities between Bernstein's analysis and the links between psychological theories and educational models made in chapter 2. Visible pedagogies are seen to draw on behaviourist-type theories, just as the model of *education as a technology* had links with causal mechanistic psychology theories. Invisible pedagogies are seen to draw on developmental child-centred theories as the progressive model of education linked with organismic theories. Thirdly, this sociological analysis of pedagogy presumes the dominance of teacher over the learner in the pedagogic relationship and therefore interprets the invisible pedagogies as concealing those power relations. When this is seen alongside the way in which pedagogy draws on psychological theories, questions can be asked about how much psychology leads in its relationship with education. Psychology's significance can be seen from this perspective – cultural reproduction of the social order – as providing concepts and models of teaching and learning which fit the changing dominant and social and economic processes. This point relates to the critique that psychology serves different social functions, as discussed in chapter 3. However, this congruence between pedagogic practices and psychological models, with its links to the centrality of concepts of control and causal powers, does not diminish the reality of the intra-personal and interpersonal levels of analysis or the significance of theorising about these levels of social phenomena.

The second social account that is relevant to this concluding chapter is Becher's (1989) study of intellectual inquiry and the culture of academic disciplines in terms of academic tribes and their territories. Becher based his study on interviews with academics across many different disciplines, but did not include either psychology or education. Nevertheless, he did study other social sciences and his broadly based analytic framework has relevance to the relationship between psychology and education. His framework assumes that there are connections between the cognitive aspects of intellectual knowledge and the social and professional cultures of these disciplines. In relation to the cognitive aspects, he distinguishes loosely between three levels of knowledge. At the most general level, he identifies four broad knowledge domains: hard pure, hard applied, soft pure and soft applied. These are represented as continua ranging from pure to applied and hard to soft. The disciplines which are at an intermediary level are located at various positions within these broad knowledge domains, and within disciplines there are specialisms. In relation to the social aspects, he distinguishes between convergent–divergent and urban–rural disciplinary cultures, which are also treated as continua. Convergence–divergence is about the extent to which members of a discipline share common models and practices. Sociology was considered by Becher to be a divergent discipline, much in the way that I called psychology a diverse discipline earlier in this book. By contrast, physics would be considered a convergent discipline. Convergent disciplines are tightly knit with well-defined and defended boundaries. Open-ended cognitive fields are associated with divergent communities. 'Urban–rural' refers to the proportion of academics to problems or topics. Urban communities have more academics per problem or topic and tend to be associated, according to Becher, with hard disciplines.

Becher's distinctions between kinds of knowledge in terms of hard–soft and pure–applied are particularly relevant to the themes of this book. Included in the hard–soft knowledge distinction is also the difference between restricted–unrestricted knowledge, that is, knowledge which is narrow and circumscribed compared to knowledge which is broad and loose in scope. Hard pure knowledge is considered to develop in a steady linear cumulative way. This is linked to the presence of clear criteria for knowledge claims and some predictability about topics and problems to advance future inquiry. It demonstrates what has been called contextual imperatives, in the sense that the sequence of explanations fits into place as part of a patterned whole. Hard pure knowledge exemplifies epistemologies based on analysis, precise measurement and the search for universals and generalities, which operate in impersonal and value-free ways. Soft pure knowledge is defined in contrasting terms: patterns of development go over the same ground as before, perhaps in different ways. There is no clearly articulated framework for development, but loosely knit clusters of ideas and theories. This is because there are different criteria for judging knowledge claims and because topics for inquiry are selected in a looser way. Soft pure knowledge includes epistemologies based on synthesis, holism, conceptual distinctions and a focus on particulars, which operate in a personal value-laden way. Becher identifies a hierarchy of status from hard to soft and from pure to applied. Hard applied knowledge involves trial-and-error methods and is not exclusively quantitative, as there is also a need for qualitative judgement. Its outcomes are techniques and products which meet practical needs. Soft applied knowledge is built up on knowledge about particular cases. It uses soft pure knowledge to understand the complexity of human situations and needs. Its outcomes are procedures which are evaluated in pragmatic terms.

The perceived superiority of hard to soft knowledge is related, according to Becher, to the moves within certain disciplines to increase their degree of hardness. He uses disciplines in the social sciences, like economics and psychology, where there have been internal movements to use mathematical models in theory building, to illustrate the attractions of hard knowledge. Though several of the social science disciplines, such as economics, straddle the boundaries of hard–soft and pure–applied knowledge, it is their softness and applied nature which exposes them to greater external influences from political agencies than is the case with the humanities and the natural sciences. There is also the question of how neighbouring disciplines relate to each other over areas of common interest. A topic can fall into several disciplines, especially within the social sciences, and this raises questions of territorial rights. These can be handled, according to Becher, either by disciplines adopting a different style of inquiry or by some agreed division of labour which can amount to differences in conceptual frameworks. Disciplinary overlaps also raise questions about unification or integration across disciplines and the negative effects of what has been called the 'ethnocentrism of the disciplines' (Campbell, 1969). Campbell has argued that this ethnocentrism prevents the development of an integrated multi-science, which has especial relevance to the social sciences. It does so by favouring the core areas over the peripheral ones, leaving important gaps to be filled in the overlapping areas. His proposed solution is what he calls 'the fish-scale model of multi-science', in which comprehensive coverage comes from the overlap of narrow specialities, in the way that fish-scales cover the fish.

The ethnocentrism of the disciplines, according to Campbell, produces a clustering of specialities which leave gaps at the borders of the disciplines. By contrast, the fish-scale model presents an approach to interdisciplinary coverage which avoids the task of training people to master two disciplines. Dual training can lead to shallowness, given the breadth of disciplines, and goes against the trend towards greater specialisation. In the fish-scale model, comprehensiveness in coverage can be achieved collectively when individuals develop specialisations in different but overlapping specialities. As a model which is constructive about developing broader fields of knowledge, it relies on specialities within and across disciplines as the most useful units of knowledge. But as Becher has noted, narrower specialities may be no better than disciplines. Specialities may not provide the constancy of disciplines needed as a basis for professional identity. They may represent specialisations based on social processes rather than cognitive fields, and so may change rapidly and not contribute to the coverage of neglected areas. They may represent different specialisations based not on subject matter, but on theoretical models and methods, and come to be rival not complementary specialities. Campbell recognises the extent to which the in-group and out-group dynamics associated with disciplinary ethnocentrism works against overlap and coverage by emphasising in-group virtues and out-group defects. Finding weaknesses in out-groups as a way of building in-group solidarity has been a notable feature of the social sciences. Instances of this were noted in previous chapters in the relationships between the different contributory disciplines to education and between them and education. What Campbell is presenting in his fish-scale conception is an ideal for individual academics and for professional organisations and academic organisation. There are two main problems with this model. One is that uncertainties about the stability and nature of specialities is likely to reduce comprehensive coverage of subject matter. The second is that intellectual tribalism is not only a matter of intellectual territory and its coverage, but also of conflicts over different epistemologies. It is about what kind of coverage is relevant to what fields, a point which has been made throughout the chapters of this book. Improved interdisciplinarity therefore has to address questions of epistemological co-existence, to which I will return shortly.

Psychology and education as divergent and interconnected fields

In this section I use Becher's framework for intellectual inquiry and disciplinary cultures to analyse psychology and education and their relationship. From the discussion in chapter 3 it is clear that psychology can be considered to span the four broad areas of knowledge. I will use the term 'basic' instead of 'pure' for reasons explained in chapter 4. Psychology is a broad field with parts which fall into hard basic, hard applied, soft basic and soft applied kinds of knowledge. There are traditions within psychology which aspire to cumulative scientific knowledge, and others which adopt interpretive assumptions and methods. There are, however, no simple distinctions between hard and soft psychologies, as there are degrees of hard and soft as well as changes within scientific and interpretive traditions. Associated with these different theoretical psychologies are corresponding applied traditions, which support the work of professional psychologists (who are the majority of psychologists). Overall, psychology is (in Becher's terms) a divergent discipline, forming a loosely knit professional community. It has tendencies to fragment along hard and soft and basic and applied lines, as I explained in chapter 3. However, it does have specialities which have more convergent tendencies: these are represented by sections in the British Psychological Society (BPS). There is also an experimental psychology society, separate from the BPS, which has greater convergence through its adoption of inquiry methods associated with hard knowledge. There are also other associations which represent general and specific kinds of humanistic and interpretivist psychologies. Yet the dominant image of psychology projected by organisations like the BPS is still that it is a causal science, even when there may be internal doubts about this and recognition of its diversity.

While psychology is a basic and an applied knowledge field, and has a professional service base, education is a professional service field whose academic discipline mainly consists of applied knowledge concerned with practical needs. It has some basic knowledge aspects associated with the foundations of its theoretical aspects. These originally included what were called the foundation disciplines of philosophy, history, sociology and psychology insofar as they were relevant to education. As explained in chapter 2, educational theory is no longer thought to need these as foundations, but rather as disciplinary resources for informing and guiding educational theory and practice. Whether or not one considers education to involve basic knowledge depends on whether these applied disciplines are considered to be part of education or part of the 'foundations' or part of both. One of the aims of this book has been to examine this important overlap between education as a mainly applied knowledge field and psychology as a contributory discipline to education and as a basic and applied knowledge field. Educational psychology is part of and belongs to both psychology and education and needs to be owned and nurtured by both disciplines. As regards soft and hard knowledge, education's mainly applied knowledge has had soft and hard elements. Its soft elements are associated with the idea that teaching is an art or craft activity that cannot be reduced to rules and procedures because it depends on spontaneity and creativity. Its hard elements are associated with teaching as an applied science. This is where there were originally high expectations that psychology and educational psychology would provide a scientific basis for education and teaching, as discussed in chapters 2 and 4. Therefore education, like psychology, includes the four different areas of knowledge, and as a disciplinary community is like psychology in being loosely knit or divergent.

Some of the elements of this analysis are represented schematically in figure 4, which shows the key similarities, differences and overlaps between the broad intellectual fields of psychology and education. The figure, it must be noted, only includes those aspects that illustrate certain key points, and is not comprehensive. Both psychology and education are shown as including hard and soft areas of knowledge, what are termed causal science and intepretivist kinds of knowledge in the figure. But while psychology is a field of basic knowledge concerned with explanation and interpretation with an applied knowledge dimension, education is mainly a field of applied knowledge in the sense that educational theory relates to practical knowledge in order to meet practical needs. The degree of overlap between psychology and education also shows that levels of analysis in psychology are towards the individual end of the social–individual continuum. There are areas towards the social end of the continuum which are outside the field of psychology, though the boundaries are fuzzy. Hence the use of dotted lines in the figure. Educational psychology is represented as the common area between psychology and education, and is part of both broad fields. Educational psychology is therefore represented as being situated towards the

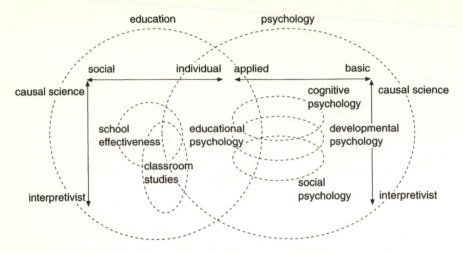

Figure 4 Relationships between psychology, education and their areas of specialism

applied end of the basic–applied continuum, but as including both hard-causal science and soft-interpretivist knowledge models. Not represented in the figure are the two branches of educational psychology, the teaching-research and professional practitioner roles. This is because these connected branches relate to different roles and employment settings (the university and the education service respectively), and this is not represented in the figure. Also included are specialisms within psychology concerned with cognitive, developmental and social psychology. These are represented as psychologies which overlap with each other and with educational psychology. They cover basic and applied aspects, but tend to include more hard than soft knowledge. However, social psychology is represented as being more towards the soft knowledge end of the continuum. Two related education specialisms are represented within education and overlap with educational psychology. The area of classroom studies is not considered a well-defined specialism with a clear identity. It is concerned with a mixed tradition of studies of classroom management, interaction and processes of teaching and learning which has a fairly long history. It is represented as including more interpretivist models associated with ethnographic studies of classroom interaction in the 1970s and 1980s. But it also includes more quantitative explanatory studies of teaching processes and outcomes which have been conducted most recently since the 1960s, especially in the USA (Gage, 1985). The other education specialism represented is school effectiveness. This is a more recent area which has developed over the last two decades and has some overlaps with classroom studies and educational psychology. Its main proponents present it as a central, if not the central, area of educational research (Mortimore, 1995; Reynolds, 1998). Though school effectiveness has been studied in terms of exploring and describing pupils' perspectives, its main model and methods are associated with generalisations and quantification.

The overlap of school effectiveness with classroom studies and educational psychology is of particular current interest. School effectiveness research has shown that the classroom level is a more powerful determinant of cognitive achievements than the school level (Reynolds, 1998). This has broadened the interest of school effectiveness researchers into effective classrooms and teaching. This expansion of interest also needs to be seen in the wider educational and political context. The government in its desire to raise educational attainment has set its sights on changes to class grouping practices and classroom teaching methods, particularly in literacy and numeracy (Barber, 1997; Reynolds, 1998). These issues were discussed in my introductory chapter and will be pursued later in this chapter, especially in relation to critiques of education research and the current interest in teaching as an evidence-based profession (Hargreaves, 1995). But it is relevant to this discussion of the relation of educational psychology to other education specialisms. Some school effectiveness specialists, though not all, have a background in educational psychology. They may no longer identify with educational psychology, nor draw on work done in educational and other relevant areas of psychology, as discussed in chapter 4. But what is important in the renewed interest in the field of classroom and teaching studies is that the overlap between effectiveness and educational psychology should not be dominated excessively by the expansion of school effectiveness models and methods. This is a contemporary example of the need for constructive and collaborative interdisciplinarity. There is a need for joint ownership and mutual co-existence where different epistemologies are in use. Any temptations towards monopolistic expansion and incorporation of educational psychology should also be resisted. This calls for the distinctive contributions from psychology to be appreciated and nurtured from within education studies. However, the temptations may be hard to resist, given the policy relevance and professional positioning which are at stake for those who take the lead in this sensitive area of education study. It may be convenient to see the wheel as having turned for educational psychology. No longer dominant as the main source of a scientific approach to education, it can be relegated to a minor role, eclipsed by school effectiveness and its wider expansion into a wider education effectiveness movement which includes teaching effectiveness. The professional rewards are great and the tone of its proponents seem to indicate that the 'school effectiveness mission has only just begun' (Reynolds, 1998).

Epistemological and value co-existence: continuing tensions and implications

Much time and effort in education studies is expended on debates and rivalries between proponents of hard and soft knowledge, or, to use Taylor's simple distinction, between correlators and interpreters (Taylor, 1985). And as I have argued previously, these debates are paralleled within psychology. But whereas in the past educational psychology was associated with the scientific base for education, this has come to be established more within areas of education which are defined in educational, not contributory discipline terms. This is important as it marks education's sole ownership of this area. But it shifts rather than resolves the pervasive question of the nature of teaching and education as art and/or applied science. What is interesting to note in the current educational context is the renewed interest in searching for systematic, explicit and generalisable knowledge about effective techniques and procedures. Evidence for this is widespread and can be illustrated by a recent study of perceptions of the research needed in special educational needs (Norwich et al., 1997). Interviews with senior educationalists, including academics, researchers, policy makers, teachers and head teachers, showed an overwhelming interest in the need for effectiveness-oriented research at various levels and settings in the system. But effectiveness questions are not simply about identifying generalisable means to ends through systematic explanatory surveys and complex statistical analyses. They are inherently about values and goals, because it is in terms of these criteria that the impact of different means is identified.

Proponents of the methods associated with school effectiveness recognise that effectiveness requires a selection among competing values (Stoll and Mortimore, 1997), but little more is said than that different value approaches can be combined (p. 10). The tendency is to avoid and even criticise the values debate on the ground that it impedes what (allegedly) really counts – a focus on effective means (Reynolds, 1998). However, concepts of effectiveness are implicit in the choice of ways to measure outcomes in effectiveness studies, because they reflect what counts as 'achievement'. It is notable that criticisms of effectiveness outcome measures have paralleled the criticisms of the early movement of behavioural objectives, which was discussed in chapter 2 (White, 1997). They highlight the fact that outcomes tend to be defined in terms of short-term and predominantly cognitive achievements, with less use of attitudinal, affective and motivational characteristics. But the point is not that short-term cognitive achievements are unimportant goals, as they clearly are important to many people with a stake in education. The problem arises from the fact that longer-term cognitive outcomes and more general affective and motivational characteristics are also important for many people. The unwillingness to engage in the values-or-goals debate means that educational effectiveness studies stick with limited but feasible criteria of effectiveness and when challenged make statements about broadening criteria – but have difficulties in doing so. The problems that need to be addressed are those of broadening effectiveness criteria.

As I argued in chapter 2 and summarised earlier in this chapter, education is inevitably concerned with multiple values and these values are in tension, thus posing us dilemmas. The way in which the tensions are treated and the

balance is struck between these values underlies the different kinds of educational models discussed in this book. It is not a question of whether schools
should have as a goal either self-directing citizenship (White, 1997, p. 53)
or basic academic skills in numeracy or literacy. It is a question of how far
they can meet both these and other important goals. This is a question of
establishing priority and maintaining a balance while holding on to several
values, not of splitting and focusing on single values and then setting up
false oppositions. However, decision making in practical situations, given
limited resources, can often entail choosing some outcomes and not others.
In this connection, I have argued that issues in the field of special educational needs give rise to basic value dilemmas about how learner differences
in general are treated in education (Norwich, 1993, 1995).

These dilemmas apply across all education, but are especially acute for
pupils with significant learning difficulties. The dilemmas emerge in decisions about identifying some children, rather than others, as having special educational needs; in curriculum planning and differentiation for such
children; and in the organisation of schooling and grouping of pupils within
schools (the inclusion issue). More recently I have extended this value diversity idea to teaching by arguing that from a commitment to broad and
balanced educational aims, especially when life-long learning is important,
teachers will need to identify multiple learning objectives (Norwich, 1997).
Affective characteristics, such as positive liking for a subject or activity, or
motivational characteristics, such as high self-perceived competence in a
subject, would also be objectives. Along with cognitive objectives they should
inform the selection of teaching techniques, relationships, materials and
settings. In some situations this may, I argued, require a reduction or change
in the content of cognitive objectives. This arises from the balancing of
different educational goals. The point is that an exclusive focus on a single
goal can have negative learning impacts because non-cognitive values can be
overlooked or suppressed. Some years ago Judge (1981) also noted that there
had been a failure to address fundamental questions about the purposes of
schooling and education. He also identified unexamined and conflicting
purposes in the form of five dilemmas: goals of utility or culture; assessment
goals which were fair or accountable; provision which was common to all
or diverse (another expression of dilemmas of difference); management or
autonomy; and teaching as a function or profession. Judge also argued that
we are at one and the same time unwilling to abandon and to fully reconcile these purposes. Like myself (above) he recognised the need to balance
purposes and principles in decision making and saw that this would have
important consequences for policy and practice.

I have argued elsewhere for the principle of value balancing, in terms of
the inevitability of ideological impurity (Norwich, 1996). I contend now, as
I come towards the end of this book, that the principle has positive and
general implications for educational policy and practice and for education as
an academic field. On one hand, it reminds us to bear in mind the diversity

of educational goals and not unnecessarily to oppose different kinds of goals against each other, for example, cognitive measurable short-term goals against more qualitative longer-term affective or motivational goals. That is, the principle is idealistic in expanding rather than narrowing educational horizons. On the other hand, it also reminds us to moderate any over-eagerness to achieve one kind of goal at the risk of ignoring other kinds of goals, possibly resulting in counter-productive outcomes. For example, the systematic, technical and rational planning of narrow learning outcomes might not be the most effective way of raising attainment levels. Here the principle calls for realism to moderate excessive idealism. If teaching techniques are prescribed for mindless use, this can reduce the morale and commitment of teachers and then undermine the enthusiasm of learners. Short-term gains may not be maintained in the longer term, and other important educational goals could be ignored.

This analysis evidently has relevance to recent and current government educational policies. Though raising standards is important, the way in which standards have been defined and monitored almost solely in terms of short-term cognitive performance indicators raises doubts about their basic and broader educational relevance. Part of the problem is that the National Curriculum is used to define these indicators, when its programmes embody overly cognitive learning goals. This is not to argue against accountability pressures on schools nor to deny that support for teachers, in the form of detailed teaching programmes, could be beneficial in broadening teachers' repertoires of teaching skills. But teaching is ultimately about what teachers do in classrooms, based on how they judge the needs of the situation, given the learners, the materials and their own teaching knowledge, skills and attitudes. As argued in chapter 2, teaching can and does involve following explicit rules of action and using acquired techniques. But the judgement, commitment and initiative of the teacher are all-important. We have good reason to doubt whether ignoring or reducing the art or craft element, and reducing teaching to action rules and procedures, is really going to raise standards. This is where Judge's dilemma of autonomy or control is relevant. Concepts of effective teaching need to include professional judgement and some autonomy. Too much emphasis on external control and management can be counter-productive. Educational effectiveness (even in narrow terms) will not be attained through excessive controls.

It is relevant that even in business management, which has been used as a model for schooling over the last two decades, there is a respected view which questions whether pure profit objectives result in the sought-for success and excellence. Regarding this, John Kay has proposed what he calls the *principle of obliquity*, which states that some objectives are best sought indirectly. This is the principle that direct instrumental action is often counter-productive in the business field (Kay, 1998). This principle also has relevance in education, as the cognitive processes of learning to read and use number, for example, are known to be connected to the emotional and motivational processes of learning. It is these connections which would probably underlie the operation of an obliquity principle applied to overly prescriptive teaching techniques which were guided mainly by narrow and short-term measurable cognitive goals.

If we acknowledge multiple educational goals, then effectiveness must not be defined solely in terms of short-term measurable outcomes: it must also include longer-term outcomes and more general and qualitative outcomes. This is a position with significant implications for the specialism of school effectiveness and the wider field of education studies. At this point in the discussion, value or ideological impurity becomes related to assessment and epistemological questions. Both education and psychology have to decide whether to assume that all characteristics and processes can be measured. We are back here to the question of epistemological co-existence or dominance by correlators and critiques by interpreters. Following the co-existence position which I outlined previously, I consider that there are powerful reasons for limiting and qualifying the extent to which all things that matter in education can be considered measurable. This is not, I repeat, an either–or situation: some things *can* be measured, even if the measures have known and unknown error. The logic of this position is that if a characteristic can be defined, in the objective sense that it has meanings which are publicly shared and intersubjective, then it can be measured. Measuring might be of a simple yes/no kind, through ordering of responses or use of some continuous scale. But the kind of measure is less important than the point that measurement is the implementation of a definition. An objective definition in the above sense might be generated from shared recognition, expert pronouncements or some replicable use of a standard instrument. However, the crucial point is that the scope of measurability depends on the extent to which we can generate objective definitions in the above sense. If there are important aspects of learning and performance which are not definable in these terms, then measurement is no longer relevant. This is a matter of degree too, in that there are different ways of generating measurement-relevant definitions. Thus it is the status and possibility of objective definitions which sets the balance of co-existence between correlators and interpreters.

Such a balance is not easy to set, as shown by the continuing controversy over the concept of intelligence, probably the most significant concept in education and psychology. Correlators have foreclosed on definitions of general abilities which relate to the dominant Western school and cultural tradition and to generated standard testing procedures of linguistic-logical abilities. These have been criticised by interpreters as ignoring cultural and sub-cultural differences when defining what counts as ability, and even as ignoring wider concepts of intelligence in dominant Western cultural circles. But wider objective definitions of intelligence can be and have been developed more recently (Gardner, 1993, with multiple intelligences), as have different models of assessment procedures (Feuerstein, 1979, with cognitive modifiability and dynamic assessment). These broader conceptions and techniques are presented as providing the basis for individually focused, qualitative descriptive assessments. Yet they can be given a more individual, comparative and quantitative treatment from a more purist correlator or 'scientific' position. They can also be criticised as being too objectified and restrictive of the diversity of intelligence – a more purist interpreter position. In contrast, the co-existence position which I have been arguing for recognises the need to balance the objectifying of human abilities with their diverse interpretations relative to cultural contexts. Over this we can expect continuing differences, but at least the co-existence position excludes the untenable purity of what has been called scientism, on one hand, and a slide into the relativism of a radical cultural interpretivism, on the other.

I illustrated in chapters 3 and 4 the extent to which these epistemological issues are played out within psychology generally, and within educational psychology in particular. But they are also central to the field of education studies, though dealt with in different ways in respect to the impact of social and political conditions. For some time there has been continuing government concern about the relevance of social research, which has come to influence the allocation of research funding. This has become especially acute more recently within educational research. The current government wants to find ways of making educational research contribute to the improvement of classroom practice and policy development. This needs to be seen in the context of the consistent hopes and expectations that research will provide the technical solutions to difficult educational problems. These expectations become intensified when governments adopt policies which aim to raise educational standards and take an interest in influencing teaching practices. Educational research can be seen as under threat, and this comes not only from low levels of external funding, but also from internal differences within the education research community. This is where Hargreaves's criticisms of the community are relevant to this chapter (Hargreaves, 1996). What is revealing about his call for a more research-based teaching profession, which draws on evidence-based research on teaching effectiveness, is that it comes from someone who had previously made a notable contribution to more illuminative and interpretive kinds of educational research. His critique of education research is that it is neither cumulative nor relevant enough to teachers' practical concerns. He draws critical comparisons with medical research and the role and use of evidence-based medicine.

I do not intend to discuss this debate about education research in detail in this concluding chapter. But I do want to show how it is part of a continuing debate about the nature of the social sciences, which is pervasive in both education, psychology and other similar disciplines. Hargreaves's non-cumulative critique has some point against once-off studies which do not relate to previous work, but it is not clear how far he is simply promoting a position which adopts the assumptions of hard knowledge or 'positivist' science (cf. Hammersley, 1997). As Hammersley notes, much educational research in this century, especially before the 1960s and 70s, involved the scientific testing of effective teaching. The moves to more interpretive and qualitative styles of research were prompted by unresolved problems with this sort of research. At the core of this current debate is, therefore, the extent to which there can be a causal science of education. That critics like Hargreaves, who can be assumed to know about them, continue to fail to mention these issues illustrates the powerful professional, political and educational forces operating and their conceptual complexity. Hammersley does not deny that some cumulative knowledge about causal relationships can be generated, but he wishes to remind us of the problems with defining teaching in experimental and quantitative designs and measuring important kinds of learning. He also reminds us that educational research can become too focused on generating information which shapes current policy and practice. This point links back to the tensions between science or theory and practice discussed in chapter 4: it will be recalled that two decades ago Hargreaves was critical of educational psychology for being over-responsive to service needs.

This debate can be seen to reflect the continuing question whether teaching can be subjected to a technical analysis; whether research can tell teachers what techniques are best for what kinds of tasks and problems. This is the question, discussed in chapter 2, whether teaching is about generalisable techniques based on action rules which can be derived from research into causal relationships, or whether it is about practices based on judgements in particular situations. Though Hargreaves states that neither education nor medicine involves the simple application of techniques, but rather a skilled process 'in which sophisticated judgement matches a professional decision to the unique needs of each client' (Hargreaves, 1996, p. 1), much of what he asserts seems to contradict this. Hammersley maintains the more historically grounded and comprehensive argument in this debate, by stressing the importance of not setting up a false dichotomy between technical and practical activities in teaching. He asserts that teaching is not a single activity but involves a range of activities along a continuum from technical to practical. Following theorists like Stenhouse (1975), he believes that teaching beyond basic educational skills lies towards the practical end of the continuum. But Hammersley also reminds us that accepting the practical nature of teaching is still compatible with seeing a research contribution. This is the illuminative or enlightenment model of research whereby research generates accounts which challenge and correct assumptions, or reveals hidden aspects of teaching practices.

The contrast between education and medicine in this debate is instructive, partly because it gives a reference point for education in the form of a higher-status professional group which makes greater use of causal science. But it also shows where there may be common ground between the opposing positions. Hargreaves, for example, represents Hammersley as 'taking the view that teaching is not a technical activity, but one which involves judgement' (Hargreaves, 1997, p. 406). That is not Hammersley's position, a fact that Hargreaves seems to recognise later when he refers critically to the continuum idea. Hargreaves wishes to point out the similarities between teaching and medicine in order to model the use of science and research as a professional knowledge base for education. Hammersley wishes to point out the differences in the nature of intervention in teaching and medicine, in terms of differences in the research base of the two professions.

Medicine is based on the biological sciences, which constitute more of a causal science than any science of teaching which identifies causal relationships involving 'symbolic treatments'. Hammersley claims that there are doubts about such a science of teaching. Hargreaves's response is to identify three levels of knowledge base relevant to medicine:

1   at the base, the biological sciences;
2   built on these, the clinical or medical sciences;
3   studies of what works.

He recognises that there may not be a basic science for education, as the biological sciences have been for medicine, but he says that we may yet achieve such a science in the development of cognitive science (Hargreaves, 1997, p. 417). His call for evidence-based teaching is for 'what works with whom under what conditions and with what effects' (p. 414). But it is not clear whether this corresponds to his level 2 (clinical sciences) and/or his level 3 (what works) knowledge base in medicine. I consider that he has no grounds for distinguishing between levels 2 and 3. As I argued in chapter 4 in relation to psychology, there is a general distinction between basic and applied science (levels 1 and 2): applied science involves systematic explanatory and empirical studies of what works with what effects under what conditions. There is no further level of knowledge about what works, other than illustrative case studies, which cannot provide the kind of technical knowledge which Hargreaves is calling for. Hargreaves is correct to point out that doctors use applied clinical scientific knowledge with particular patients, and this calls for complex judgements and decision making. But Hammersley's technical–practical continuum is not about the process of using technical knowledge in particular cases, but about the extent to which we can generate technical effectiveness knowledge given the nature of teaching. It is also worth noting that when doctors' interventions are not at the biological level, but are focused at the psychological level – on mental health troubles – they are confronted by the same issues as teachers. The question is whether psychotherapeutic and counselling actions are equivalent to the technical or practical activities we find in teaching.

Both Hargreaves and Hammersley consider teaching to involve craft/art and science elements. But some confusion arises in the debate, because no distinction is made between the actual practical decision making in relation to a client, whether patient or pupil, and the considerations that enter into the deliberations when these decisions are being made. Both seem to agree that professional judgement based on traditions, personal experiences and intuitions is central to both kinds of professional practice. This judgement and practice involve some creative artist elements. But, while Hargreaves believes that these sophisticated judgement skills can be enhanced by evidence-based knowledge about what works in teaching, Hammersley questions whether we can expect to find the extent of generalised technical know-how sought by Hargreaves for enhancing practice. His approach is based on an analysis of the diverse nature of teaching and its implications for the kinds of knowledge that can inform the practical deliberations of teachers. Hargreaves's approach seems to be responding positively to the calls from current policy makers and practitioners for kinds of research which are only available to a limited degree. Here we have a political context where policy agendas are influencing educationalists to re-examine how far, in what ways and over what time scales research can inform practice. This can be welcomed as introducing incentives to reappraise the nature of the relationship between theory and practice. But, following the themes of this book, I would conclude that it needs to be done in a way which recognises historical and continuing issues and uncertainties about the nature of human phenomena and knowledge about them. Though it is attractive to serve the policy makers and secure short-term influence, the effects can distort the complex nature of the relationship between theory and practice, and even the practical outcomes can be counter-productive.

In supporting a co-existence approach to theoretical models and epistemology in education and psychology, I realise that it will not satisfy the need for closure and definitiveness amongst many who specialise in theory and practice. As I have argued previously in this section, there are links and parallels between value and epistemological diversity. Just as commitment to multiple values means having to resolve tensions by balancing values, so the appreciation that human phenomena can be treated from internal and external perspectives leads to different and rival epistemological positions. The main thrust of the argument in this book is towards the recognition and welcoming of these differences. Tolerance of different knowledge interests is needed by professional and academic communities and individuals specialising in these different traditions. They also need to acknowledge the connections of their knowledge specialisms with other rival specialisms. Scientists need to recognise that objectifying human phenomena in the search for causal relationships cannot eliminate the human subject and find some subject-free, God-like absolute perspective. Scientism needs to be resisted, while pursuing an informed and connected science. Similarly, interpreters need to recognise that in focusing on the particular while seeking to make sense of how others make meaning out of ambiguity and uncertainty, they need to assume some common intersubjective reality so as to avoid the isolation of solipsistic individualism. But the interplay of the competing conceptions and models can also have positive and constructive outcomes for the different specialisms. Idiographic and interpretive studies can suggest phenomena to be defined and subjected to causal analysis, while nomothetic studies of causal relationships can suggest illuminative case studies of the process of meaning-making. Co-existence is therefore presented as promoting constructive tensions between competing models. Its implication for our conception about the nature of teaching is to affirm a limited scientific basis, but one which respects artistic elements in professional practice. This is where Gage's notion of the science of the art of teaching is relevant (Gage, 1985). But experience has shown that not all educational research is relevant to teaching by providing action rules from applied science; some is relevant to practice through being illuminative. A constructive tension will be maintained by avoiding the purism of objectivism or subjectivism: by recognising the interrelationships between the particular and the general, and between what is humanly constructed and what is 'given'.

The distinctive contribution of educational psychology

In the last section I explored epistemological diversity and value balancing in relation to, and from the perspective of, education. In this section I will return to the position of psychology in relation to education. I have set out in figure 5 the broad elements by which psychologists using their theoretical and practitioner knowledge interact with educationalists and their theoretical and practical knowledge, and how both relate to teachers and their professional discourse and knowledge. The figure also sets these relationships in interaction with policy makers and their prescriptions and procedures.

The figure represents these broad professional groups schematically in their institutional spheres. The psychologists and educationalists have university and training bases for their intellectual fields as well as their professional associations. In the case of psychologists this also includes psychology services which are involved in in-service teacher training. And of course there are some educationalists who are also psychologists. The various areas of psychology (educational psychology in both research and practitioner areas, and other areas of psychology relevant to education) are presented to educationalists, to teachers and to policy makers involved in education at central and local government. This is through the medium of courses, workshops, conferences and written texts. For educationalists this might be in relation to various areas, such as special educational needs, personal and social education, literacy, etc. As I suggested in chapter 4, the influence of psychologists on teachers can be either direct or indirect through the interchange between psychologists and educationalists. Though two-way, this impact has been stronger from psychologists to educationalists than the other way round. The direct influence of psychologists on teachers, though weakened in initial training, has persisted in in-service training from practising and academic educational psychologists, as well as from other kinds of psychologists. As regards the relationship between psychologists and policy

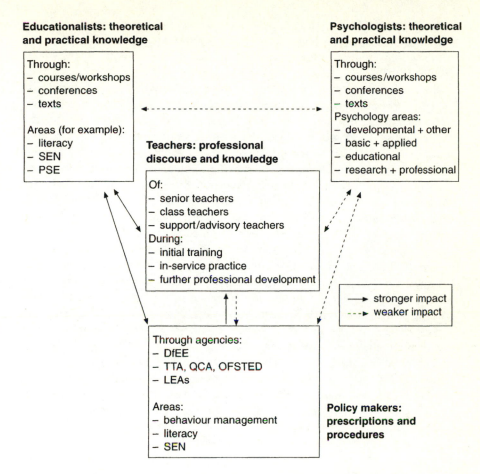

Educationalists: theoretical and practical knowledge

Through:
- courses/workshops
- conferences
- texts

Areas (for example):
- literacy
- SEN
- PSE

Psychologists: theoretical and practical knowledge

Through:
- courses/workshops
- conferences
- texts
Psychology areas:
- developmental + other
- basic + applied
- educational
- research + professional

Teachers: professional discourse and knowledge

Of:
- senior teachers
- class teachers
- support/advisory teachers
During:
- initial training
- in-service practice
- further professional development

→ stronger impact
--→ weaker impact

Through agencies:
- DfEE
- TTA, QCA, OFSTED
- LEAs

Areas:
- behaviour management
- literacy
- SEN

Policy makers: prescriptions and procedures

Figure 5 Relationships between educationalists, psychologists, policy makers and teachers

makers, the impact on central government agencies may be weaker now than it was in the early part of the twentieth century. But in local government it has continued through the work of educational psychology services and psychologists moving into officer and inspector positions. But just as psychologists' influence on teachers is through educationalists, so is their influence on policy makers. There have been some notable recent examples of ideas and practices with their origins in psychology which have come to influence policy through their uptake and promotion by educationalists: two of them are reading recovery in the literacy area and behavioural techniques in the special educational needs area. Stainthorp (1997), for example, has noted that the new National Literacy framework and the Teacher Training Agency's training curriculum for English have drawn heavily on recent theoretical models of reading and literacy generated by psychologists. These contributions, however, tend to remain unattributed to psychology.

I have represented teachers as distinct from educationalists in that their professional knowledge is less explicit and more part of their everyday professional discourse. They are influenced by educationalists at the initial and in-service training stages, and especially (at present) by policy prescriptions and procedures. But much of their discourse and knowledge reflects the conditions of their work, which does not give enough time for explicit analytic formulations of their knowledge and understanding. This is a point which can be easily overlooked in the plans to make teaching a more research-based profession. Though this picture of psychologists in relation to education puts psychology in a fairly weak position, it must be remembered that while educationalists may have more direct channels of communication with teachers and policy makers, they have also been subject to major policy interventions. They have been cast at times by some policy makers as the source of the problems in education, not as leaders offering solutions. But the persistent questions for educational psychologists is whether they have enough of a distinctive contribution to make to education to justify their current positions in university education departments and in the education service. I have set out in figure 6 seven broad areas where educational psychologists make their current contribution.

This analysis shows where the contributions of practising educational psychologists and academic research and teaching educational psychologists overlap. Given the long-standing divisions between the two branches of this applied area of psychology, it is relevant to note at least five common areas: teacher education and training, policy advice, human resources consultation and interventions, research and publications. However, only teacher education and training constitute a major part of the work of both groups. The groups also undertake these common activities in different spheres. Academic educational psychologists are involved in some initial teacher training and higher degree in-service courses, while practitioners are mainly concerned with local in-service courses. Policy advice, which is a minor part of both groups' work, tends to be for local government by practitioners, but for local and sometimes for central government by academics. Research by practitioners tends to focus on evaluating service and development matters, while academic educational psychologists are also involved in applied and sometimes basic research. This overlap reinforces the points made in chapter 4 that given the relatively small numbers of these representatives of educational psychology compared to teachers and other educationalists, they would do well to forge better working links with each other. This is especially important in view of concerns about their future occupational security. It is a point which continues to be made by other educational psychologists (Lindsay, 1998; Lunt, 1998).

But, as I argued in chapter 4, educational psychologists, whether academic or practising, need to make distinctive contributions which arise from

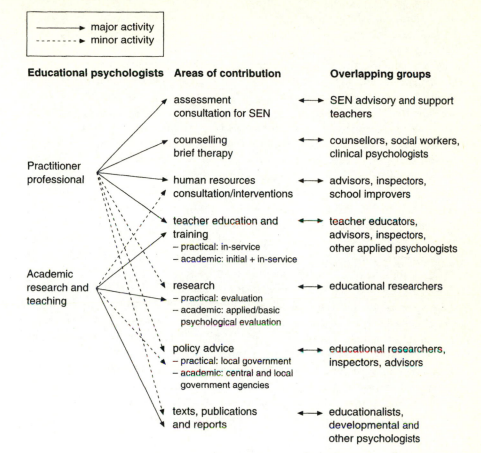

Figure 6 Contributions of educational psychologists to education and overlap with the work of educational and other professional groups

psychology and cannot simply be done by specialist teachers, other educational practitioners or other psychologists. The problem for applied and professional psychologists wanting to 'do psychology' is that their professional activity is defined in terms of knowledge and understanding of human experience and action. It is defined primarily in terms of theory, whether as causal explanations or interpretations. It is not like education or medicine, which are defined in terms of practical goals. Unlike education, which is a practical field (with educational theory as practical theory concerned with means and ends), psychology is a basic field of knowledge whether cast in causal scientific or some other mode of thought. I have argued that its practical field, applied and practitioner psychology, may have had a long history of ideas and techniques which arose in different practical fields, but it has also derived more recently from applying basic psychology. Nevertheless, practical psychological work overlaps significantly with the work of other professionals in these various practice areas. In education, the overlaps go back to the origins of educational psychology, but with other changes there have been changing overlaps.

Starting with practising educational psychologists and their main involvement in the assessment of and consultation over special educational needs, I have already commented on how this overlaps with the work of SEN advisory and support teachers, based in schools and in LEA teams. However, professional educational psychologists have a distinctive and protected role in advising LEAs about whether to issue a statement of SEN. I have suggested that there needs to be a thorough review of the statementing process with a view to reducing, but not eliminating, this protected psychological assessment. This would enable psychologists to provide more distinctively psychologically based assessments which cannot be easily replaced by external generic educational assessments done by special needs teachers. This would also enable professional educational psychologists to train to broaden their work beyond special educational needs. They could specialise more in counselling and brief therapies and human resources consultations and interventions. But even here these two areas of work are and can be done by other professionals. Counsellors, social workers and clinical psychologists can and do undertake counselling and therapy work, while advisors, inspectors and school improvement consultants can and do undertake human resources consultations and interventions. In the three other areas of professional educational psychologists' work we also find overlaps with other professional groups. In-service training as done by psychologists can be and is being done by advisors, inspectors and other teacher educators and trainers. Evaluative research work can be and is being done by educational researchers from various different settings, and policy advice at LEA level is central to the work of educational researchers, inspectors and advisors.

It is possible to conceive of a review of the work of professional educational psychologists which switches the funds spent on educational psychology services into the training and employment of an enlarged SEN advisory and support service. This could provide the generic external assessments needed by LEAs. Professional psychologists could work within such a support and assessment service, as some psychology graduates already work in SEN support services. Money would be released to purchase more counselling services and the human resource work, teacher training and research work could be covered by expanding the role of inspectors, advisors, consultants, teacher educators and educational researchers. My purpose in considering this is not to recommend the simple abandoning of professional educational psychology, but to raise the question whether the professional knowledge and skills of educational psychologists require a distinct educational psychology service and professional identity. This is prompted by the desire to find better ways in which educational psychology can develop. Underlying these issues is the question whether professional educational psychology is closer to education or to psychology. Under the current system of training and entry into the profession, professional educational psychologists are in the unique position of needing dual qualifications and experience, in teaching and psychology. If the professional group were to move closer to psychology it would no longer require teaching qualifications (though it could retain the need for prior experience of education service settings), and it would share in more generic applied psychology training. This would bring it closer to other applied psychology practices such as clinical, health and occupational psychologies, and enable it to broaden beyond its current specialisation in special educational needs. This might mean that it would focus less on curriculum and teaching matters and more on social-emotional, professional support, family and training matters. But the major determinant of its role is the future of the statutory work for LEAs in identifying significant difficulties in learning. The funding base for professional training is also important, as this is currently dependent on government recognition of the statutory SEN role. Unless government can be convinced that the education service needs the more broadly based services of educational psychologists with a reduced statutory SEN assessment role, the funding base for initial training will be threatened.

Gale has proposed a radical reconstruction of educational psychology (discussed in chapter 4) which maps out an integration of psychological provision based round schools or institutes of psychology (Gale, 1997). This proposal is modelled on medical schools which have a university base but incorporate hospitals across an area. The idea is to bring together under such an organisation undergraduate and post-graduate research and professional training psychology courses, different kinds of psychology research and the provision of psychology services to the various public services and to commerce and industry. This is a model of professional educational psychology which is closer to other applied psychologies, is better connected to basic and applied research relevant to education, and is no longer based in LEA educational psychology services. It assumes that the demand for professional educational psychology services outside the educational psychology training schools will come from other schools, which is consistent with these schools having charge of their own finances. But whether LEAs would purchase these outside professional educational services for statutory SEN assessments or other needs depends again on the future of the SEN identification and resource allocation system. It also depends on whether LEAs would want to continue to employ their own educational psychologists.

It is clear from this discussion that the professional base and balance of work for professional educational psychologists is open to several radical alternatives. But what is important, whatever their work base or specialisation, is that professional educational psychologists retain and develop new practices which are based on continuing links with applied and basic psychology. Otherwise their direct work with children, teachers and parents will no longer be distinctive compared to the other educational professionals, as set out in figure 6. This distinctive role is also undermined because part of educational psychology practice is the training of teachers and others in educationally relevant psychological ideas and methods. There are also other channels of dissemination into education, as outlined earlier in this section. The other way of retaining a distinctive contribution is to confine the use of certain kinds of techniques to professional psychologists, as is done with particular types of ability tests. This is a well-known form of professional protectionism, which can be justified if the value of the procedures can be justified and an intensive and lengthy training is required to avoid misuse. This is, however, a line of justification which is not open to those practitioners who have doubts about making any use of these ability tests. There is also the question why specialist teachers cannot be given the necessary intensive training to use and interpret the tests, without becoming professional psychologists. But there is another line of justification for the distinctive contribution of professional educational psychologists, which does not look for a genuinely unique area of specialism. It is to see the distinctive contribution in the unique pattern of different kinds of work which professional educational psychologists can provide. I have represented six broad specialist areas, all of which are or could be provided by other professional groups. But there is not one other specialist group in education which can offer this range and have the links with a different but connected discipline and professional practice outside education. Here lies the uniqueness of professional educational psychologists. However, this can only be a genuine uniqueness if professional psychologists have broad links with their psychology base and are appropriately trained in the relevant professional skills so as to provide this range of specialisms. And that depends on central and local governments being willing to review the SEN statutory assessment needs and educational psychologists' role in the in-service identification of SEN.

Figure 6 also shows the five areas of work of psychologists who work in university departments of education which can be and are also carried out by other professional groups. In the main area of initial and in-service teacher training and education, some of this work can be carried out by teacher educators, advisors and inspectors. If more psychologically focused teaching is required, then this can be done by psychologists based in university psychology departments. Similarly, for research work, other researchers can and do carry out similar kinds of research. Evaluation research into education practices and evaluation of educational developments are central to the work of non-psychologist educational researchers, especially as quantitative research methods have become well established within educational research. Science-to-technique psychology research and the empirical testing of psychology theory in educational contexts can be and is done by developmental and other psychologists based in university psychology departments. The other main activity of psychologists in university departments of education – the publication of texts and reports – is related to research and teaching activities and can also be done by educationalists and other psychologists.

The two minor activities of policy advice and human resource consultation can similarly be covered by other educational researchers, inspectors, advisors and school improvers.

Gale's model of a more integrated psychology based round university schools or institutes of psychology, putting educational psychology closer to other areas of basic, applied and professional psychology, would also undermine the position of psychologists in education departments. These schools of psychology could employ research and teaching educational psychologists and sell their services to university departments of education, as they would sell the services of professional educational psychologists to LEAs or schools. This would mean that education departments might no longer need to employ educational psychologists as psychologists, as their interest would be in specialists in (for example) SEN, literacy or personal and social education. Such specialists may be psychologists, but they will not be employed as psychologists: specialists in these education areas would not need to have direct psychology qualifications, though psychology would be relevant to their educational specialism. From the perspective of university departments of education, it would depend whether they wanted teaching and educational research services from psychologists based within their departments or purchased from psychology departments. But whichever organisational arrangement is preferred, what is more important, especially with the decline in the number of psychologists and in the contribution of psychology in educational departments, is whether educationalists value the contribution of psychology to education. One of the main messages of this book is that education is connected to and therefore needs psychology. With respect to teacher training and education, the position of this book is similar to that of Notterman and Drewry (1993), two US educational psychologists who represent psychology and education as parallel but interacting fields which should be respectful of each other and which should be brought together. Their view is that 'It is unquestionably reasonable that for those who teach, included in the grasp of what the process involves should be a sound knowledge about psychological theory and its implications for the teaching–learning process' (Notterman and Drewry, 1993, p. 6).

On this basis psychology should be a required part of professional education programmes whether this is at the initial and/or the in-service stage. As chapter 4 indicated, there are strong economic and professional factors operating here, but it is important to establish needs and principles, even if they cannot be put into operation easily.

But education also needs research which is both educational and psychological, when educational techniques are developed from psychology applications. It also needs to welcome psychological research which generates psychological theory from questions and issues which arise from education practice, and which tests psychological theory in education contexts. These kinds of psychology-led research maintain the interaction between the fields and can also have positive spin-offs for education. However, the question here is whether there is a need for a group of educational psychologists or psychologists in education who specialise in teaching and research. As with professional educational psychologists, the question is whether their work could be taken over and incorporated into expanded allied groups. This is an important question for educationalists, particularly as many have psychology backgrounds and have diversified their interests into educational areas, being less actively involved in 'doing psychology'. My position here, as on professional educational psychologists, is that although there is no one unique activity which these psychologists do compared to educationalists and other psychologist groups, the combination of the pattern of their teacher training, research, policy advice, publications and consultation work forms a unique contribution. But, as with professional educational psychologists, for this to be a genuine contribution, these educational psychologists need to maintain strong links with basic psychology overall and to make better connections with professional educational psychologists, with whom they have so much in common. This depends on the support from other psychologists in psychology departments and from educationalists in education departments. What needs to be avoided is the kind of marginalising at the borders and overlapping between disciplines that Campbell (1969) identified as the outcome of excessive disciplinary ethnocentrism.

Concluding comments

Writing this book has been a project with personal significance, as my motives for undertaking it come partly from my personal position as someone who has struggled to make sense of his professional interests in psychology and education. In the process of writing the book I have worked at clarifying and developing ideas while I was preparing, planning and actually doing the writing and reviewing of the text. For me it has been a slow but satisfying process of sorting out confusions, coming to understand and appreciate new and different arguments and positions. My wish is that reading the book will also be useful and intellectually stimulating for the reader – though I know that many readers may have started with this last chapter. For them, it may have been easier to start by leaving out the detail in the middle chapters. But I hope they will consider going through the middle chapters too.

I have been challenged to find the right words when asked by colleagues, friends and family to explain the contents of and reason for writing the book. I have not found this easy, tending to say that it is about psychology and about education and how they relate to each other, which may sound fairly dry and abstract. I also realise that my style has been detailed and critical in examining different conceptions about education and psychology in order to show their inherent connections, but also their differences. This has led me to deal with some basic human questions about what we can know and what we value about human well-being and fulfilment. My wish is that my attempt to deal with these in an open and critical way has not obscured my passionate commitment to the fields I have analysed. When I explain the contents in more detail to others, I also refer to the main themes and it is these which capture the essence of the book: that psychology and education are connective specialisms and that education involves multiple values which require balancing. This means that we have to confront ideological or value dilemmas and impurity, that there is no avoiding of the diverse natures of education and psychology which arise from epistemological uncertainty, that there is value in epistemological co-existence and that exclusive positions deny connections and pose false oppositions.

If I were pressed about what all this means for teachers, educationalists, psychologists and others interested in human and social development and well-being, I would say this. In being committed and enthusiastic we need to be analytic and cope with uncertainty, while being mindful of the difficulties of finding and maintaining a balance. I have been impressed over a long period by Kurt Lewin's dictum that 'there is nothing as practical as a good theory' (Lewin, 1951). But I have come to realise that what we call a good theory comes to reflect our own, sometimes hidden, professional culture and background, unless we can move beyond them. Since my background is in psychology, I tended to see this as meaning good scientific psychology theory. Now I realise the restricted nature of this perspective. What is good theory is itself problematic, both within the different disciplines relevant to our human and social practices, and between them. Though psychology and education are political in the sense of depending on values and practices over which there are differences and conflicts of interest, they are prone to being pressed into the short-term and narrow service of party political needs. This can have restrictive and damaging effects on these practices and the thinking which informs and sustains them. When we search for the causes of our current social, personal and educational problems we should consider more than the 'usual suspects' and look at how we frame and attribute these problems. We would do well to consider our different ideals and ways of knowing. We should examine the degree to which they are contrary and compatible and then find honest and practicable ways of seeking to integrate them.

References

AEP (1995) *Pressures on educational psychology services and educational psychologists in England and Wales*. National Perspective Paper. Durham: Association of Educational Psychologists.

AEP/DECP (1996) *Statutory advice to the LEA: guidance for educational psychologists*. Durham: Association of Educational Psychologists; Division of Educational and Child Psychology.

Ainscow, M. and Tweddle, D. (1978) *Preventing classroom failure: an objectives approach*. Chichester: Wiley.

Alexander, R. (1992) *Policy and practice in primary education*. London: Routledge.

Allport, G.W. (1961) *Patterns and growth in personality*. New York: Holt, Rinehart, and Winston.

Allyon, T. and Azrin, N.H. (1968) *The token economy: a motivation system for therapy and rehabilitation*. New York: Appleton-Century-Crofts.

Ausubel, D. (1978) *Educational psychology*. New York: Holt, Rinehart, and Winston.

Bain, A. (1922) *Education as a science*. London: Kegan Paul, Trench, Trouber and Co.

Bandura, A. (1977) *Social learning theory*. Englewood Cliffs, N.J.: Prentice Hall.

Barber, M. (1996) *The learning game*. London: Victor Gollancz.

—— (1997) *The implementation of the National Literacy Strategy*. London: DfEE.

Becher, T. (1989) *Academic tribes and territories: intellectual inquiries and the cultures of disciplines*. Buckingham: SRHE and Open University Press.

Belbin, E. (1979) 'Applicable psychology and some national problems'. *Bulletin of the British Psychological Society*, 33, 241–244.

Bem, S. and de Jong, H.L. (1997) *Theoretical issues in psychology: an introduction*. London: Sage.

Berlak, A. and Berlack, H. (1981) *Dilemmas of schooling: teaching and social change*. London: Methuen.

Berlin, I. (1990) *The crooked timber of humanity*. London: Fontana Press.

Bernstein, B. (1990) *The structuring of pedagogic discourse: class, codes and control*. Vol. 4. London: Routledge.

Bhaskar, R. (1979) *The possibility of naturalism*. London: Harvester Press.

Bigge, M.L. (1987) *Learning theories for teachers*. New York: Harper and Row.

Biggs, J.B. and Moore, P.J. (1993) *The processes of learning*. Englewood Cliffs, N.J.: Prentice Hall.

Billig, M., Conder, S., Edwards, D., Gane, M., Middleton, D. and Radley, A. (1988) *Ideological dilemmas: a social psychology of everyday thinking*. London: Sage.

Brewin, C. (1993) *Cognitive foundations of clinical psychology*. London: Lawrence Erlbaum.

Broadbent, D.E. (1973) *In defence of empirical psychology*. London: Methuen.

Broadfoot, P. and Pollard, A. (1997) 'PACE and Bernstein's pedagogic device: from competence to performance'. York: symposium paper given at British Education Research Association Conference.

Bruner, J. (1976) 'The ontogenesis of speech acts'. *Journal of Child Language*, 2, 1–19.

—— (1997) *The culture of education*. Cambridge, Mass.: Harvard University Press.

Budoff, M., Meskin, J. and Harrison, R.H. (1971) 'Educational test of learning potential hypothesis'. *American Journal of Mental Deficiency*, 72, 404–411.

Burden, R.L. (1992) 'Educational psychology: a force that is spent or one that never got going?' *The Psychologist*, 5, 3, 10–11.

—— (1994) 'Trends and developments in educational psychology'. *School Psychology International, Special Edition*, 15, 293–347.

Burden, R.L. and Hornby, T.A. (1989) 'Assessing classroom ethos: some promising developments for the systems oriented educational psychologist'. *Educational Psychology in Practice*, 5, 1, 17–22.

Burkitt, I. (1991) *Social selves: theories of the social formation of personality*. London: Sage.

Burman, E. (1994) *Deconstructing developmental psychology*. London: Routledge.

Burns, R. (1982) *Self concept, development and education*. London: Holt Education.

Burt, C. (1937) *The backward child*. London: University of London Press.

—— (1962) 'Francis Galton and his contribution to psychology'. *British Journal of Statistical Psychology*, 15, 39–42.

Campbell, D.T. (1969) 'Ethnocentrism of disciplines and the fish-scale model of omniscience', in Sherif, M. and Sherif, C. (eds.) *Interdisciplinary relationships in the social sciences*. Chicago: Aldine.

Carr, W. (1989) 'The idea of an educational science'. *Journal of the Philosophy of Education*, 23, 3, 29–37.

Cattell, R.B. (1937) *The fight for our national intelligence*. London: King.

Chomsky, N. (1959) 'Review of B.F. Skinner's *Verbal Behaviour*'. *Language*, 35, 26–58.

Clark, C., Dyson, A., Millward, A.J. and Skidmore, D. (1997) *New directions in special needs: innovations in mainstream schools*. London: Cassell.

Claxton, G., Swann, W., Salmon, P., Walkerdine, V., Jacobsen, B. and White, J. (1985) *Psychology and schooling: what's the matter?* Bedford Way Paper 25. London: Institute of Education, London University.

Cline, T. (1992) *The assessment of special educational needs: international perspectives*. London: Routledge.

Crews, F. (1997) *The memory wars: Freud's legacy in dispute*. London: Granta Books.

Davidson, D. (1980) 'Psychology as philosophy', in Davidson, D. (ed.) *Essays on actions and events*. Oxford: Oxford University Press.

Davidson, M.A. (1977) 'The scientific/applied debate in psychology: a contribution'. *Bulletin of the British Psychological Society*, 30, 273–278.

Dawkins, R. (1989) *The selfish gene*. Oxford: Oxford University Press.

Dearing, R. (1993) *The national curriculum and its assessment. An interim report*. London: National Curriculum Council and Schools Examination and Assessment Council.

DECP (1994) *Core curriculum for initial training courses in educational psychology*. Leicester: DECP/BPS.

Dennett, D. (1995) *Darwin's dangerous idea: evolution and the meanings of life.* Harmondsworth: Penguin.

—— (1996) *Kinds of minds: towards an understanding of consciousness.* London: Weidenfeld and Nicolson.

DES (1978) *Special educational needs.* Warnock Report. Cmnd 7212. London: HMSO.

—— (1990) *Psychological services in England.* Report by HMI. London: DES.

Desforges, C. (1985) 'Training for the management of learning in the primary school', in Francis, 1985.

Dessent, T. (1992) 'Educational psychologists and the "case for individual casework" ' in Wolfendale, S., Byrans, T., Fox, M., Labran, A., and Sigston, A. (eds.) *The profession and practice of educational psychology: future directions.* London: Cassell.

DfEE (1997) *Excellence for all children: meeting special educational needs.* London: Green Paper. London: HMSO.

—— (1998a) *Meeting special educational needs: a programme of action.* London: DfEE Publications Office.

—— (1998b) *Excellence in research on schools.* Research Report no. 74. (Hillage Report). London: DfEE Publications Office.

Dewey, J. (1929) *The sources of a science of education.* New York: Horace Liveright.

—— (1934) *Art as experience.* New York: Minton, Blach and Co.

Dixon, N.F. (1981) *Preconscious processes.* London: Wiley.

Donaldson, M. (1978) *Children's minds.* London: Fontana.

Doyle, W. and Ponder, D.A. (1977) 'The practicality ethic in teacher decision-making'. *Interchange*, 8, 3, 1–12.

Dweck, C. (1986) 'Motivational processes affecting learning'. *American Psychologist*, 41, 1040–1048.

Edelman, G. (1992) *Bright air, brilliant fire: on the matter of the mind.* Harmondsworth: Penguin.

Edwards, D. and Mercer, N.M. (1987) *Common knowledge: the development of understanding in the classroom.* London: Methuen.

Egan, K. (1983) *Education and psychology: Plato, Piaget and scientific psychology.* London: Methuen.

—— (1997) *The educated mind: how cognitive tools shape our understanding.* Chicago: University of Chicago Press.

Eisner, E. (1979) 'On the art of teaching', in *The educational imagination.* London: Macmillan.

Eraut, M. (1995) 'Schon shock: a case for reframing reflection-in-action?' *Teachers and Teaching: Theory and Practice*, 1, 1, 9–22.

Esland, G. (1977) *Diagnosis and testing, unit 21. Schooling and society.* Milton Keynes: Open University.

Eysenck, H.J. (1972) *Psychology is about people.* Harmondsworth: Penguin.

—— (1985) *Decline and fall of the Freudian empire.* Harmondsworth: Viking.

Farr, R. (1987) 'The science of mental life: a social psychological perspective'. *Bulletin of the British Psychological Society*, 40, 1–17.

Fenstermacher, G.D. (1988) 'The place of science and epistemology in Schon's conception of reflective practice,' in Grimnet, P.P. and Erikson, E.L. (eds.) *Reflections in teacher education.* New York: Teachers College Press.

Feuerstein, R. (1979) *The dynamic assessment of retarded performers: the learning potential assessment device, theory, instruments and techniques.* Philadelphia, Penn.: University Park Press.

Feyerabend, P.K. (1975) *Against method*. London: NLB.

Finegold, D. (1993) 'Breaking out of the low skill equilibrium', in *Briefings for the National Commission on Education*. London: Heinemann.

Fletcher, R. (1991) *Science, ideology and the media: the Cyril Burt scandal*. New Brunswick, N.J.: Transactions Publishers.

Fontana, D. (1995) *Psychology for teachers*. London: Macmillan, BPS Books.

—— (1996) 'A role for psychology in teacher education? Comments on Hazel Francis's paper'. *Education Section Review*, 20, 2, 6–8.

Foucault, M. (1980) 'Truth and power', in *Power/knowledge: selected interviews and other writings, 1972–77*. Brighton: Harvester Press.

Francis, H. (1984) *Minds of their own*. Inaugural lecture. London: Institute of Education, London University.

—— (ed.) (1985) *Learning to teach: psychology in teacher education*. London: Falmer Press.

—— (1989) *Individual approaches to learning*. London: FEU Report.

—— (1993) *Teachers listening to learners' voices*. Vernon-Wall Lecture. Leicester: BPS Education Section.

—— (1995) *Reflections on psychology and education*. A valedictory lecture. London: Institute of Education. London University.

—— (1996) 'Role for psychology in initial teacher education?' *Education Section Review*, 20, 2, 2–4.

Frederickson, N., Webster, A. and Wright, A. (1991) 'Psychological assessment: a change of emphasis'. *Educational Psychology in Practice*, 7, 1, 20–29.

Freire, P. (1973) *Education for a critical consciousness*. New York: Continuum.

Fromm, E. (1939) 'Historical and ethical psychoanalysis: selfishness and self-love', in Reutenbeck, H.M. (ed.) *Varieties of Personality Theory*. New York: Dutton.

—— (1956) *The sane society*. London: Routledge and Kegan Paul.

Gage, N.L. (1985) *Hard gains in the soft sciences: the case of pedagogy*. Bloomington Indiana: CEDR Monograph.

—— (1991) 'The obviousness of social and educational research results'. *Educational Researcher*, Jan.–Feb. 10–16.

—— (1996) 'Confronting counsels of despair for the behavioural sciences'. *Educational Researcher*, April, 5–15.

Gale, T. (1993) 'A task analysis of educational psychology: is educational psychology up to the task?' in Lunt, I. (ed.) *Whither educational psychology? Challenges and changes for the future of our profession*. Leicester: DECP/BPS.

—— (1997) 'The reconstruction of British psychology'. *The Psychologist*, 10, 1, 11–15.

Gammage, P. (1996) 'A role for psychology in initial teacher education'. *Education Section Review*, 20, 2, 5–6.

Gardner, H. (1993) *The unschooled mind: how children think and how schools should learn*. London: HarperCollins.

Gergen, G. (1985) 'The social constructionist movement in modern psychology'. *American Psychologist*, 40, 266–275.

Gillham, B. (1978) *Reconstructing educational psychology*. London: Croom Helm.

Gillie, O. (1978) 'Sir Cyril Burt and the great IQ fraud'. *New Statesman* November 24, 688–694.

Gipps, C. (1994) *Beyond testing: towards a theory of educational assessment*. London: Falmer Press.

Goodman, P. (1964) *Compulsory mis-education*. Harmondsworth: Penguin.

Gregory, P. (1993) 'Two decades of EP work: progress or just change?' *Educational Psychology in Practice*, 9, 2, 67–72.

Grey, J. (1981) *Four psychologists on psychology*. DS 262. Milton Keynes: Open University.

Guthke, J. and Wingenfeld, S. (1992) 'The learning tests concept: origins, state of the art and trends', in Haywood, H.C. and Tzuriel, D. (eds.) *Interactive assessment*. London: Springer-Verlag.

Habermas, J. (1978) *Knowledge and human interest*. London: Heinemann Education.

Hammersley, M. (1989) *The dilemma of qualitative method*. London: Routledge.

—— (1993) 'Opening up the quantitative–qualitative divide'. Paper given at the BPS Education Section Conference.

—— (1997) 'Educational research and teaching: a response to David Hargreaves' TTA lecture'. *British Educational Research Journal*, 23, 2, 141–161.

Handy, J.A. (1987) 'Psychology and social context'. *Bulletin of British Psychological Society*, 40, 161–167.

Hargreaves, D. (1978) 'The proper study of educational psychology'. *Association of Educational Psychologists' Journal*, 4, 9, 3–8.

—— (1986) *Psychology and teaching: a view from the side lines*. Vernon-Wall Lecture. Leicester: Education Section of the British Psychological Society.

—— (1996) *Teaching as research based profession: possibilities and prospects*. London: TTA Annual Lecture.

—— (1997) 'In defence of research for evidence-based teaching: a rejoinder to Martin Hammersley'. *British Educational Research Journal*, 23, 4, 405–419.

Harre, R. (1972) *Philosophies of science*. Chicago: Chicago University Press.

—— (1995) 'Discursive psychology', in Smith et al., 1995.

Harre, R., Clark, D. and De Carlo, N. (1985) *Motives and mechanisms: an introduction to the psychology of action*. London: Methuen.

Harrington, B. (1989) 'Alexander Bain: a reappraisal.' *History of Education Society Bulletin*, 44, 46–51.

Hearnshaw, L.S. (1979) *Cyril Burt*. London: Hodder and Stoughton.

—— (1987) *The shaping of modern psychology*. London: Methuen.

Herbart, J.F. (1802) *The science of education: its general principles deduced from its aims and the aesthetic revelation of the world*. London: Swann Sonnenschein.

Hernstein, R.J. and Murray, C. (1994) *The bell curve: intelligence and class structure in American life*. New York: Free Press.

Hilgard, E.R. (1970) 'A perspective on the relationship between learning theory and educational practices', in Stones, E. (ed.) *Readings in educational psychology: learning and teaching*. London: Methuen.

Hirst, P.H. (1983) 'Educational theory', in Hirst, P.H. (ed.) *Educational theory and its foundation disciplines*. London: Routledge and Kegan Paul.

Hobsbawm, E. (1997) *On history*. London: Weidenfeld and Nicolson.

Holt, J. (1964) *How children fail*. London: Pitman Publishing.

Hunt, E.B. (1987) 'Science, technology and intelligence', in Ronning, R.R., Glover, J.A., Conoley, J.C. and Witt, J.C. (eds.) *The influence of cognitive psychology on testing*. Hillsdale, N.J.: L. Erlbaum Associates.

Illich, I. (1971) *Deschooling society*. London: Harper.

Ingleby, D. (1985) 'Professionals as socialisers: the "psy complex"', in Scull, A. and Spitzer, S. (eds.) *Research in law, deviance and social control*, vol. 7. New York: JAI Press.

—— (1986) 'Development in social context', in Richards, M. and Light, P. (eds.) *Children of social worlds*. London: Polity Press.

James, W. (1899) *Talks to teachers on psychology and to students on some of life's ideals*. London: Longmans Green.

Joynson, R.B. (1989) *The Burt affair*. London: Routledge.

Judge, H. (1981) 'Dilemmas in education'. *Journal of Child Psychology and Psychiatry*, 22, 111–116.

Kaufman, A.S. (1979) *Intelligent testing with the WISC-R*. London: Wiley.

Kay, J. (1998) 'Good business: adapted inaugural lecture at Oxford University Said Business School'. *Prospect*, March, 25–29.

Kelly, A.V. (1989) *The curriculum, theory and practice*. 3rd edn. London: Paul Chapman.

Keynes, J.M. (1936) *General theory of employment, interest and money*. London: Macmillan.

Knoff, H.M. and Batsche, G.M. (1991) 'Integrating educational psychology to meet the educational and mental health needs of all children'. *Educational Psychologist*, 26, 2, 167–183.

Knox, H.M. (1962) 'Simon Somerville Laurie'. *British Journal of Educational Studies*, 10, 138–152.

Koch, S. (1959) *Psychology: a study of a science*. New York: McGraw-Hill.

Koestler, A. (1972) 'Beyond atomism and holism – the concept of the holon', in Koestler, A. and Smythies, J.R. (eds.) *Beyond reductionism. The Alpbach Symposium*. London: Radius Books.

Kohut, H. (1978) *The psychology of the self: a casebook*, (ed.) A. Goldberg. New York: International Universities Press.

Kuhn, T.S. (1970) *The structure of scientific revolutions*. 2nd edn. Chicago: Chicago University Press.

Kyriacou, C. (1986) *Effective teaching in schools*. London: Routledge.

Lakatos, I. (1970) 'Falsification and the methodology of scientific research programmes', in Lakatos, I. and Mulgrave, A. (eds.) *Criticism and the growth of knowledge*. Cambridge: Cambridge University Press.

Lawton, D. (1989) *Education, culture and the National Curriculum*. London: Hodder and Stoughton.

Lewin, K. (1951) *Field theory in the social sciences*. Chicago: University of Chicago Press.

Lindsay, G. (1988) 'Educational psychology: a critical view from a practitioner'. *Education and Child Psychology*, 5, 1, 23–32.

—— (1991) 'The educational psychologist in the new era', in Lindsay, G. and Miller, A. (eds.) *Psychological services for the primary school*. London: Longman.

—— (1995) 'Values, ethics and psychology'. *The Psychologist*, 8, 493–498.

—— (1998) 'The practice of educational psychology: partnerships in the development of theory and practice'. *The Psychology of Education Review*, 22, 1, 4–11.

Lindsay, G. and Lunt, I. (1993) 'The challenge of change'. *The Psychologist*, 6, 210–213.

Lindsay, G., Quayle, R., Lewis, G. and Jessop, C. (1990) *Special educational needs review 1990*. Sheffield: City of Sheffield Education Service.

Lokke, C., Gersch, I. and Frederickson, N. (1997) 'The resurrection of psychometrics: fact or fiction?' *Educational Psychology in Practice*, 12, 4, 222–233.

Lunt, I. (1993) 'Training applied psychologists in education: future trends and directions', in Lunt I. (ed.) *Whither educational psychology? Challenges and changes for the future of our profession*. Leicester: DECP/BPS.

—— (1996) 'The role of psychological theory in the training of educational psychologists'. PhD, Institute of Education, London University.

—— (1998) 'Why so tenuous? The links between academic and professional educational psychology'. *The Psychology of Education Review*, 22, 1, 4–11.

Lunt, I. and Farrell, P. (1994) 'Restructuring educational psychology training in the UK'. *The Psychologist*, 7, 6, 268–271.

MacBeath, J. (1998) 'The intelligent school'. *Education Review* (special edition): *A curriculum for the 21st century*, 11, 2, 68–73.

MacDonald Ross, M. (1975) 'Behavioural objectives: a critical review', in Golby, M., Greenwald, J. and West, R. (eds.) *Curriculum design*. London: Croom Helm.

McGilchrest, B., Myers, K. and Reed, J. (1997) *The intelligent school*. London: Paul Chapman.

Maliphant, R. (1994) 'School psychology'. *The Psychologist*, 7, 6, 263–267.

—— (1997) 'Tomorrow will also be history'. *Educational Psychology in Practice*, 13, 2, 101–111.

Manicas, P.T. and Secord, P. (1983) 'Implications for psychology of the new philosophy of science'. *American Psychologist*, April, 399–433.

Marland, M. (1976) *The craft of the classroom: a survival guide*. London: Heinemann.

Masson, J.F. (1984) *The assault on the truth: Freud's suppression of the seduction theory*. New York: Farrar, Straus and Giroux.

May, R. (1967) *Psychology and the human dilemma*. New York: Van Nostrand Reinhold.

Middleton, D. and Edwards, E. (1985) 'Pure and applied psychology: re-examining the relationship'. *Bulletin of the British Psychological Society*, 38, 146–150.

Miller, A. (1991) 'The contribution of psychology', in Lindsay, G. and Miller, A. (eds.) *Psychological services for primary schools*. London: Longman.

Mill, J. (1818) 'Essays on education', in Burston, W.H. (ed.) *James Mill on education*. Cambridge: Cambridge University Press.

Mischel, W. (1979) 'On the interface of cognition and personality: beyond the person–situation debate'. *American Psychologist*, 44, 741–754.

Mortimore, P. (1995) *Effective schools: current impact and future potential*. The Director's Inaugural Lecture. London: Institute of Education, London University.

National Commission on Education (1993) *Learning to succeed: a radical look at education today and a strategy for the future*. London: Heinemann.

Nicolson, P. (1995) 'Feminism and psychology', in Smith, J.A., Harre, R. and Van Langehove, L. (eds.) (1995) *Rethinking psychology*. London: Sage.

Nisbet, J. (1983) 'Educational psychology', in Hirst, P.H. (ed.) *Educational theory and its foundation disciplines*. London: Routledge and Kegan Paul.

Norwich, B. (1985) 'Aspects of the professional socialisation of teachers', in Francis, 1985.

—— (1986) 'Assessing perceived self-efficacy in relation to mathematics tasks: a study of reliability and validity of assessment'. *British Journal of Educational Psychology*, 56, 180–189.

—— (1988) 'Educational psychology services in LEAs: what future?', in Jones, N. and Sayer, J. (eds.) *Management and the psychology of schooling*. London: Falmer Press.

—— (1990) *Reappraising special needs education*. London: Cassell.

—— (1993) 'Ideological dilemmas in special needs education: practitioners' views'. *Oxford Review of Education*, 19, 4, 527–545.

—— (1995) 'Statutory assessment and statementing: some challenges and implications for educational psychologists'. *Educational Psychology in Practice*, 11, 1, 29–35.

—— (1996) *Special needs education, inclusive education or just education for all?* Inaugural Talk. London: Institute of Education, London University.

—— (1997a) 'The role of education in motivating children and adolescents to be empowered learners in the next millennium'. Invited key-note talk at Brunei International Conference.

—— (1997b) 'Retaining a contribution for university schools of education', in Harland, J. and Lambert, D. (eds.) *Exploring the role of educational studies: perspectives from the academic board*. Academic Board Occasional Paper no. 1. London: Institute of Education, London University.

Norwich, B., Leo, E. and Lunt, I. (1997) 'Research users' views about research needed in special needs education'. Paper presented at British Education Research Association Conference. University of York.

Noss, R. and Hoyles, C. (1996) *Windows on mathematical meanings: learning cultures and computers*. London: Kluwer Academic Publishers.

Notterman, J.M. and Drewry, H.N. (1993) *Psychology and education: parallel and interactive approaches*. New York: Plenum Publishing.

O'Connor, D.J. (1957) *An introduction to the philosophy of education*. London: Routledge and Kegan Paul.

Ogborn, J., Kress, G., Martins, I. and McGillicuddy, K. (1996) *Explaining science in the classroom*. Buckingham: Open University Press.

Ollsen, M. (1993) 'Science and individualism in educational psychology: problems for practice and points of departure'. *Educational Psychology*, 13, 2, 155–172.

Overton, W.F. (1980) 'World-views: Kuhn–Lakatos–Laudan'. *Advances in Child Development and Behaviour*, 18, 191–226.

Overton, W.F. and Reese, H.W. (1973) 'Models of development: methodological implications'. in Nesselroade, J.R. and Reese, H.W. (eds.) *Life-span developmental psychology: methodological issues*. New York: Academic press.

Palmer, S. (1997) 'Orthodoxy is no dancing matter'. *Times Educational Supplement*, June 27.

Pastore, N. (1949) *The nature–nurture controversy*. New York: Kings Crown Press.

Pepper, S. (1943) *World hypotheses*. San Francisco: University of California Press.

Phillips, D.C. (1985) 'The uses and abuses of truisms', in Fisher, W.C. and Berliner, D.C. (eds.) *Perspectives on instructional time*. London: Longman.

—— (1996) 'The good, the bad and the ugly: the many faces of constructivism'. *Educational Researcher*, 24, 7, 5–13.

Pinker, S. (1997) *How the mind works*. Harmondsworth: Penguin.

Popper, K. (1963) *Conjectures and refutations: the growth of scientific knowledge*. London: Routledge and Kegan Paul.

—— (1979) *Objective knowledge: an evolutionary approach*. Oxford: Oxford University Press.

Pressley, M., Harris, K.R. and Marks, M.B. (1992) 'But good strategy instructors are constructivists!' *Educational Psychologist*, 4, 1, 13–31.

Putnam, H. (1990) *Realism with a human face*. Cambridge, Mass.: Harvard University Press.

Quine, W.V. (1960) *Word and object*. Cambridge, Mass.: MIT Press.

Ravenette, A.T. (1988) 'PCP and practitioners who work with children', in Fransella, F. and Thomas, L. (eds.) *Experimenting with personal construct psychology*. London: Routledge and Kegan Paul.

Reich, R. (1991) *The work of nations: preparing for the 21st century*. London: Simon and Schuster.

Reynolds, D. (1998) 'The school effectiveness mission has only just begun'. *Times Educational Supplement*, February 20.

—— (1998) *Numeracy matters. Preliminary Report of Numeracy Task Force*. London: DfEE.

Reynolds, D. and Farrell, S. (1996) *Worlds apart? A review of international surveys of educational achievement involving England*. London: OFSTED.

Riger, S. (1992) 'Epistemological debates, feminist voices: science, social values and the study of women'. *American Psychologist*, 47: 730–740.

Rogers, C. (1983) 'The goal: the fully functioning person', in *Freedom to learn for the 1980s*. Columbus: Merrill.

Rorty, R. (1979) *Philosophy and the mirror of nature*. Princeton, N.J.: Princeton University Press.

Rose, N. (1985) *The psychology complex: psychology, politics and society in England, 1869–1939*. London: Routledge and Kegan Paul.

—— (1990) *Governing the soul: the shaping of the private soul*. London: Routledge.

Rycroft, C. and Gorer, G. (eds.) (1968) *Psychoanalysis observed*. London: Pelican Books.

Ryle, A. (1990) *Cognitive analytic therapy: active participation in change. A new integration in brief psychotherapy*. London: Wiley.

Salmon, P. (1995) *Psychology in the classroom: reconstructing teachers and learners*. London: Cassell Education.

Sampson, E.E. (1981) 'Cognitive psychology as ideology'. *American Psychologist* 36, 7, 730–743.

Schon, D. (1983) *The reflective practitioner: how professionals think in action*. London: Maurice Temple Smith.

Schonpflug, W. (1993) 'Applied psychology: newcomer with a long tradition'. *International Journal of Applied Psychology*, 42, 1, 5–30.

Schunk, D.H. (1990) 'Self concept aand school achievement', in Rogers, C.G. and Kutnick, P. (eds.) *The social psychology of primary schools*. London: Routledge.

Schwieso, J.J. (1993) 'Educational psychology and its failings: a reply to Ollsen'. *Educational Psychology*, 13, 2, 173–181.

Schwieso, J.J., Hastings, N. and Stainthrop, R. (1992) 'Psychology in teacher education: a response to Tomlinson'. *The Psychologist*, 5, 3, 112–113.

Searle, J.R. (1992) *The rediscovery of the mind*. Cambridge, Mass.: MIT Press.

—— (1995) *The construction of social reality*. Harmondsworth: Penguin.

Sellars, W. (1963) *Science, perception and reality*. London: Routledge and Kegan Paul.

Sharp, R. and Green, A. (1975) *Education and social control: a study of progressive education*. London: Routledge and Kegan Paul.

Shulman, L.S. (1988) 'The dangers of dichotomous thinking in education', in Grimnet, P.P. and Erikson, E.L. (eds.) *Reflections in teacher education*. New York: Teachers College Press.

Simon, B. (1978) 'Psychology and education', in *Intelligence, psychology and education: a Marxist critique*. London: Lawrence and Wishart.

—— (1981) 'Why no pedagogy in England?', in Simon, B. and Taylor, W. (eds.) *Education in the eighties – the central issues*. London: Batsford.

Skilbeck, M. (1984) *School-based curriculum development*. London: Harper Education Series.

Skinner, B.F. (1971) *Beyond freedom and dignity*. Harmondsworth: Penguin.

—— (1984) 'The shame of American education'. *American Psychologist*, 39, 947–954.

Smedslund, J. (1995) 'Psychologic: common sense and the pseudo-empirical', in Smith et al., 1995.

Smith, J.A., Harre, R. and Van Langehove, L. (eds.) (1995) *Rethinking psychology*. London: Sage.

Smith, L. (1992) 'Psychology in education'. *The Psychologist*, 5, 3, 114–116.

Snow, C.P. (1969) *The two cultures and a second look*. Cambridge: Cambridge University Press.

Stainthorp, R. (1997) 'What teachers need to know: empiricism not rhetoric'. Paper given at the Conference on Integrating Research and Practice in Literacy. London: Institute of Education, London University.

Stenhouse, L. (1975) *An introduction to curriculum research and development*. London: Heinemann.

Stoll, L. and Mortimore, P. (1997) 'School effectiveness and school improvement', in White and Barber, 1997.

Stones, E. (1979) *Psychopedagogy: psychological theory and the practice of teaching*. London: Methuen.

Stringer, P., Elliott, J. and Lauchlan, F. (1997) 'Dynamic assessment and its potential for educational psychologists'. *Educational Psychology in Practice*, 12, 4, 234–239.

Sullivan, E.V. (1984) *A critical psychology: interpretation of the personal world*. New York: Plenum Books.

Sulloway, F.J. (1992) *Freud, the biologist of the mind: beyond the psychoanalytic legend*. London: Fontana.

Sully, J. (1892) 'The service of psychology to education'. *Education Review*, 4, November, 314–315.

Summerfield Report (1968) *Psychologists in education services*. London: HMSO.

Sutherland, G. (1984) *Ability, merit and measurement*. Oxford: Oxford University Press.

Sutherland, M. (1988) 'Educational psychology: the distracted handmaiden'. *Educational and Child Psychology*, 5, 1, 13–19.

Sutton, A. and McPherson, I. (1981) 'Psychological practice in a social context', in McPherson, I. and Sutton, A. (eds.) *Reconstructing psychological practice*. London: Croom Helm.

Tanner, D. and Tanner, L.N. (1980) *Curriculum development*. New York: Macmillan.

Taylor, C. (1964) *The explanation of psychology*. London: Routledge and Kegan Paul.

—— (1985) 'Peaceful coexistence in psychology', in Taylor, C. (ed.) *Human agency and language: philosophical papers*. Cambridge: Cambridge University Press.

Tawney, R.H. (1922) *Secondary schools for all: a policy for Labour*. Education Advisory Committee for the Labour Party. London: Hambledon.

Thomas, G. (1985) 'What psychology had to offer – then'. *Bulletin of the British Psychological Society*, 38, 322–326.

Thomas, J.B. (1996) 'The beginnings of educational psychology in the universities of England and Wales'. *Educational Psychology*, 16, 3, 229–244.

Tomlinson, P. (1981) *Understanding teaching: interactive educational psychology*. London and New York: McGraw-Hill.

—— (1992) 'Psychology and education: what went wrong or did it?' *Psychologist*, 5, 104–109.

—— (1996) 'Role over psychology?' *Education Section Review*, 20, 8–9.

Tomlinson, P., Edwards, A., Finn, G., Smith, L. and Wilkinson, E. (1993) 'Psychology aspects of beginning teacher competence'. *Education Section Review*, 17, 1, 1–19.

Tooley, J. and Darby, D. (1998) *Educational research: a critique*. London: OFSTED.

Trickey, G. (1993) 'Measurement technology UK: fad, fashion and phoenix'. *Division of Educational and Child Psychology*, 10, 4, 7–14.

Vygotsky, L.S. (1978) *Mind in society: the development of higher psychological processes*. Cambridge, Mass.: MIT Press.

Walkerdine, V. (1981) 'Sex, power and pedagogy'. *Screen Education*, 38, 14–21.

—— (1984) 'Developmental psychology and the child-centred pedagogy', in Henriques, J., Holloway, C., Urwin, C., Venn, C. and Walkerdine, V. *Changing the subject: psychology, social regulation and subjectivity*. London: Methuen.

—— (1988) *The mastery of reason: cognitive development and the production of rationality*. London: Routledge.

Warnock Report (1978) *Special educational needs. Report of the Committee of Inquiry into the education of handicapped children and young people*. London: HMSO.

Waterman, A.S. (1981) 'Individualism and interdependence'. *American Psychologist*, 36, 7, 762–773.

Watkins, C. and Wagner, P. (1987) *School discipline: a whole school approach*. London: Blackwell.

Watkins, C., Carnell, E., Lodge, C. and Whalley, C. (1996) *Effective learning. SIN Research Matters*. London: Institute of Education, London University.

Watts, F. (1992) 'Is psychology falling apart?' *The Psychologist*, 15, 11, 489–493.

Wedell, K. (1982) 'Educational psychology services', in Cohen, L., Thomas, J. and Manion, L. (eds.) *Educational research and development in Britain, 1970–80*. Windsor: NFER-Nelson.

Webster, R. (1995) *Why Freud got it wrong: sin, science and psychoanalysis*. London: HarperCollins.

White, J. (1988) 'Educational psychology: science or common sense?' *Educational Psychology and Child Development*, 5, 1, 5–12.

—— (1993) 'What place for values in the National Curriculum?', in O'Hear, C. and White, J. (eds.) *Assessing the National Curriculum*. London: Paul Chapman.

—— (1997) 'Philosophical perspectives on school effectiveness and school improvement', in White and Barber, 1997.

White, J. and Barber, M. (eds.) (1997) *Perspectives on school effectiveness and school improvement*. Bedford Way Papers. London: Institute of Education, London University.

Wilkinson, E. (1992) 'Turn back the tide'. *Psychologist*, 5, 3, 120–122.

—— (1993) 'Psychology, psychologists and teacher training'. *Education Section Review*, 17, 1, 20–25.

Winch, C. (1997) 'Accountability, controversy and school effectiveness research', in White and Barber, 1997.

Wiseman, S.J. (1952) 'Higher degrees in education in British universities'. *British Journal of Educational Studies*, 2, 54–66.

Wittgenstein, L. (1953) *Philosophical investigations*. London: Blackwell.

Wolfendale, S., Byrans, T., Fox, M., Labran, A. and Sigston, A. (eds.) (1992) *The profession and practice of educational psychology: future directions*. London: Cassell.

Wolpert, L. (1992) *The unnatural nature of science*. London: Faber and Faber.

Wood, A. (1997) 'What do EPs do?' Contribution to the SENCO Forum on Internet. 25 November.

Wood, K. (1994) 'Towards national criteria for special educational needs: some conceptual and practical considerations for educational psychologists'. *Educational Psychology in Practice*, 10, 2, 85–92.

Woodward, W.R. (1987) 'Professionalisation, rationality and political linkages in twentieth century psychology', in Ash, M.G. and Woodward, W.R. (eds.) *Psychology in twentieth century thought and society*. Cambridge: Cambridge University Press.

Wooldridge, A. (1994) *Measuring the mind: education and psychology in England, c. 1860–1990*. Cambridge: Cambridge University Press.

Wylie, R.C. (1979) *The self concept*, vol. 2, *Theory and research on selected topics*. Lincoln, Ne.: University of Nebraska Press.

Young, M. (1958) *The rise of the meritocracy, 1870 to 2033*. Harmondsworth: Penguin.

Young, M.J.F. (1995) 'A curriculum for the 21st century? Towards a new basis for overcoming the academic–vocational divisions', in Maudsley, E. and Dee, L. (eds.) *Redefining the future: perspectives on students with difficulties and disabilities in FE*. London: Institute of Education, London University.

Index